Strategies for Adult Education

Strategies
for
Adult Education

Practices in
Western Europe

COLIN TITMUS

Follett Publishing Company
Chicago · Atlanta · Dallas · Sacramento · Warrensburg, MO

British Library Cataloguing in Publication Data

Titmus, Colin
    Strategies for adult education,
    1. Adult education-Europe-Case studies
    I. Title
    374'.94   LC5256.A2

ISBN 0 - 695 - 81642 - X

Contents

CHAPTER 1

Introduction: structures and organization of adult education

Purpose and scope of this book

The purpose of this book is, through a number of case studies, to give some picture of the practices used over the range of adult education in Western Europe. It is not a country by country survey of the region. It would be impossible to attempt that in the space at the author's disposal and is, in any case, being done in the series *Adult Education in Europe*, now appearing, which includes countries of both east and west.[1] Nor is it an overall conspectus of trends, of the kind already undertaken a decade ago by J. A. Simpson.[2] That way abstraction lies. Here the emphasis is on the concrete. By selecting individual examples of types of practice, it has been possible to treat each one at some length.

The choice of examples has been made to cover a wide range of institutions and organizational arrangements. It would not claim to be comprehensive: there are, no doubt, certain types of association, forms of provision, of learning experience, of outreach or incentive, which are omitted. One hopes, however, that there are few aspects of the structured provision of learning opportunities for adults in Western Europe that are not at least touched upon, and a large number that are examined in some depth.

The examples have been chosen not because they are unique, although the Italian '150 hours' scheme is, nor because they are innovatory, although the Swedish outreach experiment was. They have been chosen because they are representative or exemplary of aspects of contemporary provision, of responses to problems — for example, how one attracts the non-participant —, of approaches that may be used in pursuit of the goal of universal adult education. To that their relevance is unquestioned, as each one has attracted interested comment outside its own country and some have inspired imitation or related initiatives. One hesitates to say they represent best practice, that would be too contentious a claim, as the agreed criteria for evaluation do not exist. They are, however, certainly outstanding.

The body of this book is composed of case studies, but it is important that they shall not be seen as isolated instances. An attempt has been made to set each one in the context of its national adult education and society, while relating it to other practices of the same kind in Western Europe. Thus the place of Swedish voluntary organizations in adult education and national life is discussed and their status and function are compared with those of other bodies fulfilling a similar role in other countries.

It has also seemed valuable, in this introduction, to offer a more general conspectus of adult education process and provision, to offer a broader context by discussing in particular how and why the phenomenon of organization and structure of adult study, of which these case studies are manifestations, has occurred. One has, therefore, proceeded from the general, through the national, to the particular, and, in concentrating on this last, one has endeavoured never to lose sight of the fact that it belongs to a larger whole.

Growth and identity of adult education

In Western Europe, the third quarter of the twentieth century has seen an expansion in the range and quantity of adult education activity such as has never before occurred. As the nineteenth century's essential educational contribution may now be seen to have been universal, compulsory schooling, and that of the mid-twentieth century secondary schooling for all, so it was beginning to appear that the second half of this century would be known as the age of adult education. The economic difficulties of the 1970s have slowed and distorted development sharply, so that the prospect is no longer so clear, the optimistic forecasts of a decade ago not so plainly justified. There may, indeed, be only limited further expansion in the next few years. Even if there is, the importance of the adult sector in education does not seem to be in doubt, except in the short term. What is emerging is that to adult, or continuing, education new tasks are coming, have indeed already come, as a result of changing socio-economic circumstances. There may be contraction, even disappearance of traditional practices, but they will almost certainly be replaced by others, better or worse, but seen to be more appropriate to contemporary needs.

Even the popularity of lifelong education can be said to be largely due to growing interest in adult education. For the last twenty years international discussion in education has somewhat misleadingly been dominated by the idea of the former, the integration of all learning, purposive or incidental, from the cradle to the grave, into one ongoing process. Such a grand design seemed appropriate to the prosperous 1960s, but less so in the last decade, when, more in some countries than others, educational thinking has become focused on apparently more pressing and concrete concerns, notably the unemployment or unemployability of young school leavers. In fact, from the time of its first formulation, lifelong education has often been imperfectly understood, or its full implications have been ignored. There have been some countries, as may be apparent in this book, that are seeking to realize it fully, but in many others, when politicians and even educators have spoken of it, they have been jumping on a bandwagon. They have not been concerned with the vertical integration of all stages of education, or integrating the whole range of educational activities into one learning experience. They have used the broad term to denote only a part of the concept, the continuation of learning opportunities after the completion of initial education. They have meant adult education.[3]

Apart from the fact that they have been cashing in on the

popularity in educational circles of a particular term, they have had some justification for avoiding the expression 'adult education'. In countries where it has been in common use for any length of time, as in the United Kingdom, it has acquired a limited meaning and attempts to extend that have led to confusion.[4] Other countries have not thought in terms of a distinct sector of education, delimited by the age or maturity of the people who participate in it, as in *adult* education. Most frequently their thinking has been in terms of provision aimed at a specific class and therefore not restricted to people above a certain age; *éducation populaire*, popular education, in France, *scuola popolare*, people's school, in Italy, for example.

Consideration of post-initial education throughout life as a distinctive sector, with its own characteristics, problems and possibilities, because of the age, social and economic status and life experience of the participants, has indeed only become general in Europe since the Second World War, as its importance has become accepted. Even then there has been a reluctance to call this sector *adult* education, because of the implications of age and maturity associated with the word adult. In English the expression 'continuing education' is considered by a growing number of people to be less confused by historical associations. In Germany, where *Erwachsenen-bildung*, adult education, did not replace *Volksbildung*, popular education, in general usage until 1945, *Weiterbildung*, further education, has replaced the former in many contexts. In France *éducation des adultes* has never been a common term. Nowadays the most widely used one, if not *éducation permanente*, lifelong education, is *formation continue*, continuing education.[5]

Whatever it has been called, there has been some misunderstanding about what is to be comprehended within the post-initial sector. In an effort to clarify the situation and improve communication, a number of attempts have been made to define in an internationally agreed way what in this book is called 'adult education'. The latest and most detailed attempt is that of UNESCO:

> . . . the entire body of educational processes, whatever the content, level and method, whether formal or otherwise, whether they pro-

long or replace initial education in schools, colleges and universities as well as in apprenticeship, whereby persons regarded as adult by the society to which they belong develop their abilities, enrich their knowledge, improve their technical or professional qualifications or turn them in a new direction and bring about changes in their attitudes or behaviour in the twofold perspective of full personal development and participation in balanced and independent social, economic and cultural development.[6]

As far as it goes it is acceptable, but since, like other attempts, it defines process, it is incomplete. If one talks of Norwegian adult education, Italian adult education, or that of any other country, one refers not to the processes but to the collection of institutions and organizational measures that are intended to make them possible. This is not a matter of two different ways of looking at the same thing, but two different things, and for many people adult education means the institutional structure.

Clearly, as the history of auto-didacticism shows, some adults would undertake purposive, sequential learning without it. It is also true, however, that these would in all probability constitute only a small minority of the people who currently do so. It is often said that man is naturally a learning animal, particularly by those who believe that it must be the faults of the system and not the characteristics of people that prevent more adults from participating in education. It may even be true, but it is much less certain, that contemporary man is a studying animal. Whether it be a matter of genes or of the circumstances of modern life, in which so many demands are made upon interest and time, it seems that most adults have only the resources, the ability, the self-discipline or motivation to undertake limited sequential and continuing learning activities on their own initiative. It is because of the machinery of facilitation and encouragement, which has been built up over many years, that so many adults now engage in such a wide range of learning activities.

Without it, most adults would not study. Therefore, since it is not itself of infinite dimension, it not only enables and stimulates adults to study, it in effect also sets limits to the nature and extent of their participation in adult education. By its nature it determines what is taught and consequently learned, for what purpose, to whom learning opportunities

5

shall be offered, by whom, under what conditions. It determines when the study may take place, where, how it shall be organized and who pays. It is therefore of critical importance to the educational process. Both educators and learners need to know and to understand this machinery, if it is to be moulded to serve their ends and not they to it. That is why elements of it will be the concern of this book.

Determining factors of organization and structure

Many factors help to decide what are the parts of it and how they work. There are, for example, certain broadly agreed principles, which animate adult education today. Every adult has a right to adequate opportunities of education and needs to continue his education in adult life. Society not only needs him to do so, but has a duty to ensure that he can. Learning opportunities should be organized to meet both the wishes of the learners and those of society. Any individual, having passed the age of compulsory schooling, should be free to decide whether to undertake further education or not. Adult education should form an integral part of a lifelong process of education. The purposes and practices of adult education should conform to, and/or be animated by, the fundamental principles on which society is based.[7]

These principles have in them a certain amount of *post facto* systematization and rationalization of existing practice, much of which was already firmly rooted when they were formulated. One may in fact see in the structures and organization the influence of past, present and future. First that of history. Both British university adult education and Scandinavian folk high schools, for example, are products of particular times and places. If they did not already exist, it would be difficult to conceive of their being created today, at least in their current form. Second, current pressure of society. It is the combined pressure of adults, employers and government, that creates for vocational education its present position of pre-eminence in adult learning provision. Third, society's aspirations for the future. The Italian '150 hours' agreements are an example of provision motivated by one section of the population's aspirations. Swedish municipal adult education and laws relating to mature entry to higher education exemplify measures introduced to help achieve a nationally agreed goal of a socially just and equal society.

Motivation for provision

That there is any machinery of provision at all derives only to a limited degree from the demand for educational opportunity by those for whom provision is destined. Some present-day institutions may have begun as a response to such pressure, it sometimes becomes evident again if the survival of provision is threatened, but demand to create an apparatus of adult education provision where none exists remains inarticulate, or rather it is latent, not active. For the most part the means whereby opportunities to learn are offered are organized on the initiative of people who, having enjoyed such opportunities themselves, believe that others should have them.

Their motives are various. The employer who arranges training for his workforce may be inspired by self-interest. but it is not always beyond his calculations that trainees benefit too. Conversely, the provider of second-chance education, acting on the altruistic principle that lifelong education is the right of every citizen, may also have at the back of his mind that educational inequality is a source of social discontent and thus a threat to himself. Provision may be for the benefit of the provider, the participant, or third parties, frequently identified as a society or class, to which one or other of the first two belongs. It is always intended to change the learner, but often its purpose is to maintain the economic or social *status quo*. Even where it is envisaged that change may be expedited, as in some political or citizenship education, the assumption is made that it will remain within generally approved limits. Where that cannot be assumed, provision of education for change is made reluctantly, if at all.

Attracting the adult to study

The adult, unlike the child, enjoys freedom to participate in further study or not, as he pleases. This exerts a major influence on the organizational forms of adult education. It is under pressure to operate when, where and how the learner is able or willing to use it. Its content and methods must be those its clientele will accept, although perhaps not the ones they would actively choose. Nor is it enough to provide opportunities to study, however well calculated they may be to appeal to adults. Experience shows that, left to themselves, the majority of them exercise their freedom by choosing not to take them up.

A significant number of adults claim ignorance of educational opportunities. Given the amount and nature of publicity that adult education puts out these days, it is unlikely that the ignorant have physically never seen or heard any of it. More probably it has not been registered. The message has been blocked from the consciousness, which can handle only a limited number of impressions at a time, by others. Registration and retention of information seem to be a function of the strength of the information signal and of the individual's predisposition to receive it. For example, out of the babble of conversation in a crowded room, one picks up those remarks that are loudest and that most appeal to one's interest. Apart from the loud shout of greater publicity, since organizational measures taken to make the learning experience pleasurable and valuable in itself do not appeal sufficiently to adults, other inducements to draw people into participation have to be tried. These practices are becoming increasingly general and systematic.

They are the more necessary because, although it may be considered valuable for all adults to undertake any further education they choose, there are some adults and areas and purposes of study that are considered more important than others, both by providing bodies and by other powerful groups, notably employers and the State, with an interest in what is taught and learned. Mechanisms of inducement have therefore been devised, directed at all adults, but more specifically at certain categories, encouraging any kind of study, but some kinds more than others, and aimed at persuading providing bodies to offer these kinds of study and to cater for the priority categories of student.

Problems of scale

The earlier reference to the motivation of providers as though it was that of an individual or a small group may be misleading. There may be provision by individuals, but in national terms it has long since become insignificant. Large organizations dominate adult education today and students of it find organization theory helpful to an understanding of its operation. Decisions are officially made by a collective, separated from those who execute them, and the effectiveness of the collective policy depends to a not inconsiderable extent on its congruence with the aims of the executants. Moreover, the freedom of anybody to exert his will is restricted by the characteristics of the organization itself, which acquires its own momentum or inertia, only partially controlled by the management. These points are even true in the case of such local and independent institutions as residential folk high schools, of so-called voluntary bodies, as well as of public ones.

Beyond a certain order of size the practices of adult education require full-time, paid personnel to run them. That stage can be reached very rapidly, as the British adult literacy scheme has shown. For all its thousands of unpaid volunteer tutors, it could only be run by professional staff. Even in voluntary associations, of which they are employees, it is professionals who control policy more and more. The large scale of adult education organization, which has removed policy-making far from the learning experience itself, and the growing influence of the professional expert go against a principle of adult education, established on both educational and political grounds, that effective control of the learning process should be taken at local level, where the views of the adult public may be adequately represented. To counter this tendency one finds regulations being written, as in Norwegian and Danish laws, and attempts being made in practice, as in community colleges, to keep some real decision making at local level, and to involve adult students in it beyond the confines of their own class or learning group, as is laid down in the constitution of some evening folk high schools.

European practices show evidence of the tension between the principle of permitting learners to choose what they will learn and the requirements of organization on a national scale, at which level it is inevitable that they be viewed as categories — workers, the educationally disadvantaged, the unemployed — rather than as individuals. In spite of efforts to achieve otherwise, within the educational system the adult can find the study he wants only in so far as he conforms to a group for which provision is made. The operation of study circles in Sweden is an exception.

The problems of scale are associated with concern to maintain a balance in the machinery of provision between private and public control. There is some tendency to believe that, despite the fact that some of them too are affected by the remoteness of administration on a national scale, voluntary associations are more sensitive to the shifting needs of the learner, less likely to impose their own ideas of what should be offered, than the State. In a number of countries there is also distrust of central government authority on political grounds. The State, on the other hand, becomes more conscious of the importance to it of adult education because of its cost and its value as an instrument of policy, notably in the development of the economy. Government, therefore, becomes more interventionist, not only in vocational education, as in France, but in general education, as in the case of Swedish municipal adult education. The Scandinavian countries, in particular, and others too, have tried in their procedures to preserve a balance between the claims of voluntary bodies and the needs of the State. To a certain extent the difficulties are reduced or complicated, according to context, by a fairly recent tendency on the part of government, to decentralize its power to local authorities, as the Dutch government has done with educational networks and the French with socio-cultural animation.

Growth of legislation

The structures and processes of provision and promotion grew with a minimum of regulation and planning. Its scale, the State's involvement in it, the general need to impose some order, to bring about present efficiency and encourage further growth, have resulted in a spate of legislation in the last two decades. There have been attempts, through one law or another, to solve each of the problems discussed in this chapter, even to the extent of using legislation to protect voluntary bodies against the State. One might say, indeed, that an analysis of the measures passed would give a fairly clear picture of the way Western European adult education seeks to go and of the organizational steps that are being taken to get there.

Types of providing body

Providers of adult education can be classified as public or private organizations, as national or local ones, and as organizations for which adult education is the primary purpose of their existence, or is an incidental to their main function. This book includes discussion of all types. Direct provision of central government is rare, but in Sweden two State adult schools, in Norway vocational training as part of labour market policy, are examples. Local government provision is much more common — Swedish municipal adult schools, British community colleges, German evening folk high schools, all fall into this category. In no case can one say that adult education is the prime reason for existence of public authorities, but it is not so difficult to find instances where this is the case in the private sector — the various organizations that go under the name of Workers' Educational Association in the Scandinavian countries and the United Kingdom, for instance. For others, such as the Educational Association of the Temperance Movement and other Scandinavian organizations, the primacy of adult education in their aims depends on the extent of their independence from their parent body. For trade unions, employers, churches or political parties, it is an instrument for the achievement of their chief purpose. The nearest one gets to private local organizations is in discussion of residential folk high schools, both in Denmark and the Federal German Republic, and of members of the Working Group of German Educational Centres.

Range of provision

Institutions and organizational forms are devised to specialize in particular purposes and levels of education. All learning experiences, whatever objective they may have, contribute to individual self-enrichment, but there are also courses whose only aim is the development of the individual, without reference to his social or economic function. It is, however, difficult to identify an institution whose sole purpose is to provide such courses. The ones that are most active in this area, British local authorities and university extra-mural departments, Swedish voluntary associations, German evening folk high schools, tend to be almost comprehensive in their range, offering second-chance, role, and even vocational education as well. Specialized organization for second-chance or remedial education is exemplified by municipal adult education and outreach work in Sweden, the Italian '150 hours' scheme, the adult literacy scheme in the United Kingdom. Role education, for citizenship, is the purpose of the institutions of the Working Group of German Educational Centres, and agencies and arrangements specifically for vocational education are to be found in every country.

In the level of education for which it caters, provision lies between the extremes of adult literacy campaigns and higher education for adults, as exemplified by the Open University, or the organization of mature student entry in Sweden. In many cases it is not possible to classify by the usual criteria of primary, secondary, further or higher levels, as UNESCO's International Standard Classification of Education discovered. It would in fact be improper to categorize most study circles or non-vocational, non-certificate evening classes by level, as they are open to all adults. On the other hand Swedish municipal adult education and the '150 hours' programmes are specifically secondary provision, and residential folk high schools may be said to be explicitly geared to post-compulsory, if not post-secondary, standard.

Forms of learning experience

The ways in which the learning experience itself is structured are various. There is the face-to-face encounter of students with teacher, as in evening institutes and evening folk high schools. There is the study circle, equally face to face, but in principle not requiring a teacher. Norwegian correspondence schools and the Open University provide examples of institutions specializing in a specific form of learning experience, distance education, which may mean correspondence alone, correspondence combined with broadcasting, or may, as in the case of both institutions mentioned, be supplemented by some face-to-face teaching. Residential education, as offered by the Danish folk high schools or the Working Group of German Educational Centres, may appear to be less a distinctive organization of the learning experience than a structuring of the context in which it takes place. The same might be said of adult education work in community colleges. It is, however, argued by their proponents that being in such contexts is an integral part of the experience.

Mechanisms of facilitation and inducement

The gift of concrete rewards for taking part in adult education is normally limited to the grant of diplomas, such as the degrees awarded by the Open University, or to job promotion. In both instances the reward is for attainment rather than for participation alone. Money payments, such as those tried in the Swedish outreach experiment, are rare. To offer some kinds of study free of charge, when for others a student is required to pay a fee, as happens in the case of priority study circles in Sweden, is clearly an inducement. So is the allocation of paid leave in order to attend some courses, but only unpaid leave for others, which happens under French law. Paid educational leave in general may be intended as a positive inducement to participation, but it only operates as such if the person to whom it is offered would prefer study to work at his job. There is plenty of evidence to suggest that that assumption cannot universally be made. It is perhaps more realistic to see educational leave, paid or otherwise, as facilitating participation rather than rewarding it. It comes in the same general category as the offer to mature students of entry to higher education without educational qualifications,

13

made in Sweden and by the Open University. Like the adult literacy scheme in Britain, it is designed to make it easier for adults to study, but not to reward them. The Swedish outreach experiment was a combination of facilitation and inducements, because the persons invited to take part were offered more favourable conditions than ordinary circle members.

Scope of legislation

Legislation points the way in which the State, if not adult education itself, believes it should go. To a large extent the laws mentioned in this book legitimize existing practice. Provincial laws in the Federal Republic do, so did the 1944 and 1945 Education Acts in the United Kingdom. They seek to protect some interests and make obligations of what was being done optionally. They usually have the intention of bringing order, protecting the different interests involved, including the public purse, laying down principles for financial support from public funds and, invariably, promoting growth. These are both the intentions and the effect of the Norwegian Correspondence School Act, of the German provincial ones, and those of the United Kingdom.

Legislation is never merely regulatory, it always changes the existing situation. To an increasing extent it is used to create entirely new provision or structures, as in the laws decreasing municipal adult education and reforming higher education in Sweden, and the regulation setting up local education networks in the Netherlands. Perhaps the most outstanding example of an entire sector brought in to being essentially by legislative fiat is French vocational adult education, which was made by the implementation of a series of laws, decrees and orders, beginning in 1958 and still continuing.

These are clear examples of partial laws, that is, they treat a limited part of adult education, as indeed do nearly all the others. Whether they set out to specialize, as the correspondence school law (Norway), German paid educational leave laws, or the municipal adult education measure (Sweden) do, or are wide ranging, like the United Kingdom laws of 1944 and 1945, or the German provincial adult education laws, they are always incomplete in their coverage. Only the Norwegian Adult Education Act, 1976, really tries to be comprehensive, which is why it has been singled out for discussion.

The overall picture of the structures and organization of adult education in Western Europe is complex, some would say inordinately so. It is against the background of this and of the factors that produced it that one should view the case studies examined in the following chapters. To a lesser extent each country and case mirrors this complexity. Each example was chosen because it illustrates or exemplifies one aspect of structure and organization, but the intrusion of other elements complicates the study of each one. That is the reality and it would be false to pretend otherwise. On the other hand it is important to remember that all the elaboration of provision is fundamentally a response to a few simple facts. Some adults want to study. Some want others to study. An adult is free to refuse the opportunity to do so. He is not free to study unless the opportunities are created, by himself or others, to enable him to do so. These opportunities must compete with all the other demands upon his time and interest.

References

1. European Centre for Leisure and Education, Prague.
2. J.A. SIMPSON, *Today and Tomorrow in European Adult Education*, Strasbourg, Council of Europe, 1972.
3. COLIN TITMUS, PAZ BUTTEDAHL, DIANA IRONSIDE, PAUL LENGRAND, *Terminology of Adult Education*, Paris, UNESCO, 1979.
4. ibid.
5. ibid.
6. *Recommendation on the Development of Adult Education*, General Conference of UNESCO, 19th session, Nairobi, 26 November 1976.
7. COLIN TITMUS, 'Proposed theoretical model for the comparative study of national education systems in Europe', *Society and Leisure*, vol. VIII, No. 2, 1976, Prague, European Centre for Leisure and Education.

CHAPTER 2

The United Kingdom

Not long ago it was not uncommon for Britons to believe that they invented adult education as it exists in Europe today. They did not and the attitude has become rare, but it is true that adult education spread widely in the United Kingdom sooner than it did in other European countries, and that British practice was influential, just as it was in most areas of human activity associated with the Industrial Revolution.

Professor Kelly reports educational work with adults in England as far back as the Middle Ages,[1] but the roots of contemporary practice lie fixed in the nineteenth century. In the first half of the century the United Kingdom was the wealthiest power in Europe. The victories of its navy in the Napoleonic Wars had given it a command of the seas that was not challenged for a hundred years. It used this power to continue to build an already considerable overseas empire, right up to the peace treaties after the First World War. A major trading nation for centuries, it had become, by a fortunate coincidence of natural resources, access to markets, a suitable political system and, dare one suggest, a concatenation of mechanical talents, the inventor of the Industrial Revolution and the most advanced manufacturing nation in the world.

At the beginning of the nineteenth century Britain was already ruled by a two-chamber parliament, of which the lower house was elected on a limited franchise. Slowly through the century the suffrage was extended until it became universal for men in 1918 and women in 1928. With the extension of democracy political power shifted from the landed gentry to the business and professional classes and nowadays it alternates between the Conservatives, representing essentially the interests of the latter, and the Labour Party, representing those of the organized working class.

Although in the heyday of Britain's industrial domination it was believed that State intervention would hinder the free play of the market on which national prosperity depended, democratic pressure for a more equitable distribution of industrialization's profits and for the removal of its worst abuses to ensure tolerable conditions of life and work for all has compelled continually greater State regulation of economic and social activity. To some extent the consequent concentration of authority into the hands of central government, which was inimical to British tradition, was mitigated by devolving considerable executive responsibility and powers of local taxation and decision making to municipal and county councils.

By the 1820s, when trade unions ceased to be illegal, working class organization for the defence of economic interests, better social conditions and the pursuit of political rights was already widespread. The Chartist Movement in the 1830s and 1840s was a national one which was taken as a serious revolutionary threat. Its failure, largely as a result of its own internal weaknesses, put back the British labour movement for decades and no doubt helped to discredit revolution as a means of achieving its aims. Today's unions and the Labour Party grew out of the last decades of the nineteenth century and have adopted a gradualist approach to the achievement of a socialist society, working within existing institutions.

That they did so was in some degree due to the social climate of the country, in which the dominant classes, confronted by the rise of worker demands, were confident enough not to defend themselves by repression but to seek to assimilate them into the prevailing social ethos, basically sure that workers would learn to appreciate its essential rightness. The enlightened self-interest of both sides would ensure its maintenance.

By the middle of the nineteenth century it was clear to many that other countries were catching up on Britain's economic lead. The Government was aware of it and, with hindsight, it is now clear that by that time the enterprise and dynamism which had made the country's wealth was already giving way to complacency. The United Kingdom got richer for the rest of the century, but in fact it was embarked on the decline which, accelerated by the stresses of two world wars and the loss of empire, has continued to the present day.

Much of the United Kingdom's drive had a religious inspiration. Many of the new business classes belonged to nonconformist sects, not the established Church of England. They derived much of their strength from their ability to combine high moral principles with a shrewd sense of commercial advantage. Their energies were canalized into business because their non-adherence to the established Church barred them from public office. This disability, like the disfranchisement of Catholics, was removed in the 1820s and the opening up of other fields to their talents may have contributed to the weakening of Britain's economic performance. Religion fed the social conscience of the Victorian Age, impelling the labouring classes to mutual assistance and the middle classes to support political emancipation and the improvement of the workers' conditions of life. In the twentieth century, however, it has greatly declined as a force in national life.

Perhaps the fatal weakness of the United Kingdom has been snobbery. There is a strong tendency for each class to seek to express its admiration of the one above by aping its culture. Trade was despised by the landed gentry, so families successful in business gave it up in imitation of their betters. This trend had a significant influence on education. The so-called public schools, in fact private institutions for the sons of gentry, spread widely through the nineteenth century. They offered character building and a curriculum based on Greek and Latin, which was believed to be the correct general education for gentlemen who would rule the Empire. Technical or vocational subjects were rejected as beneath consideration. This attitude, strong in the universities, spread down through the classes, as the middle class began to send its sons to public schools and the State secondary schools, which multiplied in the first decades of the twentieth century, tried to imitate their traditions. Although technical subjects were taught, the brightest pupils were directed to the more prestigious classics and arts subjects.

It had long been accepted that an industrial society required a literate work force, but reluctance to countenance government intervention in education meant that primary schooling was not made available for all by law until 1870 in England and Wales. They thus caught up with Scotland, which had had a school in every parish for more than a century.[2] Responsibility for schools, where they were not provided by churches, was laid on a local authority. In 1902 the provision of State education became a duty of the county councils and councils of large towns, who were empowered for the first time to provide secondary as well as elementary schools. The widespread increase in such institutions offered opportunities to the children of small businessmen, minor civil servants and clerical workers, but working men's sons and daughters were not assured of secondary education until the Education Act of 1944 (1945 in Scotland). This measure was part of the wave of social legislation, inspired by idealism at the end of the Second World War, which established a social democratic welfare state in Great Britain. Comprehensive schooling for all to the age of sixteen was made the policy of the Labour Government in the 1960s, but the independence of local education authorities (backed, admittedly, by the Conservative Party) is shown by the fact that a decade later some authorities still maintain a two-tier secondary system, with selective entry to certain schools.

There was considerable progress in university education, including a major reform of Oxford and Cambridge, the only universities in England at the beginning of the nineteenth century. They still set out to educate gentlemen and were slow to admit sciences to the curriculum. In response to increasing demand for higher education, new universities were created to meet local needs, a number in the last years of the nineteenth century and a new wave after the Second World War. Some of them were direct outgrowths of university extension work, for example, Reading, Sheffield, Nottingham. They have strong scientific and technical departments, but they have also subscribed to the liberal education principles of the ancient universities, whose prestige remains pre-eminent, both socially and intellectually.

In most Western European countries entry to higher education is a right for all those young people who have passed the national entrance examination. This is not the case in the United Kingdom where universities admit only as many students as they consider they can accommodate and make their own selection of applicants, often taking into account factors other than academic performance. As a result many fewer young people than in other countries enter university, but many fewer also, once accepted, drop out. In fact, whereas elsewhere the proportion of entrants obtaining degress may be less than fifty per cent, in the United Kingdom it is more than eighty per cent.

Adult education became a social phenomenon in Britain so early that already in 1851 a history of it was published.[3] It was supplied both by the upper for the labouring classes and by the workers themselves. Much of it was organized as a means of bringing people to salvation, as in the Sunday school movement. It was seen as a means of creating the literate and skilled labour force the economy needed. Some of the middle classes believed that through education the urban proletariat could be brought to that orderliness and conformity to social norms that life in the new industrial cities required. Workers themselves hoped through education to learn to achieve economic, social and political emancipation. The Mechanics' Institutes, which originated in the 1820s and 1830s, some founded by workers, others by upper class initiative, set out to teach 'useful arts' for work and for civic respectability. The Chartist Movement had a strong educational element, which declined with it.

In the first half of the century there was no clear-cut distinction between education as an instrument and education for its own sake. There was however, an important development of adult education in the United Kingdom in the second half. Conscious of the growing competition from abroad, the State, which had no direct power over schools' curricula, offered subsidies for scientific and technical courses. In 1889 the new local education authorities were empowered to devote part of local taxation to technical education, some of which was spent on adult instruction. Adult vocational education became part of the national system of technical instruction.

On the other hand the Christian Socialist clergyman, Frederick Maurice, deplored the tendency he perceived in young men to pursue education for material benefit. When he and his friends founded the London Working Men's College in 1854 they set out to offer learning for living, not for earning a living. Vocational studies were discouraged in favour of those — history, literature and the arts — that were held to enrich the mind. This attitude, which was in keeping with the public school and university view that occupational studies were inferior, was adopted by the Workers' Educational Movement, founded by Albert Mansbridge in 1903.

As a result of the Government's Smith Report, of 1919, whose recommendations became the guidelines of its development in the United Kingdom for the next fifty years, adult education became by definition, non-vocational, non-utilitarian. All else was training or further education. The inter-war years were the heyday of liberal adult education in Great Britain, as working men sought, in joint WEA and university classes, to understand through the study of history, politics and economics the forces which brought about wars and depressions to afflict their lives. Its continuing popularity in the armed forces during the Second World War and the provisions of the Education Act, 1944, (Scotland 1945) relating to adult education, raised hopes for further development after the war. Growth there was, in spite of economic difficulties, but not very much in social and political subjects and rather among middle class adults than in the working class. Adult education became more of an intellectual leisure pursuit, feeding interest in the arts and hobbies, than the education for responsible citizenship that the 1919 Report had intended.

For the first half of the twentieth century vocational training for adults was largely confined to evening classes offered by local authorities and these were nearly all courses of initial training, producing skilled craftsmen for the engineering and construction industries. Even though there was an obvious need after the Second World War to offer updating courses, refresher courses and training in new and higher skills, as the pace of technical change increased, it was not until 1964 that the United Kingdom got its first comprehensive law to cover adult vocational training: the Industrial Training Act. For each sector of economic activity a semi-independent training board of employers, labour and civil servants was created to promote training and to levy a training tax on employers. The latter were encouraged to undertake training by being given a refund of tax to pay for the training they actually did. Significantly the law maintained the distinction between training, which was to be the responsibility of the Ministry of Employment, and education, the job of the Ministry of Education. In 1973, to cover the gaps and weaknesses in the training board system, a new law, the Employment and Training Act, set up the Manpower Services Commission with powers over the whole range of training and of labour planning. It has strengthened rather than reduced the distinction.

Fifty years after the Smith Report it seemed time to re-examine adult education, so the Government was at last persuaded to set up the Russell Committee in England and Wales and the Alexander Committee in Scotland to undertake the task. Vocational education was excluded from their remit, although it is clear from their Reports, in 1973 and 1975 respectively, that they found it difficult to conform to this. The Reports, on very similar data, came to markedly different conclusions. Basically, the Russell Committee recommended more money to do more of the same, but with greater efforts to reach the educationally and socially disadvantaged.[4] The Alexander Committee was far less satisfied with adult education's record and recommended it be merged with the Youth and Community Service to form a Community Education Service, which would reach all ages in conformity with the principles of lifelong education, and particularly those untouched by traditional adult course provisions.[5]

Although both reports were approved and steps were taken to implement many of their recommendations, the major one, that more money should be made available, has been ignored. The State pays lip service to the importance of adult education as an essential part of lifelong learning, but at a time of public spending cuts — and under both Labour and Conservative Governments — it has suffered a disproportionate share of the reductions in education expenditure. As in so many other areas, in adult education the United Kingdom appears to have lost its way. Thirty years ago it could justly claim to lead Europe, but now in many aspects of provision it has long been surpassed. There is no overall national policy and little sign that, like other countries, it is moving towards one. It may still have something to contribute to European practice, however, since even in the latest decade such initiatives as the Open University and the adult literacy scheme have been developed, to set alongside older features of British adult education, including local authority provision, university extra-mural work and community colleges.

Local authority adult education in the United Kingdom

Traditional British concern to keep control over matters affecting local life in local hands and out of those of the Crown has had a significant effect on the national education system. It helped to delay compulsory schooling, which even today is not uniform throughout the country, since the curriculum of a school is determined locally and teachers are local employees, not civil servants. Even the public examination system is not a national one, but in the hands of different universities.

When, therefore, the Government, alarmed at foreign threats to Britain's industrial lead, wished to increase the teaching of science in the country, as it did on successive occasions in the second half of the nineteenth century, it would have been considered beyond its powers to decree that this should occur. Instead it encouraged those bodies which did decide what should be taught — private associations, for example, Mechanics' Institutes, and later local school boards — by offering subsidies to science classes. There was further encouragement in 1889 when local authorities were empowered to levy taxes to finance technical education. These were the first authorizations of public expenditure on the education of adults and brought local authorities into this field of activity.

The 1902 Education Act made county councils, and those large municipal councils that were given county status, into local education authorities, responsible for all publicly-provided education in their localities. It also had an important effect on adult education in that it empowered the LEAs, whose provision had hitherto been restricted to technical and manual instruction, to offer evening classes without limitation of subject. There was some development before the First World War, and the Smith Report of 1919 gave a further boost by recommending both that LEAs should form joint committees with universities and the Workers' Educational Association to provide liberal adult education, and that they should also create evening institutes for social, recreational and educational activities, especially for young people.[6]

There were variations in the nature and extent of authority involvement between the wars, but nearly all voluntary organizations, including universities and the WEA, received assistance in accommodation and funds. In some cases LEAs organized and maintained classes for voluntary bodies, a precedent which was not without significance for the survival of the voluntary contribution to adult education. Up to the middle 1920s local authorities' own evening classes were mainly restricted to continuation of the school curriculum, vocational preparation and, on the non-vocational side, basic instruction in reading and writing, together with practical and hobby classes, such as dressmaking, cookery, woodwork. From that period an increasing number of them offered literary, cultural and scientific classes of a non-vocational nature.[7]

This provision was optional. The 1944 Education Act (England and Wales) laid down, however:

> It shall be the duty of every local education authority to secure the provision for their area of adequate facilities for further education, that is to say:
> (a)   full-time and part-time education for persons over compulsory school age;
> (b)   leisure time occupation in such organised cultural training and recreative activities as are suited to their requirements, for any persons over compulsory school age who are able and willing to profit by the facilities provided for that purpose.[8]

In 1945 a similar Act covered Scotland. From that time adult education has been understood as an obligation of local education authorities.

Provision under (a) above was made by colleges of further education (FE), principally providing courses leading to public certificates of general education and to occupational qualifications over the whole range of economic activity. Their principal clientele is in the sixteen to twenty years age range, but they also attract a large number of older adults, seeking to improve their general or vocational education. Some institutions offer courses leading to degrees, validated by the Council for National Academic Awards. In the last decade many local education authorities have established polytechnics, colleges of higher education, providing full and part-time courses intended to lead to more vocationally-oriented degrees than those of universities. They mostly attract young people straight from school, but they also have a proportion of mature students.

It is in the field of non-vocational, non-certificate courses that the legal obligation laid upon local authorities has had the greatest effect on the pattern of adult education provisions. The law said they were 'to secure provision', not necessarily to provide it themselves. They could have subsidized voluntary bodies to undertake the task, as happens in other countries, they were indeed required by the law 'to have regard to the expediency of co-operating with voluntary societies or bodies'. Without exception however, interpreting the latter requirement very loosely, local education authorities fulfilled their obligation by making provision themselves. They have done so to such an extent that they are now the dominant providers, the number of students participating annually in LEA courses, around 2,500,000, being over nine times those in courses offered by the only other significant organizations, the universities and the WEA.[9]

Non-vocational adult work is done in three different types of institution. First there is the adult centre which may be a programme of classes during the evening in what is a school during the day, under the direction of a part-time evening principal, or it may have its own premises, under a full-time principal, and give both daytime and evening classes. Second, there is provision in FE colleges, which in some cases have their own department of adult education. Third, there is the community college, which is discussed on page 29.

The kind of activities provided is much the same as in the 1930s, with some broadening of scope to meet the higher expectations of the post-war generation. Practical arts and crafts and hobbies, among which one may include foreign languages, are the most popular. Large centres in the main urban areas also offer literacy, cultural and scientific studies, role education, such as courses in child rearing for parents, or training in chairmanship for officials of voluntary associations, and courses which examine issues of public importance, for example, race relations. Subjects taught are decided by the principal, largely on the basis of what there has been a demand for in the past. Some take a more positive approach, seeking to reach out and attract people who have not previously been drawn to adult education, offering seminars, lectures, and organizing activities in response to what they detect as being of current concern in the community that the centre serves. An increasing number of centres involve representatives of the student body in the planning and management of programmes.

Participants have, until recently, been required to pay only a small percentage of the cost of activities. The rest has been met by the local education authority, out of local taxes and out of the general grant from national taxation made by the State to each local authority to help pay for all local services. Most staff are part time, but, in England and Wales at least, there has grown up a cadre of full-time administrators and teacher—organizers for non-vocational adult education. Some senior full-time staff have had training in adult education, but it is not compulsory. Local authorities themselves frequently organize short training courses for part-time teachers and administrators.

The wide variations from authority to authority in the range and quality of adult education provision are largely due to the freedom each has to decide what constitutes 'adequate facilities' and the differing degrees of interest in adult education shown by its senior education administrators. The law gives little guidance; most assistance has come in very general terms from the civil servants of the education ministries in London and Edinburgh. According to the Russell Report, the total expenditure on non-vocational adult education in 1968—9 in England and Wales, of which local education authorities spent £16,000,000, was £17,400,000. This total was barely one per cent of national expenditure on education and the proportion has not improved since then.

In fact it has probably got worse. Not only are the provisions of the 1944 Act and its Scottish counterpart vague but there are legal loopholes in them by which local authorities can avoid altogether the obligation to provide adult education. These were first used in the 1960s at a time of economic crisis[10] and have been used again in 1979—80. The Conservative Government, for economic and ideological reasons, imposed large cuts in both central and local government spending. Of the reductions made by LEAs in education a disproportionate amount fell on adult education. Some counties announced their intention of abolishing non-vocational provision completely. In part they acted in this way because the imprecision of the law gave them more freedom of action in adult education than in other sectors, where their obligations were precisely defined.[11] It must also be said that declarations of some in authority have made it clear, if it needed to be, that non-vocational adult education is regarded, if not as a luxury, then as desirable rather than essential. This is clearly the view of the State, whose wielding of its subsidy support as a weapon to impose its will on LEAs not only has exposed the grace and favour nature of their independence, but has shown too the State's intention to intervene, whereas in the past it has largely refrained from doing so. It is, for example, pushing local authorities to raise the full cost of non-vocational adult education from student fees, an action which goes directly against the principle that no adult shall be barred from adult courses by financial considerations.

Adult education is always likely to be a marginal concern of bodies whose main responsibility is for schools and colleges. One may therefore regret that local education authorities have so effectively taken over adult education from voluntary bodies during the century. It might have been defended if it had been provided, as it is in the Scandinavian countries, for example, by organizations for which it is their prime reason for existence. One is led to ask why the United Kingdom is the only country in Western Europe, having so extensive a provision of non-vocational activities, where it is in fact if not by law, a virtual monopoly of public authority (only the Workers' Educational Association remains a private provider of national importance and its provision is smaller, not only than that of local authorities, but of universities too).

As in other matters, it can be in part explained by the fact that Britain was first in the field. Voluntary bodies in other European countries, although rooted in the nineteenth century, established themselves as *the* providers in the non-vocational sector during the first half of the twentieth century, partly because there was no competition from public authorities. For economic reasons British local authorities were already providing technical classes by the end of the nineteenth century and the extension of their work to non-vocational courses, while it shows early enlightenment by Government, was facilitated by this precedent. By the time other governments came to consider intervention, the voluntary associations were too well entrenched for it to be practical politics to change them. Besides there had developed a theory of the value of self-help and local decision making in meeting adult needs, which made them appear more appropriate as providers.

In the United Kingdom this argument had less force, because of the greater devolution of authority in public education to local level. On the mainland of Europe adult educators were suspicious either of the State's remoteness, or its tyranny. In Britain there was nothing in the recent national past to inspire fear of State tyranny and local authorities were given their considerable powers to keep decision making close to those affected by the decisions, so that the latter could influence them and feel responsible for them.

In the first half of this century voluntary bodies were too pleased to see adult education grow through local education authorities to fear replacement by them. There were no signs of the alarm displayed by their Swedish counterparts, for example, in the 1960s, or by the French after the Second World War. The result is that the voluntary element in British adult education is smaller than in any other Western European country. As local authorities have grown larger and more remote, the effective say of the adult in what is provided for him becomes less. There is a potential for voluntary action, as the adult literacy scheme has shown, but in the hungry 1970s, when even the State favoured private initiative to replace reduced public support, the United Kingdom did not have the firmly-based, experienced associations, which are, for example, guarantors of the continuing health of non-

vocational adult education in Scandinavia and other parts of
Europe.

British community colleges

One may mourn the current state of local education authority
adult provision in the United Kingdom, but it would be quite
wrong to decry its achievements. LEAs were largely responsible for creating a national network of adult learning opportunities sooner and on a larger scale than in any other European state. Other countries may have surpassed this provision
now, but even since the Second World War local authority
initiative and imagination have developed new institutions,
which have attracted admiration and imitation abroad. Perhaps the main example is the community college.[12]

The idea of such an institution originated with Henry
Morris, the chief education official for the County of Cambridgeshire between the wars. Believing that the village
was too small to furnish for itself the social and educational
services needed in modern conditions, he planned to group
villages together and furnish each group with what he called
a village college, 'which would provide for the co-ordination
and development of all forms of education — primary,
secondary, further and adult education — together with social
and recreational facilities, and at the same time furnish a
community centre for the neighbourhood'.[13] Only four such
institutions had been built when the Second World War broke
out.

The idea was taken up again after the war in Leicestershire.
In 1949 the scheme of further education which the county
council presented to the Ministry of Education in accordance
with the requirements of the 1944 Education Act, was
regarded by the County Education Committee 'as being
essential, if the work of the primary and secondary schools is to
bear full fruit . . .'[14] It was therefore thinking of education,
well before the formulation of the concept of lifelong education, as a continuing process and, perhaps more significantly
for the development of community colleges, further education
was conceived in terms of what it could do for primary and
secondary education. The scheme includes proposals for

institutions on the Cambridgeshire model, which, since they were to be built in urban as well as rural areas, were to be called community colleges. Over the years since the first one was opened, in 1958, twenty-five more have been established in the county, other local authorities, notably Cumbria, Nottinghamshire, Devon and Coventry have made them a major element in their policy and examples are to be found in new towns, such as Milton Keynes and Telford, and in large cities, such as Manchester and London. In Scotland the new town of Livingston has one, so has Edinburgh.

There are variations in form, idea and even name (some are designated community schools, rather than colleges) but a general picture can be drawn of the realization of the concept. The purpose is to move towards the integrated educational experience envisaged in lifelong education by bringing into close relationship school, out-of-school and post-school education, together with other socio-cultural activities; to involve the community it serves with the school and the school with the community, as a means of strengthening support for what the school is trying to achieve and making what it does more suitable for current needs and as a means of creating or reinforcing the sense of community, that is the consciousness of common interests and interdependence in inhabitants of the same locality, the disappearance of which is held to contribute to alienation and anomie, so frequent in contemporary society; and to make possible maximum utilization of school facilities and provide for the community facilities which it otherwise would not be able to afford.

Physically a community college can be seen as a secondary school building, with all the class rooms, gymnasia, laboratories and other accommodation necessary to its school function, to which have been added social and administrative rooms for adults and for out-of-school youth activities. To achieve the community purpose, however, this apparently routine architectural task must be fulfilled in such a way that each group of users may indulge its own specific interests without interfering with those of the others, and that at the same time it is not excluded from contact with the others, but this contact is encouraged so as to create an all-age community at all times of the day. Physically the focus of this meeting is the social rooms, cafeteria and library, but it also occurs through shared use of school facilities, which form the major part of the complex, and which must be suitable for, or adaptable to, this shared use.[15]

But the building alone does not make a community college. There is, for example, the question of staff. The Principal is almost invariably the Head of the school, with additional duties as head of adult and youth work. A full-time adult tutor and one responsible for youth work are normal. In some cases the tendency is to appoint community tutors, combining youth and adult responsibilities. In others adult and youth workers have some teaching in the school, which is intended to make easier their integration within, and acceptance by, the much larger school staff. In pursuit of closer integration Leicestershire is attempting to move to an arrangement whereby a proportion of the working time of all school teaching staff is allocated to youth or adult work.

Involvement of the community in the college must realistically accord it some place in its government and control of finance. This is complicated by the necessity of fitting the management of the community college with that fixed for a secondary school, whether within a college or not, and is done in a number of ways.[16] In Leicestershire the policy and general management of the college were made the responsibility of the college council. Three of its members are co-opted to the school governors and six governors serve on the council. Its other members are

> . . . two representatives appointed annually from each of the affiliated bodies; one representative elected from the individual college membership for each fifty members of the college; one representative elected from the individual membership of the youth wing for each fifty members of the youth wing; the officers of the Community College; six representatives of the teaching staff of the college and its extra-mural classes.[17]

It may also co-opt members. It was believed that this council could respond more sensitively if it managed its own funds for adult, youth and community work. Each year the council is granted by the local authority a sum intended to meet the fees of part-time teachers, youth leaders and other workers, plus a sum for materials, publicity and travelling. It has considerable freedom in the use of these monies, some of the allocation for one purpose may be used for others. If the council exceeds the budget granted to it, then it must raise the extra cash by its own efforts and this often happens, so that the community is engaged to some degree in an exercise of self-help.

A community college houses within it all the activities of a school, a programme of evening and, increasingly, daytime courses for adults, and a youth club. Participants in these are individual members of the college. In addition the college hosts many clubs and associations involved in community service and action, in social, arts, physical and other recreational activities, whose members are engaged in the college through the affiliation of the society to it. The college is a community centre, with, in many cases, a bar and cafeteria, into which local residents may drop for a meal, a drink and casual social contacts, or for a swim in the college pool, or a game of badminton, or to read in, or borrow a book from, the library. It is also engaged in and often provides the starting point of action in matters concerning the community it serves — work with the elderly and the handicapped, action to improve public transport, assistance to the unemployed, links between the community and others abroad, local debates on the Common Market and plans for new roads are only a few chosen at random.[18]

The considerable successes to which community colleges can point have reduced the opposition to them that existed in their early days, but there still exist many reasons for doubt. An independent survey of its provision commissioned by Leicestershire, which was generally favourable in its conclusions and constructively critical,[19] reported of college adult education work that it attracted a higher proportion of the population of its catchment area than conventional adult centres did, but that the cost per enrolment was nine per cent higher, both points explicable, it is to be noted, by the superior facilities on offer. The range of courses was orthodox and showed no direct attention to communal problems, such as might have been expected of an institution claiming a prime community orientation. There was the same bias in the student body towards older people, predominantly women, of above average initial education, as in other adult education centres. The survey pointed out that inherent in local budgeting and voluntary involvement in management was the danger that this bias would be reinforced, as management committees tended to arrange programmes to suit their own interests and those of people like them.

This point was taken up by a national study of adult education institutions and the people who work in them.[20] It found that institutions which had student participation in planning programmes were more likely to be conventional and less likely to be innovative than those that did not. It reported that adult educators in specialized adult education institutions, who had experience of community schools, preferred the former. There were complaints that the role of community schools was unclear. In particular the study reported staff opinion that facilities in community schools were not integrated. Far from community activities having good access to school facilities, the school often threatened to take over those designed for community use. The main reason for this seemed to be that principals gave priority in their values to the school and that the great majority of staff were by training and outlook school teachers. The study noted that when the community college arrangement was praised, it was in terms of the benefit it brought to the *school*, not to adult education or the community.

The authors point out that community colleges are operated by people who were not trained to do so and that it would be fairer to evaluate them when they are staffed by trained community educators rather than by school teachers, adult educators, or youth workers. In the United Kingdom, at least, there is no sign that this will happen in the foreseeable future. There will not be the money to build the large multi-purpose edifices that have been so admired internationally. If it is objected that the community college concept does not depend on physical plant, then one would point to the evidence in Dr Hutchinson's Leicestershire survey that it is facilities that attract affiliated associations and give the college an advantage over ordinary adult centres. There is a growing doubt, anyway, whether the edifice of the college is calculated to attract the uncommitted adult and some belief that a more modest neighbourhood facility might be more successful. And, as the different parts of the education service fight for a share of the greatly reduced national expenditure on education, the danger is that each will become more separatist to defend its own particular field.

There is little evidence that training institutions are now forming community educators, rather than the sector specialists they have produced in the past, and less likelihood that it will seem worth while for them to do so in the future.

It is all too possible that the community college in Britain belongs to an era of affluence that is past, but in that period it captured the imagination of educators in a number of European countries. France has what are called integrated facilities, much influenced by British models, as for example Yerres, Grenoble and Istres. They too combine a school, adult, youth and community provision. French experience indicates how important to the establishment of community colleges the British system of educational administration has been. In France the centralization of decision making in Paris and the division of responsibility among a number of ministries has made it difficult to get an integrated facility including a school established and, once it has been established, it has been hard to achieve that devolution of authority to the institution, without which speed and flexibility of response to local needs are hardly possible.[21] There is a further problem in France: the separation of the formal school system from out-of-school and informal post-school activities, which go under the name of socio-cultural animation. Not only do teachers, particularly secondary teachers, consider extracurricular and community activities even more marginal than their British counterparts, but to a considerable degree sociocultural animation has traditionally seen itself as a reaction against school (see Chapter 5). These attitudes may be changing, but there is a lot of life in them yet.

It is significant that the community college, or school as it is called in North America, flourishes best in those countries — the United States of America and the United Kingdom — where devolution of policy and operational decision making is considerable. Increasing central government control of British education is one factor which threatens the future of the community college and the observable fact that no Western European country has decentralized authority over schools as the United Kingdom has does not promise them a bright future on the European mainland. What one tends to find there is all the community college's other facilities, even on a grander scale, but without the school.

British university adult education

The one feature of adult education in the United Kingdom of which every foreign educator has heard is university extension. It was born of a concatenation of circumstances peculiar to the country at a time when it could provide a specially attractive example to pioneers abroad. The circumstances were that British universities had freedom of action, deriving from their status as private corporations, fixed individually by charter; there was in the mid-nineteenth century a shortage of universities in England and Wales only four, Oxford, Cambridge, London and Durham; at that time the two first and oldest were in the middle of long overdue reform and were receptive to ideas that would extend university education to a wider public; there was growing demand from the middle class, particularly the females, who had up to then been denied higher education; the working class, many of whom had achieved the vote in 1867, and whom a number of university men were anxious to educate in the exercise of their new power, had not even access to secondary education. In these circumstances Oxford and Cambridge responded to need by offering lecture courses, organized by committees of the university, in areas of the country where there had previously been no higher education. They were joined by London, by Durham and by the new university institutions which were being established, in some degree encouraged by university extension, towards the end of the century. The generally accepted date for the beginning of this movement is 1873, though experiments had been made earlier, and it attracted thousands of students.[22]

Although very successful in attracting women and older middle class men, it did not really succeed in reaching workers to a satisfactory degree until the foundation of the Workers' Educational Association, a working-class organization to reach a working-class public and articulate its needs, which entered into a long and fruitful collaboration with the universities. From 1908 began, at Oxford, the system whereby programmes in an area served by a university were administered by a joint committee of the university and the WEA, the former providing the teaching resources and the latter, through its local branches, detecting and encouraging local needs and organizing the classes.

The success of this collaboration owed much to financial support from public authorities, which became available in the first decade of the twentieth century, and to the tutorial class, limited in numbers (about thirty members), committed to studying for twenty-four meetings annually over three years and to producing regular written work. When the Smith Report appeared in 1919 it was sufficiently impressed by the work done to recommend that each university should set up an extra-mural department with full-time academic and administrative staff to develop its adult work and that a central government grant should be given to other than tutorial classes, which already received it. By the outbreak of the Second World War almost every university in England and Wales had such a department.

Association with the WEA had concentrated universities' intentions on working-class adults. Extra-mural departments wanted to widen their efforts beyond class lines, as early extension work had done, and they were encouraged in this by the 1944 and 1945 Education Acts, which offered education to all post-school persons who were 'able and willing to profit by the facilities provided for the purpose'. Since the Second World War, therefore, a process begun before 1939, whereby links with the WEA loosened and the proportion of tutorial classes declined, has intensified.

By the 1944 Act and the Further Education Regulations associated with it, universities in England and Wales were confirmed as Responsible Bodies, that is, they were entitled to receive direct subsidies from the Ministry of Education for their adult education work, at a level which was fixed just after the war at seventy-five per cent of staff salaries and teaching costs. This stimulated growth in extra-mural departments but it also had a limiting effect, for adult education was defined by the Ministry as liberal, non-vocational education and the grant could only be used for that. In Scotland, where universities were not Responsible Bodies, they had to depend on university funds and local authorities to finance their work, with the result that growth was slower but the range of activity was less restricted.

Four periods may be identified in the post-war history of university adult education: a period of rapid growth immediately after 1945; then years of comparative stagnation throughout the 1950s; a decade of considerable growth in the 1960s, associated with the general expansion of higher education; then the 1970s, in which economic pressures have called the existence of extra-mural departments, if not university adult education, into question. In these years the number of universities and university colleges having academic and/or administrative staff employed full time in adult education rose to thirty-seven. Some have only a single person, but Leeds and London each have over forty and several others more than thirty in adult education departments headed by a professor (the name 'extra-mural department' is increasingly being replaced by other titles).[23]

The United Kingdom is divided so that every part of the territory is the responsibility of an extra-mural department. Even the isolated islands to the north and west of Scotland receive their periodic university lectures. Departments have their own premises within the university, they use other university facilities, some have residential centres of their own and premises in other towns, but for most of their accommodation away from the campus they rely on the free use of local education authority schools. Through this network of provision they achieved a total student enrolment in 1978—9 of 236,000. For the most part classes meet in once-a-week courses, held in the evenings, whose duration ranges from half a dozen meetings to several years. Over the years to these have been added many held in the daytime, for housewives, the elderly, shift workers and the unemployed. There has also been a growing number of courses requiring consecutive attendance for one day, or for several weeks. Including weekend schools the latter amounted to 2,353 in 1978—9.[24]

Liberal studies still account for the major part of the work. The early classes were predominantly in economics and the social sciences but there was a swing between the wars to philosophy, psychology, literature and music, and nowadays the most popular subject areas are English language and literature, the visual arts, music, archaeology, local history, the physical and biological sciences. While most universities are attached to these courses, open to an unselected public and generally sanctioned by the award of no certificate, they have sought to go beyond them. They have argued that there are other adult education needs to be fulfilled by universities and that liberal education depends not on what subjects are taught but on the manner in which it is taught. The Universities Council for Adult Education, the national association of extra-mural departments, has quoted as the aims of its work those set out for universities as a whole by a government commission of enquiry on higher education, the Robbins Committee, in the early 1960s:

> . . . what is taught should be taught in such a way as to promote the general powers of the mind. The aim should be not to produce mere specialists, but, rather, cultivated men and women. And it is the distinguishing characteristic of a healthy higher education that, even when it is concerned with practical techniques, it imparts them on a plane of generality that makes possible their application to many problems — to find the one in the many, the general characteristic in the collection of particulars. [25]

To an increasing extent, calling on other sources of finance — the Ministry of Health and Social Service, employers, professional associations and other vocational training funds, trade unions — not merely to pay for courses, but also staff salaries, they offer study for specialized groups, frequently leading to diplomas and degrees. They have rejected the distinction between the vocational and non-vocational. Extramural departments have been pioneers in social work training, have contributed to the education of magistrates, police, prison officers and the armed services, have been active in trade union training and industrial relations education and have offered high-level post-experience education for scientific, professional and business personnel. A number have been particularly active in the study of adult education as a discipline and in the training of adult educators, both full and part-time.

Extra-mural departments have diversified their programmes as a principle, following the tradition of extending university education to meet specific needs and to make it available to all those able to profit by it. Increasingly in these last years they have also diversified in self-defence. Liberal studies courses may be open to the whole adult public, but they have become more and more the preserve of older women having at least secondary and in many cases higher education qualifications. In the United Kingdom, as elsewhere, the bias of adult education policy is towards the economically relevant and, in the non-vocational area, to the educationally disadvantaged. Traditional university liberal adult studies serve neither of these. In Great Britain the belief has grown that the predominance of liberal education and the consequent devaluation of vocationally-oriented studies has contributed to the country's economic decline. As a result the value of universities as a whole is being questioned, with further pressure on their extra-mural departments.

The universities, on the defensive, threatened by a decline in the number of registered students because of smaller age cohorts rising to university age, are seeking to prove themselves more relevant to society's needs and to make up for the drop in undergraduates by expanding their work in continuing education. They too question the liberal studies work of extra-mural departments. On the other hand, while they approve of the latter's specialized social and economic role education, they are increasingly of the mind that all departments of the university must undertake such work as an integral part of their function. If the whole institution is involved in the community in this way, some are wondering, will a specialized extra-mural department be necessary? The temptation to say 'no' is very great at a time when universities, hard hit by cuts in their budgets, are having to make greater savings than at any time in this century.

The era in which British university adult education had most influence on other European countries spanned the last years of the nineteenth and the first of the twentieth centuries. France, Germany, Scandinavia, the Netherlands, Austria, even Italy were affected. It was not their universities which followed the British example, however, but private associations, evening folk high schools and people's universities, in which university staff were often active as individuals. The reasons are many, but several stand out. There was not the unsatisfied demand for higher education among the middle class, which was to be found in Britain. There was hostility to universities for political, social and pedagogic reasons among workers.

Above all, universities refused to accept any responsibility for the public outside their walls. They saw themselves primarily as centres of scholarship, with a secondary function of passing on the knowledge they had gained to those who were intellectually advanced enough to understand it. In Oxford and Cambridge, whose traditions informed subsequent British universities, the reverse was the case. European universities had no commitment to the community, as the British had, and they continued to feel none until well after the Second World War. In 1956 Professor Wilpert, of Cologne, said: 'Looking at it [the question of responsibility to the community] from inside the university I would deny any such responsibility. A university's sole function is to do its best in its research work and to teach what its members have discovered.'

At the same meeting Monsieur Babin, Rector of the University of Strasbourg declared: 'French higher education cannot possibly be made directly responsible for adult education . . . To include such a task among the duties of a university professor would be . . . to play down to the common man, which would be of no use or benefit to anyone'.[26]

There were one or two exceptions, for example Tampere in Finland between the wars, Göttingen in Federal Germany, the universities of Norway and Denmark since the Second World War, which have offered extra-mural programmes to the general public, but they have been few. It is only in the last twenty years that adult education has been seen as an essential part of the universities' role. They have accepted this less of their own initiative than under social pressure, inspired by the principles of lifelong education and equality of opportunity, and the economic need for advanced post-experience education of a vocational nature. The Missions of Lifelong Education, promoted and financed by the State in French universities since 1972, which now number over eighty, are basically agencies for the implementation of the vocational training law of 1971. The Federal German universities, which compose the Working Group for University Adult Education, are for the most part concerned with post-experience courses for graduates of higher education. In Sweden the emphasis lies on opening full-time degree courses to adults.

It would be hard to see the influence of British practice in these recent developments and if it were to be found it would be that of post-war innovations, not of liberal studies courses.

In fact these days Britain is more likely to be influenced by continental practice than vice versa — with one significant exception, the Open University.

The Open University

The early 1960s were a time of considerable development of higher education in the United Kingdom. Because of the growth of secondary education there were many more people with the basic qualifications for entry, but, under the selective entry system, no places in universities for them. The Robbins Report (1963) recommended that there should be expansion to take all those who could profit from such an education and a number of new universities were being established. There was concern that the new places should be more equitably distributed over the social classes: only four per cent of children of working people, according to Robbins, entered higher education, compared with forty-five per cent of those whose fathers were in the higher professional classes.[27]

These proposed changes would, however, do little for those who were already adults and had missed higher education in their youth. Hardly any opportunities for part-time degree study, such as existed abroad, were offered by British universities. There was a strong feeling that the nationally adopted principle of equal educational opportunity for all demanded that something should be done for them. At the same time the success of educational broadcasting, particularly through the developing medium of television, had opened a vigorous debate on how the medium could best be used.

All these elements were brought together by Harold Wilson in a speech in 1963. He proposed a University of the Air. When, as a result of the General Election of 1964, he became Prime Minister, he appointed one of his Ministers, Jennie Lee, to realize his idea. It was the combination of power and determination in these people, plus the skill and energy of Lord Perry, its first Vice-Chancellor, that made the Open University a reality. By the time it opened to students, however, political and educational realities had changed the original concept. It was a full and independent university, on the same legal footing as other British ones, offering its own degrees. It was open in the sense that no educational qualifications were required as a condition for entry to its courses. It was a distance learning institution, in which tuition was done by a combination of correspondence and broadcasting, but there was also a small amount of face-to-face contact between students and academic staff.

The Open University has five faculties: Arts, Social Sciences, Educational Studies, Science and Technology. Other faculties, such as Law and Medicine, and subject areas, such as modern languages, were excluded at the beginning, for financial and organizational reasons, and the economic climate has never permitted expansion into these fields, although it was hoped for. Seventy-five courses were originally planned and now there are over one hundred. One basic degree is offered — Bachelor of Arts, which may be obtained at Ordinary or Honours level. Each course lasts thirty-six weeks, plus a one-week residential Summer School. Some shorter courses, worth a half credit, are also offered. To obtain an Ordinary degree a student must gain two Foundation (first year) and four other credits, for an Honours degree another two are required. Since a student can only take two courses a year, three years at least are required for an Ordinary and four for an Honours degree, although students with previous qualifications may be granted some credit for these and thus shorten their studies.

As a distance learning institution, the Open University relies to a large extent on the high quality of its course material for success. Each course is prepared by a course team, including academics, educational technologists and BBC producers. They produce a correspondence text, television and radio programmes, which are closely co-ordinated. It is an expensive way of producing a course, only justifiable with large numbers of students. There are obvious limitations on the academic freedom of the individual teacher, heightened by the political consideration that broadcasts may be seen by and influence a mass audience. Because of cost and time the course, once prepared, is difficult to change, which means that it is more rigid than the face-to-face lecture course given in a conventional university, although the latter may be inferior in quality.

By deliberate policy the correspondence text, which

contains the essential matter of each week's lesson, is expensively produced, to make the student feel he is not getting tuition on the cheap. At Foundation Level there is a television and radio broadcast every week but other courses, of which there are now over one hundred, have less, according to their need. This is due to shortage of air time and money. The BBC broadcasts Open University programmes on its regular television and radio channels and is only able to give about twenty-five hours of radio and thirty-five hours of television time each week. To enable a student to do the practical work necessary in high level science courses the university provides each science student with an advanced home experiment kit, which was devised by university staff.

It was decided early on that, from what was known about adult learning problems, pure distance teaching would be inadequate to many of the students the Open University hoped to attract. Therefore a network of local back-up services is provided, divided nationally into thirteen regions, each under a regional director. Under these work 5,000 part-time course tutors and tutor-counsellors, mostly full-time staff of other universities and institutions of higher education. Their job is to help students with their learning and other difficulties, which may affect their study. Each student has a counsellor for general guidance plus a tutor for each course he takes. The tutor marks his written assignments and conducts tutorials at study centres, of which there are 259 in schools, universities and community centres throughout the country. In these centres there are facilities for television and radio receiving, for video and radio playback, and for discussion groups. Participation in these face-to-face activities is optional and varies greatly from student to student.

Assessment of a student's work is done by a combination of continuous assessment and examination. Every three or four weeks he is given a series of multiple choice questions which on completion are sent to the Open University headquarters and there marked by computer. He also has to write an essay-type assignment, marked by his tutor. To ensure uniformity of standard samples of Tutor-marked Assignments are further marked by staff at headquarters. At the end of each course each student must sit an examination at a local centre.

Although no educational qualifications are required, entry to the university is not completely open, because of limitations in its own resources. Annually there are more applications than places available for new students. Selection is on a first come first served basis, modified by quotas set for different regions, different occupations (to favour the working class applicant) and to ensure a balance between applicants for different faculties. The selection is done by computer. In the first year, 1970, 24,200 students began the course out of 43,000 applicants.[28] In 1979 there were 21,000 admissions out of 42,764 who applied. Students, once accepted, are automatically accepted for subsequent years. In the years 1971—8 inclusive 116,696 students were finally registered, of whom 32,552 had received degrees by 1979, and others would no doubt qualify in subsequent years. Of entrants in 1971, 54.3 per cent had graduated.[29]

Although the Open University has the same legal status as other universities, its special situation is recognized in that, instead of its annual budget being recommended through the University Grants Committee, as that of its sister institutions is, it receives direct funding from the Department of Education and Science (for England and Wales, although the Open University serves Scotland and Northern Ireland too). In general eighty-nine per cent of its budget is met by ministry grant, nine per cent from student fees and two per cent from other sources, including research funds. Fees are charged by all British universities, but full-time students entering university direct from school automatically receive a grant to cover fees, from their local authority (England and Wales) or the State (Scotland). This regulation does not apply to part-time adult students, so Open University entrants have a burden, amounting to £67 per course (1980), which does not face younger full-time students.

From the beginning it was clear that there existed for single courses a public which did not wish to undertake a full degree. Many courses are now open to such people and some are specially designed for them, for the university sees it as a duty to play a leading role in the field of continuing education outside the degree field. Indeed a committee of the Open University published an influential report on the subject.[30] As a university it could only attract first-class staff if it

44

offered research possibilities and, in addition to staff research, there are a number of students working for higher degrees.

The Open University began in the face of strong opposition from both the political and educational establishments. It was argued that it would not work, that the country could not afford it and, if it could, the money could be better spent on other forms of adult education. Much of the institution, as it now exists, has been determined by the need to win public acceptance within the financial resources set.

It was argued that, if such a multi-media organization were to be created, there was a greater need for secondary education than higher. Lord Perry has conceded that this argument had force, but says that it would have lacked the prestige to gain the support. Because a university would do that, it had to be a university.[31] The institution was presented as offering the opportunity of higher learning to people who had not previously received it, and as being open to anyone who applied. Its students disappointed some people because, although they had for the most part missed higher education in youth, they were not members of the working class. A survey conducted by the Open University showed, however, that eighty-five per cent were children of working class parents and would have been disadvantaged therefore at the normal age for entry to higher education.[32]

The question of unrestricted entry was never a real possibility if the university was to give the individual care to its students that United Kingdom universities are accustomed to offer. Organizational, as well as financial, realities would have prevented it. Press publicity (not inspired by the Open University) led some people to expect teaching to be mainly done by radio and television, but this too was not a practical proposition, particularly when it became clear that a fourth television channel would not be made available. As a result the Open University is essentially a correspondence institution with extensive local back up, and it becomes more so as the number of courses rises but the amount of air time does not.

Once it had been decided that the Open University should exist, its overriding need was to achieve academic respectability; its degrees had to gain acceptance as of a similar standard to those of other universities, by the latter, by employers and by students. This concern, essential as it has been to its survival, has determined the range and kind of courses offered, and to that extent student learning need has come second.[33] Claims have been made by the Open University that it costs little more than half as much as a conventional university to take a student through to a degree. It may be cheaper to some extent, but costs are not really comparable, because the Open University depends on the premises and part-time services of staff belonging to other institutions of higher education throughout the country.[34] Without these its costs would be much higher. Without the existing network of further and higher education it is doubtful whether it could have functioned at all, at least in its present form.

The Open University has aroused much interest in Europe, but probably less there than in other parts of the world. A number of plausible reasons may be proposed for this. Since the general practice in Europe is that those who obtain a higher secondary leaving certificate are automatically assured of a university place, there was perhaps not the same pressure for second-chance higher education as in the United Kingdom. The superior quality of Open University course materials is obviously not so attractive to non-English speaking countries. There has been some doubt about the desirability of a university with national coverage, given that in a number of countries the tradition of devolution of authority from the State to the university is less well established.

In the Netherlands it was decided that secondary education for adults was the chief priority, so the Open School has been the main concern, although proposals for an Open University are now being made. Given the religio-politico-social divisions of the country, discussed in Chapter 7, it is unlikely that there will be one national institution. If there is not then the costs may be too great. Sweden rejected an Open University approach on the grounds that, with its small population and large distances, a virtually unrestricted entry to higher education for adults would be more cost effective (see Chapter 3). The only distance learning university now operating in Western Europe is the University of Hagen in the Federal German province of North Rhine-Westphalia. It will be interesting to see how far it will serve a federal public and, if it does not, if it is viable only on a provincial level.

What other European countries seem to have been most

impressed with is the Open University's total package of multi-media distance teaching, combined with face-to-face tutoring and local back-up on a national scale. If one may hazard a guess, few are likely to apply the lessons to a purely university institution teaching for degrees. It may even be said that the Open University itself is going beyond that in its continuing education programmes. What is more likely is an organization teaching at a number of different levels, of which degree courses will not be the chief. They are more likely to be provided through face-to-face teaching on a part-time basis, given that there is not the same resistance in continental universities to this as there is in the United Kingdom, and given the falling full-time student numbers due to smaller age cohorts in the next few years.

The preceding remarks are not intended in any way to decry the Open University. It has provided higher education to thousands who would otherwise have received none. It has stimulated interest in part-time higher education and helped to make credit transfer from one institution to another easier — it was almost non-existent before the Open University. It has, by its example, raised the standard of teaching materials and even teaching in conventional face-to-face situations. It has made a considerable contribution to thinking about continuing education. It has been, and will continue to be, worth the money and effort. On the other hand, it is, perhaps even more than most recent initiatives in adult education, a product of a particular time and place.

The adult literacy campaign in the United Kingdom

The other major British initiatives in adult education of the 1970s lay at the opposite end of the needs spectrum from the Open University. It had been widely assumed that, after a century of compulsory schooling, illiteracy as a social problem had been overcome. A few researchers had been aware for some time that this was an optimistic view of the situation and, in an *ad hoc* fashion, as is the custom in adult education, a few voluntary associations and local authorities had been providing basic education or literacy classes to meet specific local needs, to which their attention had been drawn.

47

Most people, however, believed that although there were some adults whose mastery of reading and writing was inadequate, these were exceptional.

In the early 1970s it became increasingly obvious that the situation was worse than had been thought. As a result of research and empirical observation, notably publicized by the Biritsh Association of Settlements, the figure of 2,000,000 adult illiterates began to be bandied about.[35] It was a guess, but not an uneducated one. About this time the Russell Report[36] attracted attention to the needs of the educationally disadvantaged. The Government came under pressure to make some positive response. Independently the BBC planned a project on adult literacy. From the coming together of these different elements emerged the adult literacy campaign.

It faced many difficulties. In an advanced society, it was a new problem to have to contact large numbers of people who, by definition, were impervious to written or printed messages. Even if communication was established, experience indicated that under-educated adults were resistant to education, a difficulty compounded by the fact that to come forward would be to admit illiteracy, which, on the available evidence, most were ashamed to do. If the number of illiterates were as large as suggested, it would be a major and costly organizational exercise to attract and teach them, just at a time when local authorities, which were responsible for education, were themselves undergoing major reorganization as a result of local government reform,[37] and were having to make big cuts in expenditure as a consequence of the national economic crisis. From the practical experience already gained, it appeared that the most effective method was individual tuition on the basis of one teacher to each illiterate. It was seen as a delicate task, for which training would be essential. Where would so many tutors be found and how could they be trained?

The difficulties were resolved, in so far as they were, by a threefold collaboration between the broadcasting organizations, the Adult Literacy Resource Agency (ALRA) and local authorities (with an important contribution by voluntary associations). Although commercial broadcasting had some part, the main television and radio role was played by the BBC. It broadcast series of programmes designed to teach illiterate adults and to encourage them to seek further help. It produced training series for tutors of illiterates. Above all, it helped to recruit both students and tutors, particularly by drawing listeners' and viewers' attention to the telephone referral service which had been set up. A different telephone number for each of England, Wales, Scotland and Northern Ireland was broadcast, not only in the literacy programmes but also in others of the Corporation's general output, which adults needing help, or offering their services as tutors, could ring. The referral service would then pass on the name to the appropriate local agency, which would contact the person directly. The service was financed by charitable trust.

The Adult Literacy Resource Agency was set up by the National Institute of Adult Education of England and Wales at the request of the Government, which funded it with £1,000,000 a year for three years. The money was to be used to encourage and enable local authorities to increase, or commence, adult literacy work, in response to the increased demand that was expected because of broadcast and other publicity. The agency and its funds were given a limited life, because it was intended only to stimulate local authorities into action. As the bodies responsible under the 1944 and 1945 Education Acts, it would be their duty to continue it. Initially the Agency made its main contribution in the promotion and financing of training, but it later became increasingly involved in advisory work, the publication of teaching materials for tutors, research and special projects. A similar agency was set up in Scotland.

Because of the responsibility, mentioned in the last paragraph, the principal burden of the adult literacy campaign fell on local education authorities. The State could not provide the tuition itself, under the British system, nor could it compel the authorities to do so. They had to be persuaded and enabled, hence ALRA. With some reluctance their adult education, (in Scotland, community education) services, under-manned and under-financed, took on the task. To provide one-to-one tuition on the scale expected to be required, they would have to rely on volunteer, unpaid tutors, who had not only to be recruited, but, given the sensitivity and difficulties of the students and the tutors' anticipated inexperience, would need to be trained. Since local authority staff had, for the most part, no knowledge of adult literacy work, tutor trainers would themselves have to be trained by the few people in the country who knew something about it. Much importance was attached, especially in the early days of the campaign, to matching potential students to appropriate tutors, another time-consuming task. When that was achieved, local authority staff had to maintain a close supportive relationship with both tutors and students and, if possible, monitor progress. Not surprisingly, as the scheme got under way, most authorities found it necessary to appoint full-time organizers of adult literacy schemes, with, in many cases, part-time paid supervisors and trainers of tutors.

After a period of preparation, usually inadequate for local authorities, the campaign proper ran for three years from 1975, beginning with a programme of broadcasts and the opening of the referral service.[38] By February 1976 ALRA figures showed that 45,767 students were under tuition in England and Wales (in Scotland a little under 1,300 clients had been through the referral service). By February 1978 ALRA estimated that 125,000 students had begun tuition since the start of the campaign, in Scotland figures up to March 1979 showed 11,883 persons.

As anticipated, most teaching was done on a basis of one student to one tutor, in either the student's or the tutor's home. By February 1978 about 75,000 potential tutors had come forward in England and Wales and by March 1979 4,080 in Scotland. The amount of training they received was limited, about six two-hour sessions, because of the importance of getting them into action, to meet both student needs and their own wishes. The great majority of tutors were unpaid, only those supervising groups or taking classes normally received an hourly fee. Between eighty and ninety per cent were women, mostly young and of good educational background. In 1976 a half to one-third were graduates or trained teachers. On the whole their motives were a desire for a personal interest outside home and a wish to help others become literate, the inability to read or write being seen as a great deprivation. Of every one hundred initial volunteers about fifty to sixty attended training courses and thirty-five to forty actually took up teaching.

At the beginning of the campaign four-fifths of the students were men. Women clients later rose to one-third, but always remained a minority.

Table 1   Age distribution of adult literacy students, England and Wales, 1975—6

Age group	%
under 21	16.9
21—30	32.7
31—40	27.4
41—50	15.3
over 50	7.5

Table 1 shows that the higher the age group the smaller the proportion of students, but since it is not known who are the adult illiterates, the significance of this is obscure. Between one half and two-thirds of students were or had been married, but it is not possible to generalize about occupations. Nearly a half seemed to be in relatively skilled or demanding jobs and the number of unemployed was not high. From these data few conclusions can be drawn. If there were 2,000,000 sub-literates in the United Kingdom, only about seven per cent sought help during the campaign and it is to be expected that those who did were the most strongly motivated, that is those in work or other environment where inability to read or write constituted the greatest handicap. Unskilled illiterates from the lowest socio-educational groups were the least likely to return to education, as general experience in adult education has shown.

This may account for the fact, surprising to many tutors, that only thirty per cent of students were absolutely illiterate. Forty per cent had some basic reading ability and thirty per cent could read with ease. The problems of the last group were rather writing and spelling. There were groups with special problems, for example ethnic minorities and prison inmates, for whom provision was made, and physically and mentally handicapped, the slow learners for whom the specialist medical and welfare help they needed seemed to be inadequate once they left school.

On numbers alone the literacy scheme was a success, although the privacy of the one-to-one learning situation made systematic monitoring of performance impossible. It obviously needs to continue, not as a special scheme, but as an integral part of national adult education provision. The campaign helped many people, but, besides indicating possibilities for action, it also left a number of problems unsolved.

It is clear that there are many adults with reading problems and also some with a need for basic education of a wider kind. Some came to the literacy scheme in the latter state, others were led to it by the scheme. Britain must now face the problem of how one prevents the newly literate from relapsing into illiteracy, a question which has long bedevilled work in developing countries, but is this time found pertinent for an advanced society. The privacy of individual tuition by a caring equal built up the confidence of students, for whom the lack of it was often the biggest obstacle to learning. How can the transition from private to group study, necessary for further progress, or even to prevent relapse, be achieved?

The role of voluntary associations and individual voluntary action had become almost insignificant in, if it had not disappeared from, British adult education. The adult literacy scheme showed that both could be mobilized to great effect for the right cause. The scheme was a movement, conventional adult education is an institution, which is now, for economic reasons, threatened by death from starvation. Even Government is interested in the possibility of mobilizing to its aid voluntary help since it cannot afford paid workers. It is doubtful, however, whether the response to such an emotive concept as illiteracy could be transferred to basic education, even less to second-chance secondary education which is concerning countries such as the Scandinavian ones. This is a pity, for a labour intensive, if not a one-to-one, approach might offer a better chance of reaching the chronic non-participants, the ones most in need, about whom adult education in all European countries feels guilty, and this approach could only be undertaken with voluntary labour.

Adult literacy came into being as a national project when different pressures brought central government into action. Without that intervention and the stimulus of national funds, it is questionable whether all local authorities would have responded. Yet a number of their officials believed government action constituted a dangerous precedent, an encroachment on their prerogatives. What is one to do, then, in the United Kingdom when national educational action is required?

Perhaps the most interesting question raised by the British adult literacy scheme is: how far is such action needed in other Western European countries? Except for Portugal, Spain, Italy and Greece, none admit to a problem of basic literacy on the United Kingdom scale, except in so far as they have large populations of migrant workers. Is this, however, a matter of terminology and did the adults in need of basic education, detected by Swedish outreach activity, include a number of illiterates, as the British scheme brought forward some who were under-educated rather than illiterate?

If the British problem is greater, then one is hard put to it to say why. Although English language may be more difficult to spell, it is not harder in other respects than other languages. Schooling is no shorter in the United Kingdom, but there has possibly been less emphasis in recent years on reading and writing drills than in other European countries. Judged by public library records Britons do not read less than, for example, the French. Britain does not have conscription, it is true, and it is during that period that other countries pick up and teach young male illiterates to read. In other respects British culture does not appear to be sufficiently different from that of neighbouring countries to offer an explanation.

Perhaps there is not a great difference between countries. In that case either the United Kingdom has exaggerated its problem, which, in the light of the literacy scheme seems unlikely, or else other states are closing their eyes to theirs.

References

1. THOMAS KELLY, *A History of Adult Education in Great Britain*, Liverpool, Liverpool University Press, 1970.
2. Scotland and Northern Ireland have different educational systems from that of England and Wales. On the whole though, educational legislation in the last two has been paralleled by similar laws in Scotand and Northern Ireland.

3. J.W. HUDSON, *A History of Adult Education*, 1851.
4. *Adult Education: A Plan for Development*, London, Her Majesty's Stationery Office, 1973.
5. *Adult Education: the Challenge of Change*, Edinburgh, HMSO, 1975.
6. Ministry of Reconstruction, (Adult Education Committee), *Final Report*, 1919, quoted in KELLY, op. cit.
7. KELLY, op. cit.
8. *Education Act, 1944*, Section 41.
9. *Statistics of Education 1975, vol. 3, Further Education*, London, HMSO: *Scottish Education Statistics, 1974*, Edinburgh, HMSO
10. *Adult Education: a Plan for Development*, op. cit.
11. CHARLOTTE BARRY, 'Adults brace themselves against legalised assault', London, *The Times Higher Education Supplement*, 7 March, 1980.
12. The term 'community college' has a different meaning in North America. See C. TITMUS *et al.*, *Terminology of Adult Education*, Paris, UNESCO, 1979.
13. H. MORRIS, *The Village College*, Cambridge, 1924.
14. SIR ROBERT MARTIN, Chairman of the Leicestershire Education Committee, quoted in A.N. FAIRBAIRN, *The Leicestershire Community Colleges and Centres*, University of Nottingham Department of Adult Education, 1978.
15. NICOLE CHARTIER, *Multi-Purpose Schools and Centres in Europe*, Paris, Foundation for Cultural Development, n.d.
16. *Sharing and Growing: a short account of the growth and activity of community colleges in Devon*, Devon County Council Education Department, 1977.
17. A.N. FAIRBAIRN, op cit.
18. *Sharing and Growing*, op. cit.
19. EDWARD HUTCHINSON, 'A study of the Leicestershire community colleges', in FAIRBAIRN, op. cit.
20. G. MEE and H. WILTSHIRE, *Structure and Performance in Adult Education*, London, Longman, 1978.
21. N. CHARTIER, op. cit.
22. N.A. JEPSON, *The Beginnings of English University Adult Education*, London, Michael Joseph, 1973.
23. *UCAE Annual Report 1978–79*, Universities Council for Adult Education.
24. ibid.
25. *Higher Education: Report of the Committee under the Chairmanship of Lord Robbins* (HMSO 1964), quoted in, Universities Council for Adult Education, *First Statement submitted on behalf of the Council to the Committee on Adult Education* (Russell Committee), 1970.

26. For a fuller discussion of Western European attitudes to university involvement in adult education and of the pressures impelling university participation now see JOHN LOWE, COLIN TITMUS, DUSAN SAVICEVIC, 'Widening access to university adult education in Europe' *International Congress of University Adult Education Journal*, vol. XV, No. 3, November 1976.

27. Robbins Report, op. cit.

28. WALTER PERRY, *Open University*, Milton Keynes, Open University, 1976.

29. *Report of the Vice-Chancellor, 1978*, Milton Keynes, Open University, 1979.

30. *Report of the Committee on Continuing Education*, Milton Keynes, Open University, 1976.

31. PERRY, op. cit. p. 56.

32. ibid, p. 144.

33. ibid, p. 66.

34. ibid, p. 239.

35. K.B. START and B.K. WELLS, *The Trend of Reading Standards*, Slough, National Foundation for Educational Research, 1972; *A Right to Read*, London, British Association of Settlements, 1974.

36. *Adult Education: a Plan for Development*, op. cit.

37. *The Local Government Act 1972* and *The Local Government (Scotland) Act 1973*, came into force in 1974 and 1975 respectively

38. For data relating to the campaign the author is indebted to H.A. JONES and A.H. CHARNLEY, *Adult Literacy, a Study of its Impact*, Leicester, National Institute of Adult Education, 1978, and *Adult Literacy in Scotland*, Edinburgh, HMSO, 1980.

CHAPTER 3

Sweden

The Napoleonic Wars constituted a turning point in Swedish history, as in that of so many other European nations. The country emerged with a new Constitution, a new King, who had been one of Napoleon's Marshals, a new territorial acquisition, Norway, and a policy of neutrality in contrast to the imperial ambitions it had nourished in earlier centuries.

The Constitution maintained a balance between the monarchy and the *Riksdag*, a Parliament of four Estates, Nobles, Clergy, Burghers and Peasants, dominated by the first group. Their power was declining, however, and that of the merchant and peasant classes rising. It was not until 1866 that a modern two-chamber parliament was established on a limited franchise, and even then the change in the balance of power was not great. Pressure for more reform did not build up until the last years of the century. It coincided with and was in part an expression of the rise of the labour movement, which acquired its own party of socialist persuasion, the Social Democrats. In 1909 the franchise was extended to all males over the age of twenty-four and in 1921 to all those of both sexes over twenty-three. With this last measure Sweden can be said to have attained full parliamentary democracy. The process had taken over a century, but it had been peaceful, won by moderation and realism.

In the first half of the nineteenth century Sweden was basically an agricultural economy. It was the second half of the century which saw what has been called 'the great transformation' to a modern industrial state. To a large degree it was fortuitous, triggered off by events outside Swedish control, which created an increased demand abroad for timber and iron ore, of which Sweden had plenty, at a time when it was modernizing these industries. It was also stimulated by the inventiveness of Swedes, who, among other things, invented dynamite, ball-bearings, the primus cooker and the safety match. In 1870, seventy per cent of the population gained its living from agriculture and related activities, by 1900 only fifty per cent. The urban population rose from seventeen per cent in 1870 to twenty-five per cent in 1910, that engaged in manufacturing industry doubled over the same period from fifteen to thirty per cent of the gainfully employed. It did not equal that engaged in agriculture, however, until the early 1930s.

The Swedish policy of neutrality in foreign affairs was not seriously tested until the First and Second World Wars. Diplomatic skill and the good fortune of its strategic value and geographical position, particularly during the Second World War, when Denmark and Norway were invaded, enabled it to keep out of combat. Its industry was boosted by both struggles and it emerged better off than its competitors who had been more closely involved. The inter-war years were, none the less, difficult for Sweden, as they were for other countries. They can be summarized as a story of serious labour disputes, quarrels between unions and political instability, out of which emerged in 1932 a Social Democratic administration which, apart from a short break in 1936, was to remain in office for the next forty-four years, alone or in coalition with other parties.

In the middle of the world slump the outlook appeared bleak, but the Government took the view that the crisis was due to under-consumption and decided to embark on a large programme of public investment — houses and hospitals, for example — which would stimulate demand and employment. Helped by a recovery in world trade, it worked. This fact strengthened the hand of the Social Democrats, who were able to undertake an extensive series of social works, which formed the basis of Sweden's reputation as a welfare state. In 1938, under Government pressure the Confederation of

Trade Unions and the Swedish Federation of Employers signed the Saltsjöbaden Agreement, which laid down binding procedures for collective bargaining and the settlement of disputes, and has brought Sweden industrial peace ever since.

The Second World War gave pause to social progress, but the country emerged well-equipped to profit from the post-war boom. On the foundations laid before 1939 Sweden achieved the highest standard of living in the world, the USA excepted. Full employment, even a labour shortage, meant that few labour problems cropped up to test the Saltsjöbaden Agreement, until the world recession of the 1970s.

In 1945 it was argued that a nation which had spent so heavily on defence during the war, could equally afford to pay for social measures in peace. The programme begun in the 'thirties was continued and the protection afforded each citizen was increased at all stages of his or her life, from conception to death, through maternity payments, family allowances, sickness and employment benefits and old-age pensions significantly higher than in most other countries. Taxes have had to be correspondingly high, but general prosperity and approval of welfare provision have caused them to be tolerated.

Sweden is the fourth largest country in Europe, but with a population of around eight million, the same as London, it is sparsely inhabited. Although the process of urbanization, begun in the nineteenth century, has continued, the only urban area of size by international standards is Greater Stockholm, which has over one million inhabitants. In 1910 only twenty-five per cent of people lived in urban areas, in 1940 fifty-six per cent, in 1970 eighty-one per cent.

Sweden is widely considered to be the most secular society in Europe, judged in terms of religious observance. It is by tradition a Protestant country and the Lutheran Church is still the State church, financed by a small tax on its members. By the end of the eighteenth century Lutheranism could be said to be more a part of the State bureaucracy than a religious movement, a position some would say it still holds. In spite of its legal status its influence on national life was small and declined during the nineteenth century. Formalistic and conservative, it resisted the rise of democracy, but, lacking the force of the Catholic Church in France, for instance, it never made religion a major issue in the political struggles of the period. There was, however, a religious revival whose dynamism came from other Protestant sects, introduced from abroad, such as Methodists and the Salvation Army from Britain, Baptists and Pentecostals from America. Although their numbers have remained comparatively small, their influence is considerable.

The Lutheran Church abandoned any pretension to special responsibility for education, such as the Catholic Church claims, by the early nineteenth century. The Protestant tradition has, however, strongly encouraged the development of education. It emphasized personal responsibility for salvation, to which the way was to be found through studying the Bible. In 1686 a Church Law decreed that each parish clerk should teach the children of the parish to read and each minister was to examine the literacy of parishioners. The importance of education for all was therefore recognized early. In 1842, before industrialization, a law ordered the creation of an elementary school in every parish, under a lay board, and parents were obliged to see that their children attended it. Although the elementary schools were joined in 1849 with existing secondary establishments to form a national education system, progress appears to have been slow until the end of the Second World War. Following long deliberations by a Schools Commission and an even longer trial period, nine years of comprehensive schooling, from the age of seven to sixteen, were made compulsory for all children in 1962.

According to Gunnar Myrdal, social scientist and Minister of Commerce in 1945, Sweden's rise to wealth has not been due to any special quality of its people, but rather to luck. If it is, the Swedes made good use of their luck. Their inventiveness, their shrewd concentration on quality and advanced technology made the most of their natural resources. In politics practicality has usually prevailed over ideological purity. From the views expressed before they took office, the Social Democrats might have been expected to undertake a secularist and republican policy, to extend State control over the means of production. In fact the State Church and the Monarchy were left untouched and ninety per cent of industry remains in private hands, because to do otherwise would have brought few advantages and real problems.

The country's success may be related to other factors. The Swedes are a homogeneous, some have said conformist, people, their self-confidence and sense of common national identity strengthened by their having been free from foreign occupation since the Middle Ages, unlike the other Scandinavian nations. Their Protestant heritage has taught not only personal responsibility, but social conscience. It is not surprising to find a basic national consensus, demonstrated by the fact that, when the Social Democrats finally lost power in 1976, there was hardly any discernible change in State policy.

The growth of adult education in nineteenth century Sweden ran in close parallel to the country's history. In the first half of the century, in a dominantly agricultural economy, Protestant religious thinking and liberalism were the inspiration. In the second half of the century the main effort was directed towards meeting the needs of the new urban working class. In the 1850s workers formed study groups, taking the idea from Germany, In 1880 Workers' Institutes were set up in Stockholm on middle class initiative. In 1885 students of Uppsala University founded joint summer schools with workers.

By 1914 a pattern had been established of provision by private, non-profit-making initiative, which was viewed benevolently and marginally assisted by the State. In 1923 a government-commissioned report recommended increased subsidy to certain areas of adult education activity, but it was not fully implemented owing to the economic difficulties of the time, and progress generally seems to have been steady rather than spectacular. The parallel with the Report of the Smith Committee in England is quite striking.

In 1947 Parliament accorded official recognition to voluntary adult education, together with increased financial support. A seal of approval was in effect put on the work that had been going on for decades. The results really began to show in the mid-1950s. As continually increasing amounts of money have been allocated to adult education, there has been a massive increase in the number of participants — calculations based on officially published statistics, show that annual enrolments are equivalent to two-thirds of the adult population.

The reasons for this are complex, but one may plausibly argue as follows. Swedes have traditionally valued education. The economy's concentration on quality and advanced technology has made knowledge more obviously important. That their economic policy has so obviously worked has reinforced their respect for education. The guiding principle of social policy, the pursuit of social justice, must apply in education as in other fields of activity. There should be equality between generations as well as between classes. So adult education was considered good in principle, not only successful in practice. It was also non-contentious, and, given the consensus, even conformist, nature of Swedish society, once it was accepted as a socially-approved form of behaviour, it is not surprising that the majority of citizens appear to participate in it at some time in their lives.

Over the last twenty years there has been both growth and change, as in their pragmatic, moderate way the Swedes have responded to new requirements. In the last decade, indeed, the main thrust of national education policy, as announced by the Government, has been directed towards expanding and improving learning opportunities for adults. They have become more varied, as will be seen shortly. Adult vocational training, principally undertaken by employers, has grown significantly. In 1957 the National Labour Market Board, a State agency, began providing vocational training for the unemployed, workers threatened with unemployment and handicapped persons, in other words for the same categories of the workforce and offering roughly the same sort of training as Government Skillcentres do in Great Britain and the State-funded Association for the Vocational Training of Adults does in France. In the early 'seventies over 100,000 persons were taking its courses each year.

Swedish educational associations

In the social history of nineteenth century Sweden a notable phenomenon was the proliferation of popular movements and associations. It began in the first half of the century, but acquired pace and importance under the influence of industrialization and its concomitant urbanization, continuing well into the twentieth century. Credit for much of the nation's social and political progress has been attributed to them. Today they constitute powerful pressure groups, which play a significant role in the customary process of consultation and discussion which precedes policy making.

The Swedish Temperance Movement, stimulated by British and American missionaries, was created to fight alcoholism, a major social problem in Sweden for hundreds of years. Due to its influence, from 1917 to 1955 alcohol could only be bought on presentation of a ration book and can still be obtained only from State liquor shops. Temperance had close connections with the socialist movement, and owed a lot too to the religious revival of the nineteenth century. Not only did a number of non-conformist churches take root, but some life was inspired in Lutheranism, which was manifested in the National Evangelical Foundation, formed in 1856.

The first consumer co-operative in Sweden dates from 1850, the National Co-operative Society from 1899. From the first the movement's purpose was to protect the working classes from exploitation and it has maintained ties with the labour movement. Its expansion has continued over the years and today it owns about five per cent of Swedish industry. The first trade unions were formed in the 1860s and 1870s. In 1889 representatives of trade unions formed the Social Democratic Party and in 1898 the Confederation of Trade Unions (LO), all of whose members were to be affiliated to the party. Since the Saltsjöbaden Agreement of 1938, the unions, with a membership of 2,000,000 out of 2,800,000 wage earners, closely identified with the Social Democrats, have become more and more part of the country's ruling establishment.

National party politics in the modern sense developed in Sweden, when loose interest groupings gave way to more disciplined, nationally organized bodies, beginning in 1895 with the Farmers' Party. By the time the first Parliament met after the franchise reforms of 1909 the essential political alignments of today were established.

Why did the popular movements become so powerful? To quote Sven-Arne Stahre:

One reason, surely, is that they have always appreciated the importance of knowledge; from the very beginning, they saw to it that their members were enabled to learn not only about the conditions and objectives of their own organisations, but also about the social and economic problems of society at large. They therefore came to sponsor programmes of adult education which concentrated on training for better membership and citizenship. In so doing they have been able to preserve their identity against encroachment from the outside. Further they have been able to recruit the vast majority of leaders from their own ranks, and instilled in members a sense of communion and responsibility towards their own organisation and towards the larger society.[1]

As the movements grew their educational activities became so important that separate associations, retaining links with the main organization, were created to run them. The first in 1901 was the Temperance Education Board, a co-operative venture of all the temperance societies. The earliest completely independent educational organization, the Workers' Educational Association (ABF), was founded in 1912 with the backing of the trade unions, the co-operative movement and the Social Democratic Party. In the 1920s the Farmers' Movement formed associations to take learning to the rural population, in 1930 came the Educational Association of the Swedish Church, in 1935 the Salaried Employees' Educational Association and in 1942 the People's University, to provide continuing evidence of the growth and development of the voluntary sector in the first half of this century.

For many years the associations *were* adult education. By the end of the First World War their pattern of provision and organization had largely taken its modern form. Each one is democratically structured, under the leadership of a management board elected by a national assembly. The board appoints the professional executives responsible for the actual administration. At regional and local levels there are similar structures. It was the success of the educational associations and the influence of the movements from which they derived that brought about the 1923 Report on adult education. It was to them that the Report and the Parliament order of 1947 intended major support to be given.

As the amount of government financial support increased in the 1950s, 1960s and 1970s, so did the scale of operations by the educational associations, the most spectacular period being the last two decades. They also receive financial contributions from local authorities, from organizations by which they are sponsored and from student fees. Payment of State grants is only made to bodies approved by the National Board of Education. This government department has, since 1972, had a special adult education section. In order to make grants the board must be satisfied as to the organizational stability, scope and general objectives of the association. Activities must be open to the general public, there must be no indoctrination and courses are not subject to public examinations.

Following some rationalization through mergers over the years there are now ten recognized associations:

The Workers' Educational Association (ABF): sponsored by eighteen national organizations in or allied with the labour movement.
The School for Adults (Vuxenskolan): linked to organizations of the Liberal Party, national economic and labour organizations in agriculture, the Swedish Homestead Society.
The Educational Association of the Citizens' School (Medborgarskolan): linked to organizations of the Conservative Party.
The Salaried Employees' Educational Association (TBV): linked to the Central Organization of Salaried Employees, which is independent of the LO, the main trade union federation.
The Swedish Ecclesiastical Educational Association (SKS): linked to national and district organizations in the established Lutheran Church.
The Educational Association of the Free Churches of Sweden (FKS): linked to eleven national non-conformist organizations.
The Folk University (Folkuniversitetet): linked to the National Federation of Lecturing Associations and Universities.
The Educational Association of the Temperance Movement (NBV): linked to various temperance organizations.
Study Promotion (Studieframjandet): linked to Young Farmers' organizations.
The Educational Association of the YMCA and YWCA (KFUK–KFUM): linked to the Young Men's Christian Association and the Young Women's Christian Association.[2]

The principal activity of the educational associations is the study circle, which is discussed on pages 68–76. In earlier days lectures and lecture series predominated and are still popular. Considerable sponsorship is given to cultural activities, plays, concerts and exhibitions and residential courses are offered. The subjects studied under the aegis of the different associations are not determined by their political, religious, or social affiliations, but by the interests of the public. One will therefore find the whole range of topics for which there is a demand in the programme of each association. Nevertheless, either because the organization makes a special effort, or because people associate certain subjects with certain associations, there are some significant emphases. For example the Workers' Educational Association provides nearly half of all the study circles in social sciences, law, economics and business. The two church associations, SKS and FKS, organize two-thirds of the ones dealing with religion, philosophy or psychology.

It might appear that there must be competition between associations, duplication of effort and some waste. On the whole national associations would claim that they complement each other and point to long-standing co-operation in matters of study materials, qualifications of educators, the scope of subject matter.

Nevertheless they have had causes for disquiet. Adult education has gone beyond liberal studies, the traditional provision of the associations. It is now seen as an integral part of the education system, an essential tool of economic policy. Where formal education is a State system, and manpower planning is a State concern too, as in Sweden, there has been reason to fear that the State will lay hands on the liberal education sector, as part of its efforts to tidy up, to rationalize the whole of education, to reduce to order what, through the exercise of freedom of action and choice, is diverse and, perhaps, disordered.[3]

These apprehensions were crystallized, if not sparked off, by the 1967 Bill on Certain Measures in the Field of Adult Education. It increased grants to the educational associations, but it also provided for municipal adult schools. Public authorities were thus entering, for the first time in a major way, the field of direct non-vocational provision for adults. The response of the associations was to seek a stronger common front to protect their interests. They formed the National Federation of Adult Education Associations, composed of the ten associations, the county education associations, folk high schools and libraries.

What effect their action had it is not possible to say, but in succeeding years associations' grants went up. Attention in legislation turned to the problem of reaching the under-educated, who were participating little in adult education, and for this the educational associations, with their study circle technique, were considered to have considerable advantages. Therefore, although their monopoly has been broken beyond repair, their status and security have grown. However, they are not so free as they used to be. Some of the extra funds can be used only to promote activities in areas of priority, decided by the State. Fortunately there is up to now general agreement on what these priorities should be.

In all the countries of Western Europe the beginnings of modern adult education provision are to be found in private, voluntary initiative. In some cases, as, for instance, that of Mechanics' Institutes in the United Kingdom, individuals formed groups expressly to organize the offer of study opportunities for adults. In other cases organizations formed for other purposes turned to adult education as a means of achieving their primary objectives. Sometimes by implication, but usually explicitly, these organizations directed their efforts principally at the new urban working class. By education it would be saved, politically, economically, socially, or religiously, from its ignorance, squalor and impotence. Adult education was an instrument, a means to an end. Only secondarily, if at all, was it an end in itself, undertaken for its own value in an individual's development.

The basic educational goal of European governments during the nineteenth century was to establish universal schooling for children and to improve higher education for an élite. The State did not believe adult education to be sufficiently important for provision of it to be made by public authorities. In the gap thus left voluntary bodies established themselves. Outside adult training in vocational skills, which was late to develop on a major scale, and with the notable exception of the United Kingdom, adult education became identified with voluntary initiative, which public authorities supported to a greater or lesser degree financially, but with which they did not compete. What began as an accident was elevated into a principle, as people discovered sound political and educational reasons for keeping adult study under private and, preferably, local control, rather than putting it into the bureaucratic hands of the State.

As governments have come to value adult education as an essential element in their educational policy, mainly in the last quarter of a century, they have continued, by and large, to refrain from setting up in competition with the voluntary bodies, for three principal reasons. Their own priorities have lain elsewhere, in vocational education and in opening the school and higher education curriculum to adults. It has appeared easier and cheaper to operate through the national networks which the private associations had created than to enter into conflict with them, especially as they had a significant political support. They have genuinely accepted the arguments of principle for private provision, namely that voluntary bodies were best equipped to reach those most in need of education and least likely to participate, those who had had least success in the State school system, because these organizations were more flexible, more sensitive to adult needs, gave learners more opportunity to take some responsibility for provision to meet their own learning requirements, than public authorities could, that freedom to learn what and how adults wanted, even to criticize the State, was essential in a democratic society, and could best be guaranteed outside State control.

In some countries, paradoxically, the legislative arm of the State has given voluntary initiative protection against encroachment by the executive arm. Danish law requires that certain kinds of adult study be the responsibility of private associations, municipalities shall only intervene if the former cannot undertake the task.[4] Austrian law forbids the Federal Government from setting conditions relating to the programme of activities, the methods, or the staff employed, when making subsidies to organizations.[5] The provisions of Norwegian law are discussed on pages 160—167.

Broadly, therefore, Swedish voluntary associations conform to a common pattern. They are less numerous than the socio-cultural organizations of France, of which very few, for reasons discussed in Chapter 5, are concerned with adults alone, or with systematic, purposive study. They have remained purely private, unlike the mixture of public and private institutions that form the Folk High School Association in the Federal German Republic and which will be considered later. They are as independent as those of Austria, while enjoying more generous financial support from the State. They resemble most closely those of Norway and Denmark, fellow Scandinavians.

These three countries have enjoyed a combination of circumstances from which only the United Kingdom among other Western European States has benefited. They have enjoyed continuity, have suffered no political upheavals, except for German occupation during the Second World War in the case of Norway and Denmark. There has been a steady progress towards parliamentary democracy, built on a basic national consensus, in which at no time in the last century has a significant body of public opinion or the State been hostile to their work. They have not had the political and social divisions of France, the religious ones of Holland, or the linguistic ones of Belgium, nor have they had the authoritarianism of Germany and Austria, or the local particularism of the Swiss Federation. They have been unitary, stable and relatively prosperous states.

The rise and contemporary importance of voluntary adult education associations in these countries is closely related to such factors. If those of Sweden are more strongly entrenched, attract a higher proportion of the population than those of Norway and Denmark, it is probably due to the greater prosperity of the country and to the more single-minded pursuit of social justice and equality of opportunity that it has consequently been able to embark upon.

Swedish Study Circles

Study circles are so closely associated with the image of Swedish adult education that it is easy to assume that they are unique to that country or that the Swedes invented them. Neither is true. Their absolute dominance of the field of adult learning is not even of very long date. As has already been mentioned, until well into this century lectures and lecture series were as important. Nevertheless of their current significance there can be no doubt. Their annual enrolments are equal to over sixty per cent of the whole Swedish adult population.

Study circles of a kind go back a long way, but the rise of

this kind of study organization in its present form did not begin until the twentieth century. The first one is said to have been founded in Lund, a university town in the south of Sweden, in 1902.[6] Particularly suited to the free, democratic structure of the educational associations, study circles grew with them and might have done so faster had they attracted more State support. It was not, however, until 1947, when parliament authorized increased grants to study circles, that growth really became rapid. By the middle 1950s there were 50,000 of them, that number had quadrupled by 1970 and had grown by a factor of seven in 1978, the last year for which statistics are available.

According to the Adult Education Proclamation a study circle is 'a circle of friends engaged in communal, methodically organized studies of a predetermined subject or topic'.[7] This definition permits of a wide diversity of organization and procedure. It is claimed that there are few features common to all circles — the element of comradeship, the principle that all, even the leader, shall participate in the work and on equal terms, the prior choice of a limited field of study and the planned and systematic pursuit of it.

The notion of the Swedish study circle, widely entertained outside the country, has been somewhat lyrically expressed by a Frenchman, F-R Bastide:

> There is not a village in Sweden which does not have, every evening, at least one study circle; the members of these circles meet at home after dinner, that is to say, about six o'clock, or else they put on their astrakhan hats, take their *sparks* — small individual sledges which they use as scooters to travel through the streets silent under the snow — and make their way to the town pastrycook's: in this country of semi-prohibition the pastrycook's takes the place of the cafe, where one may listen to an incredible quantity of lectures. One is among friends. Everybody is on familiar terms with the others. There may be a retired colonel, a housewife, a scholar, an employer, the station master and the lampman from the same station. People study in order not to be alone, but also in order to improve the lives of all, and to understand each other better. Everything is studied: from the mandolin and ceramics to constitutional law and Elizabethan tragedy.[8]

It is a striking feature that a circle does not need to have a teacher, only a leader, who may not be a specialist in the subject under study, nor have any professional training as a teacher. He or she is likely to have had training in study circle leadership, given either by the educational associations, or at the Linköping Training College. The course at the latter establishment lasts a year, takes sixty persons at a time and is open to study circle leaders and folk high school teachers. It is open to non-graduates, the only entry qualification required being experience in the field. Courses run by the associations concentrate on teaching methods appropriate to study circles, particularly adult leadership, the stimulation of group activities, the use of libraries and teaching aids. They are subsidized by the State.

Because the leader may have no specialized knowledge of the topic for study, emphasis is placed on the production of study materials, literature, tapes, records, film strips, films etc. Two correspondence schools owned by the popular movements, Brevskolan and LTK, specialize in the production of this material. From the very nature of the phenomenon it serves, study material is varied in amount and kind. It is seen as a principle and prime virtue of the study circle that it involves the student in active, not passive, learning. Apart from the subject, one is to learn by practice how to learn, to work with others for a common purpose, to contribute one's own knowledge and experience to the pool and to draw on those of one's comrades for new knowledge and insights. Essentially study material should provide the basis and stimulus of this process. It should offer a systematic learning guide, containing the factual data required. It should be presented objectively, for students must form their own opinions, not have them ready made for them. As far as possible it should relate to the life experience of adults likely to use it. In style and format it should be attractive and encourage the users to independent learning effort. That is to say it should promote discussion, individual or group projects. It may help this by offering a list of books for further reading, or the names of people or organizations from whom further information may be obtained, or propose assignments for homework.

In principle a study circle decides its own subject, its own method of operation to suit the needs and interests of its members. Today, in fact, as in British evening institutes and German folk high schools, programmes are offered by associations, in which the subject and method of procedure have already been determined by the organizers, working on the basis of public demand in previous years, or the requirements of public policy in the case of priority circles. In joining, members accept both the subject and procedure. Any group of adults can still, however, set up a circle, as long as it satisfies the requirements of minimum members and duration.

It seems inevitable that, as dependence on specially-produced study material grows and as it becomes more sophisticated, the majority of circles will be constrained by their material into a limited number of patterns of organization. There may be no legal compulsion to operate in a certain manner, a minority studying topics outside the usual range may go their own way, but the logic of their situation (and possibly the training of their leaders) will mould most of them.

A study circle does not require a teacher with specialized subject knowledge, but nothing prevents it having one. It was already reported nearly twenty years ago that in urban areas the most popular ones did.[9] With the increase in high-level study at the upper levels of the secondary curriculum and at university level, the number of circles taught by specialists is growing. Their pattern of practice cannot be much different from that of liberal education evening classes in other countries, which attach importance to participation in discussion by the students.

Nevertheless groups operate in large numbers without teachers. In reading circles, a very early form of activity, each member reads a book, which is then discussed in the circle. Others work in a similar way, but members undertake some other agreed preparation. Some groups base their discussion on papers prepared and presented by members. Correspondence circles use questions supplied by correspondence schools. Sometimes questions are sent to the group, a group answer is prepared and sent in for marking and comment. In other cases the circle is a supplement to courses for which members are individually enrolled. They use group discussion to help their own study and send in their own answers to the school.

Table 2   Study circles in Sweden by subject area, 1977–8[10]

Subject area	Number of circles	% of circles	Number of participants	% of participants
Behavioural sciences, humanities	25,050	7.4	260,288	8.2
Aesthetic subjects	113,629	33.4	1,105,857	34.8
Business and commercial subjects	3,459	1.0	34,522	1.1
Mathematics and natural sciences	12,027	3.5	111,367	3.5
Medical and nursing studies	2,498	0.7	25,121	0.8
Social and information sciences	75,429	22.2	706,031	22.2
Languages	78,144	23.0	672,422	21.2
Technical subjects	10,827	3.2	107,149	3.4
Miscellaneous	18,861	5.5	155,930	4.9
TOTAL	339,924		3,178,687	

Table 2 shows the number of study circles in 1977–8 and their subject distribution. The number of enrolments, it should be noted, does not mean that over 3,000,000 people participated, since some people take part in more than one study circle each year. It is estimated that about two and a quarter million of an adult population of about five million, or about forty-five per cent, joined a circle. The statistics show a predominant interest in languages, artistic studies and social studies, which has been the case for a number of years.

Table 3   Number of study hours provided by study circles in Sweden
1977–8[11]

Educational Association	Number of study hours	% of study hours
Workers' Educational Association (ABF)	3,135,684	32.1
Folk University (FU)	709,931	7.3
Educational Association of the Free Churches of Sweden (FKS)	305,678	3.1
Educational Association of the Temperance Movement (NBV)	511,669	5.2
Educational Association of the YMCA and YWCA (KFUK/M)	66,924	0.7
Study Promotion (Sfr)	677,012	6.8
Educational Association of the Citizens' School (Mbsk)	1,059,749	10.8
School of Adults (SV)	1,699,329	17.4
Swedish Ecclesiastical Education Association (SKS)	613,470	6.3
Salaried Employees' Educational Association (TBV)	999,138	10.2
Total	9,778,584	

Table 3 shows the comparative strength of the voluntary associations, measured by the number of hours put in by study circles organized by each one. The average number of hours for each circle was twenty-nine. The Workers' Educational Association is by far the largest organization, with nearly a third of all circles. The only other associations exceeding ten per cent of the total are SV, Mbsk and TBV, all with links to political parties or trade unions. The market share of the associations with religious links is small, about fifteen per cent, having declined since 1970.

The importance of languages in study circles may be attributed in part to State grant regulations. To qualify for a grant a study circle must have a minimum of five and a maximum of twenty participants. It must run for at least twenty hours spread over a minimum of four weeks. No meeting may last more than three hours. Subsidies are intended to cover seventy-five per cent of the cost of leaders' fees and study materials.[12] Certain circles, in Swedish, English, mathematics and social science conducted at a level corresponding to years 7—9 of compulsory schooling, are designated priority circles. They attract a grant intended to cover one hundred per cent of costs and may therefore be offered free. Circles for handicapped people, in trade union studies and for immigrants are also included in the priority category. Thirty-eight per cent of all circles fall into this category.

Another special form is the university study circle. About half of these are like other circles in having no examinations. The rest follow syllabuses devised by universities and students may sit a private examination in order to obtain degree credits. Group leaders must be qualified to teach the subject at university and seventy-five per cent of costs are met by subsidy as in standard study circles. University study circles amount to about two per cent of all circles.

What is distinctive about the Swedish study circle? The form is found in all the Scandinavian countries, in the German Federal Republic folk high schools, in *animation socio-culturelle* in France. It does not dominate the adult education scene in these other countries, as it does in Sweden. In this matter it should be noted, though, that in Sweden study circle is a general term, which includes other ways of organizing the learning situation, which would in other countries be called, as in Norway or Great Britain, evening classes. Therefore the extent to which a particular form predominates may be more apparent than real.

Then can one say that the Swedes use the term as a blanket one for all forms of study organization in a particular sector of adult education — that of leisure-time liberal education? Certainly the range of subject-matter is similar to that covered in correspondence courses, study circles and evening classes in Norway, by evening classes in the United Kingdom, by evening classes, lecture series and study circles in the German Federal Republic. In these other countries the range extends beyond liberal education to vocationally oriented studies, but then so do Swedish study circles to an increasing extent. They fulfil a similar function to that fulfilled in other countries by the forms of organization mentioned, but all the Swedish provision in this area is not called study circles, there are lectures and lecture series.

If one wishes to obtain some inkling of why study circles flourish to the degree they do where they do, one ought probably to look at their period of origin and growth, rather than to the present. It is to be noted that the study circle is most important in the Scandinavian countries, Denmark, Finland, Norway and Sweden, where non-vocational provision has sprung from democratic associations. Where it is made in terms of institutions, as in evening folk high schools of Federal Germany or Austria, or the evening institutes of the United Kingdom, circles account for a smaller proportion of provision. It may be argued that the spirit of the association found more natural expression through the study circle than did that of establishments finding their models in school and higher education. In the United Kingdom the Further Education regulation which made it obligatory for a learning group to have a teacher specializing in the subject to be studied in order to qualify for subsidy effectively excluded study circles almost completely.

In Norway and Sweden the growth of the study circle may have been related to geography and climate, and the difficulties of obtaining the regular services of subject specialists in the winter months, when circles were held. In support of this view one is reminded that, in Swedish urban areas, where communication difficulties are less great, the most popular circles do have specialist teachers. Another factor may have been that, as Bastide points out,[13] anti-alcohol legislation has meant that the French café, the beer cellar, or the public house do not exist. The study circle may have provided the focus for social contact which in other countries is furnished by these establishments. Certainly in Denmark, which has a less extreme climate and less draconian laws regarding the sale of alcohol, the study circle does not appear to be as important as it is in Norway and Sweden.

It seems that Swedish study circles are to be defined by spirit rather than form. Friendship and community of effort towards a predetermined learning goal are the essential principles which unite them, as Bastide[14] and the Adult Education Proclamation show.[15] In other countries they are defined by spirit, form and, for example, in Denmark,[16] the purpose the learning is supposed to serve. That difference and the arguments related to national wealth already advanced to explain the overall support of adult education in Sweden may account for the unique position of Swedish study circles compared with those of other nations.

Municipal adult education in Sweden

The introduction of municipal adult education disturbed the voluntary associations. Although the Labour Market Board, a public agency, had been making direct provision of vocational training for adults over a period of years, its courses were aimed at a narrow group and served a limited purpose. In itself it did not threaten the associations. Municipal courses, on the other hand, were not only directed at a large section of the potential public of study circles, their subject area covered a major part of the circles' range and their purpose was one that had been central to the circles. In view of the lobbying power of the popular associations, the direct intervention of public authorities into provision must be taken as a clear sign of the importance they attached to what they were setting out to do.

The initiative formed part of the government's long-standing policy to raise the general level of formal education in Sweden in order to meet the requirements of an advanced society. After years of experiment the period of compulsory schooling had been raised in 1962 from seven to nine years. It took some years to implement that and to undertake the necessary reorganization of the structure and curriculum of schools in order to achieve a national comprehensive school system, in which, in fact, over eighty per cent of young people would continue in full-time education for at least eleven years. This reform, it was perceived, had significant implications for both higher and adult education. Attention therefore turned in the late 1960s to both of these.

A statement by Sven Moberg, Minister responsible for adult education, in 1970 expresses the justification for increased State spending on adult education in general and for the creation of municipal adult education:

During the past few decades, the Government has invested considerable sums of money in the field of education and culture. A nine year compulsory school system has been introduced for all children between 7 and 16. The secondary schools now have the capacity to admit 85—90% of all 16-year olds and a high percentage of these youngsters then go on to some form of college or university education. At the same time, the opportunities for adult education have gradually been increasing. One consequence of the educational explosion, however, has been the development of a considerable gap in educational levels between the younger and older generations.

Over half of those who are gainfully employed today have had the benefit of only six or seven years of formal schooling. The disparity in education berween the younger and older generations makes it difficult for many older people to hold their own in the labour market. There is also a risk that it may help to bring about intergenerational conflicts.

To reduce the educational gap and counter the growing isolation between generations, public investments in the field of adult education must be increased . . . . In our changing society with its rapid accretion of knowledge, adult education offers a means for those who have completed their basic education to supplement it and update it. In the future, there will be even greater demands for a system of education that provides a continuous alternation between periods of education and work.[17]

That statement was made three years after municipal adult schools had been set up under the Government Bill on Certain Measures in the Field of Adult Education, 1967. In Sweden the school curriculum is determined centrally by the State and is uniform over the whole country. The new courses, which would be offered free of charge, were to cover at the appropriate level subjects taught in years seven to nine of compulsory school and in the upper secondary school, that is, years ten to twelve. The municipal education authorities were to administer this provision, which would be financed by State grants. Teaching would be in normal school premises and would be undertaken by teachers doing the same work with young people.

Most of the teaching was expected to be done during the evenings, but if the demand and facilities existed, daytime courses could be conducted. The students were not required to take the whole curriculum, but could study one, two or more subjects at a time, to permit accelerated study of each one.

Municipal adult education was promulgated without the long period of pre-planning and testing that led up to school reform. The number of modifications to regulations which appeared almost annually in the early 1970s is perhaps a consequence of this. It highlights some of the problems that arose and the State's determination to overcome them.

It became obvious early on that a large number of the adults at whom the courses were directed were either unwilling to take up the opportunity, or were incapable of making good use of it. Some of the State subsidized teaching time at compulsory school level had been allocated for individual tuition and educational and vocational counselling from the beginning. This was increased, in 1970, to twenty-five per cent of the total, in order to attract those who had not completed their formal schooling.

Since those most in need were still not being reached, further efforts were subsequently made to attract them. Courses at the compulsory school level were opened not only to those who had not had nine years schooling, but also to those who had and needed to repeat some subjects. There was a limit to the subsidies allocated to courses at the upper secondary level. Municipalities were requested to set up boards to process admissions. In thinly-populated areas the minimum number of students required for the opening of a course was reduced from twelve to eight. In these areas teachers were permitted to count time teaching municipal adult classes in their normal work load.

A little later permission was given to employ full-time or part-time educational and vocational guidance counsellors. In towns where a large number of workers worked shifts, it was proving difficult to recruit sufficient students to start courses. Therefore a hundred classes in such places were allowed to begin with only eight students, as an experiment.

Two measures, intended to facilitate participation in any kind of adult study, apply to municipal adult education. In

1975 the Act Concerning an Employee's Right to Educational Leave came into force. The leave may be for any study the recipient chooses, as long or as short as the course requires. He or she may therefore demand release in order to attend a municipal class during working hours, for a couple of hours, half a day, a whole day each week, or for a period of months.

The limiting factor is that, unlike such legislation in most other countries, the 1975 Swedish law makes no provision for maintenance of wages, or for payment in lieu of them. Instead the State offers grants to cover living costs to adults, whether employed or not, who undertake study. Full-time students in municipal adult education receive a combination of grants and loans on the same basis as students in universities and colleges. For those who undertake systematic study for short periods, or part of the day, hourly or daily allowances are paid. Leave and study grants are held to have sharply increased entry to daytime courses.

When the programme first started, secondary school staff taught the classes in addition to their normal teaching duties. It was later decided that such an arrangement was harmful to both kinds of teaching. Currently, although there are some full-time teaching posts in municipal adult schools, most staff work part-time in the adult and the rest of the time in the youth school. In addition to the teaching personnel, State subsidy to a municipal adult school provides for a principal, a director of studies and a guidance counsellor.

The Government appears to have placed these second-chance courses in municipal schools because they were specialists in the curriculum and possessed appropriate resources in personnel and teaching materials. There was criticism, however, that neither administrators nor educators had training in teaching adults, or organizing learning programmes for them. The curriculum of years seven to nine in the compulsory school and in the upper secondary school was taught unchanged, using the same materials and methods as for young people. In acknowledgement that these criticisms were valid, a training course for teachers in municipal adult schools was opened at the Stockholm College of Education in 1971.

At the compulsory school level and in the general curriculum of the upper secondary school the most popular subjects with adults are Swedish, English, German and mathematics. The most commonly studied vocational subjects — these are taught in the upper secondary school — are training courses for industry and handicraft, home economics and commercial and clerical work.

The enrolment for municipal adult education had risen to 392,000 students in 1975. Over twenty-seven per cent of them followed compulsory school courses, a little less than forty-three per cent general courses in the first two years of the upper secondary school and thirty per cent vocational courses. A little over seventy per cent of all students were over twenty-five years of age, and about thirty-five per cent over thirty-five. Women outnumbered men in almost all age groups.

Municipal adult education's work in general education at the level of years seven to twelve of school is complemented by two State adult schools, at Norrköping and Härnosänd. Intended for those who, either because of where they live or because they work unsocial hours, cannot attend municipal courses, these institutions conduct their courses either by correspondence or by a combination of correspondence with a short period of residential study. They had between them 7,692 students in 1975.

Municipal adult education is now a major part of Swedish provision and its role is likely to extend. In 1977 it was given the task of providing basic education for adults whose earlier schooling was deficient or non-existent. The goal is to afford the opportunity for all adults, Swedish born or immigrant, to acquire the minimum of knowledge and skills necessary to hold down a job and to function effectively in society.

In the context of Swedish experience it is perhaps surprising that municipal adult education should have been created at all. Adult education had grown through varied private initiative with State support. It operated in a form, the study circle, much of whose success was attributed to its informal, easy-going procedure, in contrast to the formal regimen of school. As for the school curriculum, except for the practical subjects, those that were to prove the most popular in municipal adult classes were already studied in study circles. There are nearly 150,000 circles more today than there were a decade ago and over a third of all circles are now in priority subjects and recruit more than four times as many participants as municipal adult classes do. There appears, therefore, to have been little to suggest that the educational associations could not have handled the volume of activity that it was intended to generate through the offer of free classes studying the upper end of the school curriculum.

One may wonder then why it was thought desirable to create municipal provision for adults. The answer may plausibly be sought in the purpose of the State's initiative. It was essentially an extension of the 1962 school reform, intended to offer adults equal educational opportunity with their children. The best way not only to offer equality, but to be seen to do so, might be to offer the same experience, not only in terms of curriculum, but also of learning environment. If one is thinking of school curriculum, then it will easily appear that the obvious place to teach it is school. If one is dealing with a uniform level and range of subjects, as in Sweden, then study circles by their nature might not appear the best situations to achieve them.

Whatever may have been the local reasons for the State's action, the creation of municipal adult education is an example of a trend that is spreading through Europe. Adult education is seen as an integral and major element in a policy of lifelong or recurrent education. Certain sectors of it are regarded as key instruments of social and economic policy, in which direct public intervention is required, rather than the loose supervision which is exercised as a matter of principle in many countries over provision made by private associations. This trend is already far advanced in adult vocational education and is visible in adult secondary education, for example in Norway, Finland, Denmark and the United Kingdom, as well as in Sweden.

In all the Scandinavian countries voluntary organizations are not excluded from adult secondary education. One may prepare for secondary qualifications through face-to-face instruction organized by associations, or by correspondence study. A major, if not predominant, role is, however, played by public institutions, by a whole array of them in Denmark — continuation schools, polytechnics, commercial colleges, grammar schools, and even, at the higher level by teacher training colleges and advanced technical colleges — by evening secondary schools or evening sections of youth secondary schools in Finland, by evening classes of county council schools in Norway. Some provision is made in the United Kingdom by commercial correspondence schools, but the greatest part is by local authority further education institutions.

The essential difference between Swedish municipal adult education and other countries' programmes of a similar kind is not one of purpose, or, except perhaps marginally, of content and level. It is that others make it possible for adults to achieve upper secondary standards, may even encourage them to do so, while the actions of the Swedish Government since 1967 show that it goes further. It is determined to do everything it can, short of actual coercion, to ensure that all citizens, of whatever age, have attained at least the level of the nine year compulsory school.

Mature student entry to higher education in Sweden

School reform had inevitable consequences for higher education, only some of which were foreseen. As it became the exception rather than the rule for young people to leave school before the age of eighteen so the number qualified to enter advanced studies increased, imposing upon higher education stresses which it was not equipped to meet. Enrolment in universities, which before the Second World War had been steady at 2,000 per annum, rose in twenty years to 8,000 in 1960 and then in the following eight years leaped to 30,000.

The Government's intention was to widen access to post-secondary education still more, in pursuit of equality of opportunity both within and between generations. As the average length of full-time education grew, the arguments which lay behind the creation of municipal adult schools appeared also to require the opening of higher education to adults. Its organizational structure and basic curriculum, untouched over many years, called for revision to meet the needs of the time. Virtually unrestricted and undirected growth had taken expenditure to the point where it was becoming urgent to examine the efficiency of the system. In 1968, therefore, a commission, popularly known as the

U68 Commission was set up to prepare an overall plan for post-secondary education in the 1970s.

It met over a period of five years. Then, after it had reported, there followed a further two years of debate and modification, leading to a law in 1976. The defeat of the Social Democrats in 1976, after more than forty years, brought about further changes and a new law, the one currently in force was passed in 1977, nearly a decade after the reform process had been set in motion.

Having completed its school reforms, the Swedish Government had already shifted the focus of its attention to adults when the U68 Commission was appointed. From the beginning that body conceived of post-secondary study as a recurrent process to be continued throughout life. One of its earliest papers, in 1969, presented five possible models of recurrent education, three of which would have required of individuals a period of occupational experience after secondary level and before going into higher or further education. All post-school study would in these models have been adult education.

A matter of some concern had been the apparently low motivation of many students in higher education, indicated by the number who abandoned their studies before completion, or took an overlong time to complete them. It was said that a significant proportion entered higher education under social pressure, rather than with any clear purpose of their own. In the late 'sixties and early 'seventies, like other countries, Sweden went through a period of active student discontent, although it did not take such extreme forms as in France. The number of enrolments in higher education declined and at the same time from research carried out in upper secondary schools of five European countries Sweden emerged as the only one where the aspirations of a majority of pupils involved no further education or training.[18] It also had the smallest proportion wishing to go on to higher education. These phenomena were no doubt influenced by a significant amount of graduate unemployment at the time, but there was also evidence that after twelve years of schooling many young people had had enough and were seeking other kinds of experience.

Since the concept of recurrent education stresses the enriching effect of alternation between periods of study and periods of other activity, this attitude could not be dismissed as mere perversity. On the other hand the nation could ill afford to lose from higher education some of its brightest people. It was therefore important to make it possible to enter further and higher education after experience of work or leisure had shown its relevance and revived the appetite for learning. This need gave an added spur to experiments involving the admission of adult students without the usual formal qualifications, which had already begun, inspired by the search for inter-generational equality of opportunity.

The problems of adults were not the only, nor even the main, concern of the U68 Commission and the legislation which followed it. Their aim was a thorough reorganization of post-secondary education. Since the changes introduced were meant to benefit *all* students, however, adults profited too. The whole of higher education was to form one unified system, under a National Board of Universities and Colleges. This choice was made — as opposed to a binary system, where universities are separate from other colleges and further education institutions, which had previously existed in Sweden and obtains in the United Kingdom and Norway — to avoid differences in social status and to facilitate student choice of studies, as well as to make resources allocation easier. There was to be a greater geographical accessibility of study opportunities, principally by converting former teacher training colleges into colleges of higher education. Administration was to be decentralized into six regions around the existing universities. A regional board was to be responsible for the planning and co-ordination of resources.

The programmes offered by universities and colleges were to be of four kinds. Three were to be full-degree programmes, the fourth consisted of single courses. Students could register for a single course, according to their interests and ability, and they could, by taking further single courses on a credit system, ultimately achieve a full degree. Full-degree programmes were reorganized to offer better opportunities in the labour market on graduation. Both the single courses and the revised degree programmes made it easier and more attractive for mature students to undertake higher education.

It was a new admissions policy that really offered adults a

permanent opening. There were to be four categories of entrant: those who had taken a three-year upper secondary course; those who had taken a two-year upper secondary course; those who had a certificate from a folk high school;[19] and those who were at least twenty-five years old and had had a minimum of four years work experience (including work in the home). Suitably qualified adults might obtain entry in any category, only twenty per cent of the places in each one being reserved for entrants coming directly from school. In some study programmes, for example in medicine and teacher training, the number of places had been limited for years. Where this applied, the number of candidates accepted from each category was to be proportional to the number of applications in each one. Where there was competition for places adult applicants in the first two categories would enjoy an advantage in that points for length of work experience, up to five years, would be added to school marks.

To take a full-degree programme candidates were to give evidence of general educational competence and for certain study areas competence in specific subjects would be required, for example a knowledge of mathematics for science and technology. One general requirement, English and Swedish up to the level of upper secondary school, would be met by candidates in the third and fourth categories, not by a formal examination, but by a testimonial from an employer or some other acceptable person. Candidates in the fourth category could obtain points corresponding to the school marks of other groups by sitting a voluntary study aptitude test, administered once a year. Less demanding and formal requirements were laid down for entry to a single subject course.

Relaxed conditions for adults, applied experimentally in the early 'seventies, more generous and more widely available maintenance grants, free tuition and, from 1975, the right to educational leave, had already had a double effect on entry into higher education. The number of new students aged twenty-five or over rose from twenty-five per cent in 1970 (a high proportion compared with other countries) to fifty per cent in 1976. Enrolments for 1977, after reform legislation came into effect, only confirmed the trend. Well over half, both of new entrants and of all undergraduate students, were over the age of twenty-five. This was true of both sexes.

Table 4 Swedish higher education: First year students, autumn 1977, by sex and age[20]

Age	Males %	Females %	Total %
24 and under	45	40	42
25—47	50	54	53
Over 47	5	6	5

Table 5 Swedish higher education: Total undergraduate enrolment, autumn 1977, by sex and age[21]

Age	Males %	Females %	Total %
24 and under	45	45	45
25—47	51	50	50
Over 47	4	5	5

A second development has occurred, to which the increase in mature students has contributed. The majority of new students do not now register themselves for a full degree. In the autumn of 1976 as many as seventy per cent intended to take only one or two subjects. Moreover the tendency to stay a shorter time in the college or university and not to continue study in any subject beyond one or two semesters is affecting entry to post-graduate courses and the organization of teaching. The pattern of municipal adult education is being repeated in that curriculum and methods designed for young people are proving inappropriate to adults with their particular learning problems and life experience. The complete change in the age distribution of students will require a further radical rethinking in higher education, which may be seen both as a challenge and an opportunity.[22]

Sweden was not alone in reorganizing its higher education system, indeed it was rather late to do so. In the United Kingdom the Report of the Robbins Committee on the subject, the creation of a number of new universities and then of polytechnics belonged to the 1960s. In the same decade university institutes of technology were founded and a major reform of universities was enacted in France. In 1969 Norway began to introduce district colleges and about the same time an experiment in *Gesamthochschulen*, or comprehensive universities, was begun in the Federal German Republic.

These developments were all to a large degree inspired by pressure on higher education places, a desire to achieve greater equality of access to post-secondary study, and to make the curriculum more relevant to working life, so that graduates would find it easier to get jobs and the economy would obtain the manpower it needed. There were a number of other similarities to be noted: the resemblance of British polytechnics, French IUTs and Norwegian district colleges; the adoption of a binary policy in these States; the decentralization of administration in the Swedish law of 1977 and the French one of 1968. There was also a general concern to open higher education more widely to adults. It became an obligation of French universities under the 1968 law — in polytechnics and district colleges a quarter and a fifth respectively of all students are over twenty-five years old. The Open University in the United Kingdom was intended entirely for adult students. No other Western European country has done so much, however, as Sweden to encourage mature student participation in higher education or achieved such striking results.

One might argue that this was a logical consequence of the Swedes' greater overall commitment to education and to equality of opportunity between generations. More obviously than other nations they have linked their prosperity and social advance to education and have been prepared to invest a higher proportion of their gross national product in it. Their belief in recurrent education and in the need to give adults the same chances as the younger generation has led them inevitably on from municipal adult schooling to higher education for adults. Their pragmatic concern for social justice and peace, one might contend, has overborne respect for academic standards more than in other countries to let mature students in. The build up of large-scale participation in other forms of adult education had prepared large numbers of people to take advantage of the more advanced opportunities offered.

All this could be true, although it indicates a consistency of policy planning and behaviour, not universal among nations, which might be explained by the fact that Sweden could afford it and by the existence of a national consensus of opinion about the worth of education. One should also note, however, that at the time higher education reform was being planned, Sweden experienced a sharp decline in the entry to post-secondary courses of young people direct from school, while, when other countries were introducing their reforms, demand from their population in this age group was still increasing. Sweden therefore had a reason others did not have to seek among adults so high a proportion of the pool of highly educated manpower it would need. Only now in countries such as the United Kingdom is the prospect of a similar situation engaging the attention of policy planners.[23]

Outreach activities in Sweden

From official figures it appears that annual enrolments in Government-subsidized adult education in Sweden are equal to about sixty-nine per cent of the adult population — although of course, there is double counting, due to the fact that some people participate in more than one course during a year.[24] It would not be an exaggeration to say that between forty-five and fifty per cent of Swedish adults undertake some form of systematic study every year. It may, therefore, seem surprising that Sweden should be so concerned with outreach, that is activities designed to increase awareness and utilization of adult education opportunities, particularly by direct intervention and interaction with a target population.

There are, however, significant gaps, certain groups of people who never take up the opportunities offered. These are to be found mostly in the socially and educationally disadvantaged, the very population sectors that have always been the priority target of adult education provision. To confront this problem the Government created in 1970 the Committee on Methods Testing in Adult Education (FÖVUX), in response to recommendations by the Trade Union Confederation and the Workers' Educational Association. It was to set up a project to determine what were the factors which stopped people with below average schooling from taking part in adult education and to conduct experiments to test different methods of overcoming the identified obstacles to participation, including different types of financial assistance to individuals. The cost was to be met by the State.

An experiment was undertaken, running over several years in different regions of the country. Each year a programme of study was offered to certain adults in selected occupational or social categories, or living in selected types of community. Intensive methods of recruitment were used and each sample was divided into groups, in each one of which different measures were taken to facilitate or to encourage participation. At the end of each year the results were evaluated and the subsequent year's work was planned in the light of the experience obtained.

Throughout the experiment the programme of study was the same. The adults were invited to participate in a study circle in one of four subjects, Swedish, English, mathematics, or social studies, the choice of subject being left to each student. In later years courses for some groups were supplemented by a period of residential study in a folk high school.

At different times in the project recruitment was directed towards the following occupational and social categories:

1. employees in industry working normal hours;
2. employees in heavy manufacturing industry working shifts;
3. shift workers in the mining industry;
4. employees of nursing institutions working irregular hours;
5. people living in sparsely populated areas;
6. housewives;
7. physically handicapped, particularly people having sight or hearing defects, or limited mobility.

The persons to be contacted were to be between the ages of twenty-five and sixty-seven, have had only six or seven years schooling and not previously have participated in adult education.[25]

The recruitment was undertaken by study organizers,

selected at their place of work by trade unions in consultation with local branches of the Workers' Educational Association (ABF) and Salaried Employees' Educational Association (TBV). ABF selected those who were to approach housewives and local handicapped organizations selected those who were to work with handicapped adults. The organizers were to contact as many persons as possible in each target group, either at their place of work or, in the case of housewives, at home. They were to outline the scheme and to invite them to participate, explaining the options open to them. A week's training was given to organizers and they were paid for the time spent on the task.

Groups were offered differing conditions of enrolment and study:

1. some were to study in working hours with payment in lieu of wages;
2. some were to study outside working hours, but were offered an incentive payment (300 kroner) on condition they attended seventy per cent of course meetings;
3. some were to study in working hours, with payment in lieu of wages and with the incentive payment;
4. some were to study half in and half out of working hours and to receive payment in lieu of wages;
5. some were to study outside working hours without incentive payments or payments in lieu of wages.

No charge was made for tuition or course materials and students could apply for a grant to meet the cost of travel, meals and child care.

The number of people contacted varied from year to year as the target categories changed, from 3,962 in 1970—1 to 2,069 in 1973—4. There were complex correlations between categories, subject preferences, conditions of study and year of study. It is possible to indicate some of these by taking as an example the third year of the project, 1972—3. Then 4,512 persons were contacted, of whom 2,176 expressed a wish to participate in a FÖVUX course. The target groups, the number of individuals approached and the proportion of favourable responses are shown in Table 6.

Table 6   Results of Swedish outreach activity, 1972–3[26]

Occupational or social target group	Number approached	% wishing to participate in scheme	% not wishing to participate in scheme
Employees with normal working hours	2349	40	60
Industrial shift workers	793	58	42
Personnel working duty rosters in nursing institutions	500	81	19
Women working at home	464	37	63
Persons with defective vision	82	56	44
Deaf persons	47	75	25
Persons hard of hearing	103	55	45
Disabled persons	174	35	65

The overall favourable response was forty-eight per cent, but there were wide variations from group to group, from eighty-one per cent of nursing personnel to thirty-five per cent of disabled persons. More people wanted to join the special study circles than could be accommodated and those for whom no place could be found were offered free study in regular ABF and TBV circles. Altogether the scheme ran 110 study circles with 1,045 participants. They were planned to last between forty and sixty hours, and targets were largely met, the average duration being forty-six hours. Of those who were approached and expressed a subject preference forty-nine per cent opted for English, eighteen and a half per cent for Swedish, eighteen and a half per cent for mathematics and fourteen per cent for social studies. Again, however, there were wide variations from group to group — and also variations in subject popularity from year to year.

Students were not given the opportunity to choose their conditions of enrolment and study. The effect of these and of financial assistance was, however, investigated. Study in working hours was much more popular than spare time study of any kind. Seventy-five per cent of those who were given the chance to study wholly in working hours and over fifty per cent of those who could study half in working hours said that these conditions had directly influenced their decision to participate. Help with child minding also had its effect, but the influence of the incentive allowance was negligible. Apart from these conditions the main reason given for joining a study circle was interest in the subject. The personal contact of the study organizer was also important.

The people contacted who did not wish to join the scheme were asked their reasons and again the answers given varied from group to group. Many of those in paid employment said they had not the energy to study and work. Others felt they were too old to start studying again or they did not have the time. Many handicapped could not participate through poor health, which could help to explain the small number of disabled persons who wished to do so.

In 1974, after four years operation, FÖVUX made a number of specific proposals to the Government as a result of experience in the scheme. Noting the importance of recruiting outreach workers from the groups at which the activities were aimed, it proposed that trade unions and other popular associations receive grants to finance such activities, particularly in the workplace and, in order to reach house-wives, in housing estates. The law, which had come into force in 1974, giving trade union representatives the right to carry on their union duties in working hours without loss of pay, could be used to cover adult education outreach work.

The committee disapproved of differential financing between priority and non-priority study circles, which it considered smacked of interference in the affairs of educational associations. It believed that the aim should be free study circles for all, just as municipal adult and higher education were free. In order to achieve this goal it recommended larger grants for the associations, to be adjusted annually in the light of wage and price increases. Special assistance was proposed to provide counselling services and to help educational work with handicapped people and those living in isolated areas. At the time of the committee's Report the law on educational leave was still at the stage of discussion. Assuming that it would be passed, the committee recognized that it could only help those in heavy work or working shifts to undertake study circles if they were compensated for loss of earnings. Since existing forms of study assistance grants applied only to more extended studies, FÖVUX proposed both hourly and daily grants for those joining study circles or attending short courses in folk high schools.

Whether as a direct consequence of the Report or not, much of what was recommended has been implemented — outreach activity in the workplace, higher State grants to educational associations, hourly and daily study allowances. In fact this is one of the distinctive features of the Swedish scheme — not only is the relationship between it and subsequent national policy close, but it is sufficiently near in time for the link to be apparent. In other countries one has the impression that similar experiments are conducted with little confidence, or even little concern, that national practices will be significantly influenced by the results they achieve — at least in the short term.

The same problem of non-participation has provoked outreach projects in a number of States. Although adult education has in principle set its sights primarily on those in most need — the adults who have had least education — it is everywhere the case that these have shown themselves least likely to participate. Numerous attempts have been made, usually on a short-term, experimental basis, to involve them in systematic learning experiences. More than ten years ago a project was undertaken in an area of Lorraine, in France, dependent on the coal and iron industries.[27] In the United Kingdom projects have been conducted in a working-class district of Liverpool, mining villages in Staffordshire and a modern housing estate in Southampton.[28] A number of experiments have been reported in Holland.[29] Nowhere has the effect of such schemes been so general as that of the FÖVUX project.

The people at whom the latter was directed were similar in kind to those in other schemes — in skilled or semi-skilled employment, working unsocial hours, living in isolated places or having disabilities which made participation in education difficult, and all having minimal schooling. Most other projects, however, assumed that educationally and socially disadvantaged adults might not take part in adult education because the subjects or the learning format offered were uncongenial or unsuited to their perceived needs. Much effort was expended on attempting to discover what and how they wanted to learn. That does not appear to have been the case in Sweden. The only format offered was the study circle, the choice was limited to only four standard school subjects, which might otherwise be called subjects essential to fundamental competence in society, and even the length of the courses was predetermined to a large degree. There was nothing to suggest that these limitations were imposed because of lack of resources to do otherwise, so one may assume a confidence in the suitability and/or flexibility of the study circle to meet individual adult needs. The restriction of subject choice suggests either a belief that these subjects were the ones the target groups would want, or else that the Swedes, with a practicality already noted, were concerned to get adults to participate not merely in any kind of study, but in study which would be of social value.

The scale of the Swedish experiment is important in terms of size of population. If a similar project contacting the same proportion of the adult population were conducted in France or the United Kingdom it would have to reach nearly 100,000 people. Since politicians and public opinion are not for the most part statistical scientists, the sheer numbers involved in relation to total population appear likely to have given the results weight that no other outreach activities have matched.

In that the experiment involved systematic and ongoing co-operation between the State, private social associations, trade unions and employees, already identified as the most potent organizational forces in Swedish society, conditions were already set at the outset for the results to be taken seriously. That payment of incentive grants and study allowances could be envisaged is evidence of Swedish prosperity and commitment to adult education for reasons of economics and social justice that have also been discussed.

The FÖVUX project was therefore an attempt to tackle a problem common to all Western European countries, but the methods used, the scale of operation and the consequences of it in general practice depended on conditions which did not obtain to the same degree or in the same combination elsewhere. It would therefore be unwise to relate its lessons to other States less prosperous, less united in belief in education, less successful in attracting adults to continuing study, with different social goals and even a different history.

References

1. s–v STAHRE, *Adult Education in Sweden*, Stockholm, Swedish Institute, 1966.
2. *Adult Education in the Nordic Countries*, Stockholm, Nordic Council, 1976 and R. UDDMAN, 'New developments in Swedish adult education' *Notes and Studies*, 45—46, Amersfoort, European Bureau of Adult Education, 1970.
3. P. HAMMARBERG, 'The situation and tasks of the voluntary organisations', *Notes and Studies*, 49—50, Amersfoort, European Bureau of Adult Education, 1971, and L–O EDSTRÖM, *Struktur und Reform schwedischer Erwachsenenbildung*, Bonn, George Westermann Verlag, 1969.
4. *Act Concerning Leisure-time Education*, 1968.
5. *Federal Law on the Promotion of Adult Education and Public Libraries out of Federal Funds*, 1973.
6. P. BERGEVIN, *Adult Education in Sweden*, Bloomington, Indiana University, 1961.
7. *Adult Education in the Nordic Countries*, op. cit.
8. Quoted in L. TRICHAUD, *L'Education populaire en Europe: 2, Scandinavie*, Paris, Editions Ouvrières, 1969.
9. P. BERGEVIN, op. cit.
10. Statistics provided by the Swedish National Board of Education.
11. Statistics provided by the Swedish National Board of Education.
12. According to 1977—8 figures they cover in fact about forty-five per cent of costs, no doubt due to inflation. *Fact Sheets on Sweden: Adult Education*, Stockholm, Swedish Institute, April, 1978.

13. L. TRICHAUD, op. cit.
14. ibid.
15. *Adult Education in the Nordic Countries*, op. cit.
16. *Act Concerning Leisure-time Education*, 1968.
17. B. JOHANSSON, *Adult Education in Sweden*, Stockholm, Swedish Institute, 1973.
18. E.J. KING ET AL., *Post-Compulsory Education: a New Analysis in Western Europe*, London/Beverly Hills. Sage Publications, 1974.
19. For a discussion of Scandinavian folk high schools, see Chapter 8.
20. *Higher Education in Sweden, Facts and Figures 1978*, Stockholm, National Board of Universities and Colleges.
21. ibid.
22. U. DAHLÖFF, *Reforming Higher Education and External Studies in Sweden and Australia*, Uppsala, Uppsala Studies in Education 3, 1977.
23. *Higher Education into the 1990s*, London, Her Majesty's Stationery Office, 1978.
24. Estimate based on statistics provided by the Swedish National Board of Education.
25. Information on the FÖVUX experiment is based on *Extended Adult Education*, Stockholm, Liber Tryck, 1974.
26. ibid.
27. M. LESNE, C. COLLON, C. OECONOMO, *Changement socio-professional et formation — Etude d'une Situation de Crise dans le Bassin de Briey*, Paris, INFA, 1970.
28. T. LOVETT, *Adult Education, Community Education and the Working Class*, London, Ward Lock Educational, 1975.
P. FORDHAM ET AL., *Learning Networks in Adult Education. Non-formal Education on a Housing Estate*, London, Routledge Kegan Paul, 1979.
29. *Experiments in Dutch Adult Education*, Amersfoort, the Netherlands Centre for Adult Education, Study Centre NCVO and the European Bureau for Adult Education, 1977.

CHAPTER 4

The Federal German Republic

The United Kingdom and Sweden show a growth of adult education in socially and politically stable societies, moving steadily towards democratization. The story of the Federal German Republic is very different. Until 1871 there was no unified German state and since then it has undergone such ups and downs that the continuity of its adult education tradition is quite surprising.

After 1815 Germany returned for fifty years to being a collection of independent states, autocratically and conservatively ruled, backward socially and economically. The French Revolution and the Napoleonic period had left a legacy of liberalism and nationalism, but they were repressed by the reactionary separatism of the times, surfacing briefly in the 1848 Revolution, only to be put down again. The more popular of the two was nationalism and it proved decisive in the 1860s, when Otto von Bismarck, Chief Minister of Prussia, already the strongest German state, used it as a tool to weld the motley collection into a federal empire, with the King of Prussia as German Emperor.

Apart from the ripeness of the times and his own diplomatic skills, Bismarck's success rested on Prussia's administrative efficiency, the power of its military machine, which won decisive wars against Denmark, Austria and France, and, perhaps above all, its rapid and skilful industrialization from the 1840s onward, for which it enjoyed the advantage of good supplies of raw materials. During the Empire, Germany's economic and population growth continued, so that by the beginning of the twentieth century she was challenging Great Britain as the most advanced and most powerful power in Europe, with 65,000,000 inhabitants.[1]

Although there was a parliament, the Empire was autocratically ruled. The dominant class was the nobility, particularly the officer caste. The intellectual and business middle class, wealthy and dazzled by the glamour of imperial success, accepted political impotence. The working class, whose party, the Social Democrats, was the largest in parliament by 1912, also took too much pride in German achievements seriously to challenge the existing despotism. But a rigidly class-structured society, held together only by loyalty to a Crown, which depended on prestige acquired by military victory, revealed its divisions when Germany lost the First World War and the Emperor abdicated.

The country was not dismembered, but became a parliamentary republic, with its seat of government in Weimar. It was a form of government of which the Germans had no experience and whose dullness compared ill with the colourfulness of its predecessor. Its achievements in restoring a ruined country were solid and it might have survived the resentment against it for having accepted humiliating peace terms, the pressures of disappointed nationalism and the stresses imposed by bitter struggles between political extremists of the left and right, but when to these were added the deprivations caused by the world slump of the early 1930s, it fell.

There followed the dictatorship of Adolf Hitler and his National Socialist Party, which lasted twelve years from 1933. Hitler preached the right of the Aryan race, of which the German people were the highest examples, to rule the world. He demanded the subordination of the individual to the State and ruthlessly crushed all opposition. Since he managed to restore the economy, to impose political peace and by his foreign policy achievements fed German nationalist ambitions, he carried most Germans with him. Once again they responded to success and closed their eyes to the darker side of the regime. When in the Second World War Hitler over-reached himself, he brought Germany down in greater ruin than that of 1918, with a completely demoralized people.

Recovery was, however, rapid, greatly assisted by the split between Russia and the other victors, led by the United States of America, which made Germany the main field of action in the cold war. There was one disadvantage: the country was divided into two, the east becoming the German Democratic Republic, in the Communist bloc, and the rest, the Federal German Republic, a bulwark of western parliamentary democracy. Under clever leadership the FGR embraced its role with enthusiasm. The fatal glamour of nationalism and a penchant to obey authority unquestioningly having twice destroyed Germany, it turned to the hard task of rebuilding the economy and making democracy work.

Adopting a free market approach, its success in the first part was immense and it is now the richest state in Europe. That success, the support of the Western Allies and fear of Russia, helped to establish firm roots for what is in effect a two-party parliamentary regime. Because of its strategic position in the cold war, it was soon accepted in the North Atlantic Treaty Organization and it became one of the founders of the European Community, but its foreign policy has shown none of the aggressiveness that had previously brought the country such trouble.

The size of the FGR is roughly equal to that of the United Kingdom and less than half that of France. Its population, 62,000,000, is greater than that of either. It is a federal state of ten provinces, plus West Berlin, an enclave entirely surrounded by the German Democratic Republic. To ensure against too great a concentration of power at the centre, there is considerable devolution of legislative and administrative authority to the governments of the provinces.

Bismarck made Germany a pioneer in State welfare provision and the Germans have long been accustomed to extensive social security. In the FGR the cost is largely met, not out of taxes, but by insurance premiums, a further sign of the desire to reduce the bureaucratic control of the State. Most people insure against accident, sickness, disability, to provide for retirement pensions and unemployment benefits. There is a large proportion of exemptions, however, and the cost of contributions is high.

As one of the basic institutions of democracy, the Allies recreated trade unions, banned under Hitler. They have become rich and powerful. Whereas British and French unions see their interests in conflict with those of the employers, West German ones, in their desire to become an integral part of the capitalist system, are co-operative. In much of industry and commerce there is worker participation in management. Since its creation the FGR has had an excellent record of industrial peace, which has both contributed to its economic success and been a consequence of it.

Ever since the Reformation Germany has been divided between Protestants, predominant in the north and east, and Catholics, in the south and west. In the nineteenth century neither the Evangelical (formed of a union between Calvinists and Lutherans) nor the Catholic Church was notably progressive or critical of the social *status quo*, although the latter did fight Bismarck and win on issues such as its prerogatives in marriage and education. They retained such strength in Germany, however, that Hitler dared not suppress them and they constituted the most outspoken and enduring centres of protest against Nazism. As a result, in the spiritual chaos after the Second World War the appeal of the churches was great and thousands flocked to them. Since that period their attraction has declined. Although ninety per cent of West Germans are nominally either Protestant or Catholic, in approximately equal numbers, only about a quarter go to church regularly. Nevertheless each church is allowed to levy a tax on every registered member, which gives them substantial funds, and in many areas of political and social life their influence remains considerable.

Prussia, as a Protestant country, took education seriously and it is on the Prussian system, as reformed after the Napoleonic wars, that German education is founded.[2] There was the primary school for the common people, offering basic literacy and numeracy, and secondary school, the *Gymnasium*, with teaching based on Latin and Greek, but including German, science and mathematics, which was open only to a social and intellectual élite and led on to university, where the emphasis was laid on academic freedom and scientific research.

During the nineteenth century additions to the system were made which contributed to Germany's industrial expansion. Continuation classes to the primary school, for young

100

people who had begun paid employment, helped to create a skilled, educated labour force. New types of secondary school stressed mathematics, natural sciences and modern languages, and technical universities were founded specifically to train applied scientists and engineers.

There were some attempts at democratization during the Weimar Republic, but major structural changes only occurred after the Second World War. In the FGR responsibility for education at all levels lies principally with the provincial governments.[3] In spite of the devolution of authority there is a common basic pattern. Education is compulsory from the age of six to fifteen or sixteen years, according to province. Primary, secondary and most tertiary education is free.

All children go to primary school for four years and then on to a four-year, six-year, or nine-year secondary school. It is normally through the last, the Gymnasium, that one enters university. Comprehensive education has made only limited progress and there is less pressure for equality than in the United Kingdom and Sweden. This is in accord with the competitive market philosophy of society. Following a century-old tradition there are many opportunities for vocational education at post-compulsory level, including full-time or compulsory part-time courses for those who leave school at the minimum age. It is possible, though a slow progress, to rise through the post-compulsory system to university. Higher education, a centre of high prestige and conservatism, has been difficult to reform, partly because the provinces cannot agree on a common policy. Nevertheless modernization and democratization are occurring, to meet the enormous demand for student places, but they cannot compare with those of Sweden.

Although there were numerous unco-ordinated initiatives before then,[4] popular education, as adult education was called in Germany until after the Second World War, laid down what are recognizably the roots of contemporary forms during the Empire. The origins of evening and residential folk high schools will be considered later, but there was also the Society for the Spread of Popular Education, founded in 1871, which had 7,000 local branches by 1910, offering lecture and discussion evenings and library facilities. In 1890 the People's Association for Catholic Germany was founded and in 1906 the Social Democratic Party set up its Central Education Committee.[5]

The country's ruin of 1918 called popular education to the major task of rebuilding the national morale of the whole German people, not merely the working class, and educating it for democracy. The Republic's Constitution laid down that popular education was to be encouraged by national, provincial and local authorities. Folk high schools were the major institutions, but trade unions also played a constructive role, including the foundation of a workers' academy at the University of Frankfurt on Main.

The Nazis put an end to this activity, but it was on the precedent and the survivors of the 1920s that adult education was rebuilt after 1945 as a major instrument of education for democracy. Partly because help was to be encouraged where it could be found, and partly in pursuit of the policy of reducing dependence on the State, a multiplicity of private organizations became involved in the work. Protestant and Catholic Churches run seminars, study circles and have residential centres. The German Trade Union Federation has a large, highly structured programme, laying emphasis on both union and general education, but including some vocational work. The major political parties either have their own educational organizations, or are closely linked to one.

Entry qualifications to further and higher education have not been relaxed for adults, as they have in Sweden, but there is Second Chance Education, offered in both private and public establishments. Evening secondary schools provide the way by which adults may arrive at higher education and, following a tradition going back a century they may undertake specifically vocational studies in further education or vocational training schools alongside young people.

Following, at some distance, it is true, an example set by North Rhine Westphalia in 1953, almost all the provinces have passed legislation in the last decade to regulate, protect and promote adult education. They lay down the obligation of public authorities to support it and guarantee the freedom of private provision and its right to subsidy from public funds. Some have also passed laws which oblige employers to release employees from work for short periods to enable them to follow courses of education. Provincial legislation is not intended to cover education of a directly vocational nature, as this is a Federal responsibility and is governed by two Federal measures: the Employment Promotion Act and the Vocational Training Act, both of 1969.[6]

The evening folk high schools in the Federal Republic

The German term *Volkshochschule* derives from the Danish, *folkehøjskole*. It came into use towards the end of the nineteenth century, when people in Germany were seeking an appropriate institutional form for popular education. At that time a number of educators were attracted by the Danish folk high school and also by the British university extension movement. There was some support for the adoption of elements from both, without a clear distinction always being observed between the two. In the course of time *Volkshochschule* came to denote two quite different kinds of institution, a residential one closer to the Danish model and an evening one bearing some resemblance to the British. The English version of the term 'folk high school' is closer to the Danish origin than to its German meaning, which would be more accurately rendered by 'people's university'. However, it would be pedantic to insist on correctness when usage is so firmly established, so in this book *Volkshochschule* will be rendered throughout by 'folk high school'.

The immediate predecessors of the evening folk high school belong to the Imperial period. Then there were committed middle-class efforts to provide working class adults with opportunities to undertake serious sequential study. They took two forms, private associations, like the Humboldt Academy, Berlin, and lecture courses for the general public given by universities.[7] The latter, although as popular as the former (they were cheaper), attracted criticism for their unsuitability to working class needs. Universities were seen to be following an outworn tradition in their belief in the primacy of knowledge for its own sake, without concern for its relevance or transmission to human beings in their social situation. What was required was a new direction for popular education, concerned with the individual as a member of a class, a community, a nation, as a person engaged in an occupation.

Out of these discussions, some experiments just before 1914 and intensive debate during the First World War, emerged the folk high school, which would be an instrument for the reconstruction and unification of the demoralized, disunited nation. At New Year, 1919, a circular of the Prussian Ministry of Culture defined a folk high school as an institution serving no party, group or confession, but the people as a whole.[8] The new Republican Constitution singled it out as an agency of popular education to be supported by public funds.

Robert von Erdberg, a seminal figure in folk high school history, wrote in the Prussian circular:

> . . . for the goal is not only to raise the working class intellectually, but to renew our intellectual life overall, which must draw away from the narrowness and narrow-heartedness of bourgeois thought, and from contact with the masses create new content. In a word, it is a question of the creation of a new culture, in which the upper class and the people will fuse into an organic unity.[9]

Some progress was made, since by 1932 there were 216 evening folk high schools,[10] all open to the general public, some free of ideological bias, others sponsored by churches or special interest groups. Each one was a separate, locally-controlled institution, responding to perceived local need. Most depended on local authority grant for survival. Under National Socialism they were taken over by the German Labour Front and used as agencies for the spread of Nazi ideology.

Because of the good reputation folk high schools had had internationally in the 1920s, when in 1945 the British occupying authorities sought to promote adult education, they were keen to encourage former FHS workers, who were anxious to recommence their activities. In a short time, in all the occupation zones, folk high schools were re-established. In the western zones they were strongly influenced by British ideas of liberal education for personal development and responsible citizenship. Following the example of the British WEA, close links were formed with the trade unions in a joint organization, *Arbeit und Leben*. They did not, however, follow the British recommendation to co-operate closely with universities. The latter were distrusted for their reactionary political history and, as in the early years of the century, for the narrowness and abstract nature of their academic tradition.[11]

In the late 1940s and early 1950s, organizations of folk high schools were founded at district and provincial level and then, in 1953, at Federal level, when the *Deutscher Volkshochschul-Verband*, the German Folk High Schools Association, was set up. The evening folk high school had not only become more influential than it ever had been during the 1920s, it had become the dominant form of adult education institution in the Federal Republic, embodying the animating principles of national adult education policy. In the years which have followed, its position has strengthened.

Folk high schools may be sponsored by the State, local authorities, church organizations or other private associations. From the early years after 1945, municipalities and other local authorities set up evening folk high schools and subsidized those that were privately established. As adult education came increasingly to be regarded as an integral part of the education system and the folk high school the basic form of adult education, so the number of publicly-owned ones increased, and private ones, because of their growing reliance on public funds, became more susceptible to influence by public authorities and more integrated into the official network of adult education provision.

It is interesting that this absorption into the state apparatus appears to have inspired no disquiet about the evening folk high school's independence of operation. In part this may be because most provinces have passed adult education legislation in the last decade, in which it has been customary to guarantee it: 'State promotion of adult education leaves untouched the right of an institution to formulate independently its educational programme. Institutions are free in their choice of director and staff and in their teaching.'[12] Moreover, just as there is already devolution of responsibility for education from the Federal to provincial governments, so these laws devolve responsibility to local authorities, thus placing adult education, in theory at any rate, under local democratic control. If that were not enough, the constitution of a folk high school, which has legal force, protects it from direct intervention by local politicians.

In early post-war days, under the influence of British liberal education, evening folk high schools concentrated on general and role education. There was some vocationally orientated teaching, but the award of certificates and diplomas was not encouraged. Since then the emphasis has changed to meet the demands of different social and economic circumstances. According to the Folk High School Association subjects taught comprise 'techniques of learning, society, politics, law, educational issues, psychology, philosophy, religion, literature, art, music, the media, mathematics, natural sciences, technology, economics, commercial practice, languages, home economics, health, gymnastics, hygiene, games and modelling, late acquisition of school qualifications.'[13]

The last seeks to bridge the gap between adults and young people who have had better educational opportunities. The Association has developed its own certificates in modern languages, mathematics, electronics, statistics, data processing, electro-technology, chemistry, with courses of instruction and modes of assessment adapted to adults. They have been widely recognized as proofs of competence. Liberal studies are still very popular, but specifically vocational courses, in addition to the certificate ones, are offered on a large scale.

Study is organized in a variety of ways — formal classes, study circles, discussion groups, independent working groups, lectures, forums, brains trusts, and excursions, concerts and exhibitions are arranged. The length of study varies widely, for example the 1979—80 programme of the Oberhausen Town Folk High School (North Rhine Westphalia) advertises offerings ranging from single meetings to numerous courses which last for sixty two-hour meetings.[14] Activities are no longer confined to the evenings, there are daytime and weekend courses and longer full-time ones. Some small folk high schools do not have their own premises, but others have elaborate purpose-built establishments. Oberhausen, in addition to Folk High School House, operates in forty-six different locations, schools, community centres, factories and business premises.

The constitution of Oberhausen provides an interesting

106

picture of the status and method of government of a large folk high school. It is a public institution, provided by the municipality of Oberhausen, which appoints the Director, who is responsible for its work. Under him responsibility for the programme is in the hands of the head of each subject department. There are planning and advisory committees at each level from the course upwards, and student represent-ation on each one. The folk high school assembly, which meets at least twice a year, has a heavy bias in favour of senior staff. It may make resolutions or recommendations and if the Director does not comply with these, the assembly may refer the matter to the municipality.[15]

In the period since 1962 total expenditure of folk high schools has risen from 41,700,000 deutschmarks to 329,700,000, a considerable growth, even allowing for inflation. Of this sum sixty per cent was received in subsidies, the rest mainly in student fees.[16] There is no fixed scale for the latter: the factors which determine the charge made for each course or series of meetings appear to include the cost of the course, the number of students it is expected to attract and the extent to which it is felt desirable to attract students by low fees. This may be affected by the social importance attached by the institution's management to certain topics or groups. In Oberhausen courses for foreign workers are free, a study group for parents of handicapped children has a fee of 5 deutschmarks for fifteen two-hour meetings, for a course of sixty meetings in Spanish it is 90 deutschmarks.

Since 1962 the number of courses per annum presented by evening folk high schools has more than trebled, the number of enrolments nearly so, and the number of meetings has increased by a factor of six, so that participants now study on average twice as long each year. Table 7 shows the growth in courses and enrolments by subject group since 1970. In addition to enrolments for courses there are currently about 4,000,000 people per annum attending single meeting events. By far the most popular subjects are languages and practical activities. Perhaps the most significant information, in view of the immediate post-war purpose of the evening folk high schools is the decline, both absolute and relative, in the interest in society and politics, the subject matter of citizen-ship education.

Table 7 Evening folk high schools: Courses and enrolments by subject[17]

Subject	1970		1977	
	Courses	Enrolments	Courses	Enrolments
Society & Politics	5,957	181,838	6,269	141,833
Education, philosophy, religion, psychology	3,170	95,269	8,628	158,780
Art	4,511	84,522	4,810	118,803
Regional and local studies	1,718	50,224	1,638	50,988
Mathematics, science, technology	7,009	141,801	9,452	155,410
Administrative and commercial practice	11,077	219,312	18,704	329,860
Languages	31,033	566,566	73,791	1,202,817
Manual and musical activities	15,630	224,859	47,496	622,512
Home economics	8,925	124,469	19,231	253,741
Health care, inc. physical educ.	14,148	323,676	27,755	553,172
Preparation for school leaving certificates	2,435	53,274	2,881	56,203
Other	4,270	161,441	4,176	113,360
Total	109,883	2,227,251	224,831	3,757,479

The influence of folk high schools is strengthened by the German Folk High School Association. This organization represents their interests and provides back-up for their activities. In particular the *Pädagogische Arbeitsstelle*, Educational Centre, in Frankfurt, provides resource and documentation services. It conducts seminars and conferences for provincial or district groups of folk high schools on programme planning, adult learning and teaching methods. The Association also maintains the Adolf Grimme Institute, to promote co-operation between adult education and television, and a Centre for International Co-operation to support adult education in developing countries. From its very early days the Association has joined with the German Trade Union Federation (DGB) in *Arbeit und Leben*, Work and Life, a joint body which, with DGB financial support, arranges lectures, seminars, one-day, weekend and week schools, aimed at promoting the political consciousness of participants, their judgment and knowledge in matters relating to the world of work, politics and social life.

It has been suggested that the evening folk high school owes its pre-eminent position in the Federal German Republic to the fact that it fulfils a role, that of a comprehensive institution of adult education, open to all, which a number of countries appear to have found it necessary to fill. One may ask, then, in what ways does it differ from institutions elsewhere which appear to occupy a similar position, such as British evening institutes and Swedish study circles?

Like the former, but unlike the latter, evening folk high schools have as their essential ingredient, an organizational structure centred on the teaching staff. They exist before the participants arrive, whereas there is no study circle without them, they and they alone are its constituents. Folk high schools and evening institutes, although their identity does not lie in buildings, are, by the names 'school' and 'institute', closely tied to physical facilities, again unlike study circles. The latter cease to exist when the learning process for which they were formed is completed, folk high schools are permanent frameworks set up to accommodate any number of learning experiences.

The evening institute differs from the evening folk high school in that it has no private providing bodies and no guarantee, either in constitution or in principle, to protect it from the direct intervention of the local authority in its teaching programme. The positions of both are determined by systems which make local authorities responsible for ensuring that adequate provision of adult education is made, if not for providing it themselves. The two types of institution are alike in that they are modelled on establishments of formal secondary and tertiary education. The study circle is not. To some degree, in fact, it has developed in reaction against such a model. The British and German practice makes the teacher, who should be a specialist in subject knowledge, responsible for the learning experience, in spite of some limited introduction of student representation in the decision-making process. In principle study circle members are the only arbiters of their learning, there need not be a teacher at all.

Certain points may be made about German history and society, which are likely to have affected the development of the evening folk high school to its present form and position. State suspicion and occasional repression have inhibited the growth of popular associations, except under the Weimar Republic and the present regime. The Prussian tradition of State responsibility for education, making schools and universities institutions of the State, has long ago become the German one. In had become a highly structured system with a high reputation in the nineteenth century. There is evidence to suggest that the Germans are as conformist as the Swedes, but whereas the latter have a tradition of conformity to democratically arrived at norms, the Germans, under the monarchy and National Socialism, have looked for discipline and system imposed by authority.

It is not surprising in these circumstances that popular associations, although some, particularly the Society for the Spread of Popular Education, made a contribution, did not pre-empt the field of adult education to the extent they did in Sweden. Nor, given the well-established academic tradition, is it out of keeping that what was thought to be necessary for adults, at the turn of the century, was an opportunity for serious, systematic study, with the emphasis on the transmission of knowledge from the specialist to the learner within a structured institutional framework. Whether a predilection for formal study and institutional organization was reinforced by British university extension and the Danish folk high school or whether these foreign phenomena helped to establish these tendencies is not clear, but their influence at the beginning of the twentieth century is indisputable. It was undoubtedly the nature of the German university and its relationship with the community, as indeed was the case in Sweden, which ensured that its links with adult education would become tenuous, so that the evening folk high school avoided association with it.

There was not under Weimar that suspicion of central power of the State, that existed after the Second World War. There was need to build a strong State, establish democracy and keep Germany together. Adult education had its part to play in working for both goals and, if it was to do so, it needed public authority support. It was therefore in keeping with the conditions of the time and German educational tradition that evening folk high schools should work with, even under the wing of, public authorities.

In the late 1940s the Weimar situation was to a large extent repeated. The evening folk high schools had, however, extra advantages over any other forms of adult education. Allies and Germans were seeking anything from the past that had not been tainted by Nazism and that was solidly rooted in German life, to serve as foundation for rebuilding. The folk high school, evening or residential, had impeccable credentials from Weimar, its ethos was close to that of the British university/WEA tradition, it had been strongly implanted and a number of its workers had survived the Hitler period and were still alive.

It is plausible to see the current status of the evening folk high school as a resolution of two potentially conflicting forces, on the one hand a policy initiated in 1945 of breaking the educational monopoly of the State and encouraging a plurality of democratic private organizations, on the other a German tradition of ordered study, of respect for scholarly authority, of public authority responsibility for and control of education. Even with the legal and constitutional safe-guards built into the structure, the fact that the system works without friction may in large part be due to a national inclination to accept the system of authority as it is, to adapt oneself to it, rather than to attempt to change it. Private pro-viding bodies, folk high school staff and students tend to conform to local authority, not only because it furnishes the money, but because to do so is seen as good citizenship.[18] In the Federal Republic today one is tempted to ask whether it

111

would make any real difference if the private providers handed over their evening folk high schools to local authorities.

Residential folk high schools in the Federal Republic

The term *Heimvolkshochschule* means a residential people's university. In this book it will be translated by residential folk high school, because that is the accepted English expression. Over the years the institution so-called has developed into something very different from the evening establishments which have just been discussed. It has remained closer to the Scandinavian models from which the term 'folk high school' derived, since its purpose, by definition, is to offer extended residential courses to young adults of both sexes.

At the end of the nineteenth century the Danish folk high school was not only attractive in theory to German popular educationists, it impinged directly on German experience. Danish-speaking inhabitants of Schleswig-Holstein, won by Prussia from Denmark in 1864, used to cross the border to attend Danish folk high schools. In the first decade of the twentieth century, therefore, several establishments were created in Schleswig-Holstein to act as German counter-attractions to these.

There was a rapid resurgence after 1918, when the term *Heimvolkshochschule* came into use to distinguish them from the evening folk high schools. A 1919 Prussian decree, while recognizing that both are covered by the term 'folk high school' says, 'The construction of real folk high schools, which are linked with residential centres, remains the longer term goal'.[19]

Residential folk high schools spread from Schleswig-Holstein to other frontier areas, such as East Prussia, Württemberg and Hanover. The provision of opportunities for extended education, of which living together was an integral part, appeared to have a relevance to the needs of urban, as well as rural, young people and the first residential folk high school for town youth was founded at Dreissigacker, near Meiningen, in 1920.

The Nazis put an end to them, but there was again a

crucial role for them to play in 1945, as the first post-war conference of folk high schools declared:

> Through the collapse of the National Socialist ideas in which they have been brought up and the needs of the present time German adolescents find themselves in an intellectual, spiritual and ethical crisis, which threatens to become a long term state. For the young men and women of 18—30 years of age we must create educational institutions, operating at a deeper level, continuous and comprehending all people, which exclusively serve a new education with independent goals. These educational institutions must be developed out of the special forms of popular education, attempted after the First World War, but only realised here and there, the Youth Folk High School and the Residential Folk High School.[20]

That there was a rapid response was due to the recollected experience of people and organizations and the survival of buildings from the Weimar Republic. Old students and staff occupied influential positions in the western zones of occupation. Churches and private bodies with confessional links enjoyed a prestige in the immediate post-war years, which enabled them to develop their evangelical, pastoral and educational work with public authority support. Rural social and occupationally oriented groups operated to further the interests and education of people living and working in country areas. To a lesser degree the labour movement supported the reopening of residential folk high schools and took part in their provision. Two schools, Husted and Göhrde, which were founded specially for workers by private initiative, created early links with trade unions.

In 1960 the German Committee on Adult Education defined residential folk high schools as centres of the boarding school kind for young adults between the ages of eighteen and thirty, where they could live and learn together. Since the purpose was basic and systematic education for intellectual clarification, inner stability and human and political behaviour, they required courses which lasted longer than four weeks.[21] The Association of Rural Residential Folk High Schools laid down that its members should offer at least one residential course lasting a minimum of four weeks each year.

Schools which fulfil these conditions are recognizably the descendants of those of the 1920s. The changes which have taken place, although major, have not altered the essential pattern. They claim freedom from bias, but in the religious ones the basis of teaching is still the doctrine of the provider. Occupational schools seek to raise the consciousness of the rural/peasant class as an independent group within society, and emphasize political, economic and social questions as they affect it. Non-denominational, non-occupational ones have perhaps the least obvious sectional sympathies, and seek to form adults capable of making their own decisions in religious and ideological matters and in their occupational lives.

There is no common syllabus laid down for residential folk high schools. Each develops its own in accordance with its staff resources and its aims. People do not attend primarily to study a particular subject discipline, but to experience the responsibilities of communal living and to develop as self-confident, independent individuals. They also seek what they did not learn at school, or what they were not sufficiently mature to study there. They do not wish, however, to be reminded of school, they wish to draw on their own experience. Emphasis is on the current world situation, seen in a historical perspective.

Residential folk high schools are centres of general, not vocational, education. They do not teach technical or agricultural subjects. They have always lacked staff competent to undertake the first and so a tradition has grown up of ignoring them. In the case of the second it is thought better to concentrate on issues of the relationship of the country with society. Since the Nazis, nationalism has been discredited in Germany, except in so far as it means the unification of the two Germanies, so that animating principle of the Weimar period is not to be found in residential schools today.

In the 1920s a residential folk high school was conducted, as in Denmark, as a family, of which the principal was the father. Now it is run as a community in which the teacher—student relationship is less important than the mutual education of the students. The atmosphere of the school is decreasingly that of a home as the stress is laid more and more on cognitive learning. Traditionally more importance has been attached to people with experience of the world than to professionally trained teachers. Now as formal teaching and serious study have become central functions, so the tendency has been to call for academically qualified subject specialists.

Rural students of the 1920s, accustomed to bowing to authority, accepted unquestioningly the almost absolute power of the principal, now most schools have written regulations and all have a council of elected student representatives, which exercises wide powers.

As they have always done, the majority of students come from rural occupations, the rest are artisans, workers and clerical staff. They are a much more mixed group than they used to be. Increased mobility of the population, intensified in West Germany by the refugee problem, the fact that residential schools no longer recruit only from their immediate locality, the breakdown of differences between country and town, all have had their effect. Most students have had a fairly low level of previous education. Over two-thirds have attended only the upper primary school and less than ten per cent have a university entrance qualification.

More obviously than most adult education institutions, it may be argued, the long-term residential folk high schools in West Germany owed their implantation to specific political circumstances. At the end of the nineteenth century, to a newly-created state anxious to promote a sense of national identity, the Danish folk high school, inspired by a similar aim and also of proven attraction to German citizens, constituted an obvious model. In 1945 the search was for any kind of democratic institution from the German past which could be used to re-educate a generation of young people entirely steeped in National Socialist ideology. For the re-creation of residential folk high schools there existed people, buildings, a tradition from Weimar of work with just that age group, so it would have been perverse not to encourage their revival.

The advocates of the schools maintain they have a justification which goes beyond that situation, that they constitute the most intensive form possible of education for young adults and that there will always be a need for institutions to provide such education. Against this it was argued by opponents, even immediately after 1945, that it was undesirable and impractical to take young people away from their home environment for months at a time in groups of thirty or forty. What was required was short courses for large numbers, because that way more people would be reached for the same expenditure.

The latter point of view appears to have been justified. The five-month courses of the beginning of the century have shortened, so that few schools offer courses of three months or more. They have to face intense competition from associations and institutions providing programmes of short courses, Protestant and Catholic academies, residential youth centres, civic education centres of various kinds, centres of trade unions and political parties. Many so-called *Heimvolkshochschulen* nowadays offer no long courses at all and almost all have important programmes of short courses.

One of the reasons for the limited success of the longer courses is that only a small number of young, mostly unmarried folk can afford the time away from family and work. The overwhelming number of students come from the lower-paid section of the community and they can neither do without wages, nor is it easy to get leave from their employer. It was hoped that educational leave legislation would help to remedy this, but where provincial governments have passed such laws they seem either to have ignored or rejected the needs of residential folk high schools. In Lower Saxony and Berlin beneficiaries are entitled to ten days leave a year, in Hamburg and Bremen ten days every two years and in Hesse five days a year.[22] They all encourage, therefore, short rather than long courses.

Traditionally residential folk high schools award no diplomas, but present-day emphasis on the award of paper qualifications has obliged them to break away from that too and to offer second chance education. Indeed they are in the somewhat ironical situation that the kind of protection in law and guarantee of public financial support which, for many years, only North Rhine Westphalia gave, has been specifically given to residential folk high schools in the last decade by a number of provincial governments, when the distinctive provision of these institutions is in doubt.[23] Their problems are not entirely unique to the Federal Republic, however, as will be seen when the Danish folk high school is examined (see Chapter 8).

Citizenship education in the Federal Republic

The last two sections have been devoted to types of institution in the Federal German Republic. This one will examine a kind of adult education defined by the purpose it is intended to serve. Any institutional form, content or organization of the learning experience is to be included as long as it is directed to one end, that of *politische Bildung*. Literally in English that means 'political education', but the English term is applied to a much narrower field than the German one. The most appropriate rendering is 'citizenship education', although even that, as commonly used in British adult education, covers too limited a range of subject matter.

That so much emphasis has been laid on citizenship education since the Second World War is due to the state of Germany and of German education in 1945, which has already been discussed. Adult educators were greatly influenced by American and British ideas, particularly by the latter. Discussing the British recommendations Professor Borinski, a German closely involved in educational reconstruction after the war, presents their implications as follows:

> According to British theory and practice, *liberal education* stands in contrast to *vocational training*. It is in this sense a disinterested and general education which concerns itself with the whole personality. It affects the totality of human existence. It teaches a person to make the most of life. Thus it is more comprehensive and goes deeper than mere preparation for a trade or profession. But if we are to get the most from life we cannot be purely concerned with the individual. Liberal education puts the individual alongside other human beings, alongside his fellow citizens in society and State. Liberal education is at the same time *education for democracy*. After the collapse of Germany, education for democracy was imperative in a situation where the anti-democratic, authoritarian regime had been destroyed and people, especially young people, had to learn how to live together in freedom and responsibility, criticism and tolerance.[24]

German adult educators were convinced that education for democracy must be the prime purpose of their activities in those post-war years, that all education for adults, whatever subject-matter or other purpose it might have, should, like liberal education, be animated by democratic ideals and contribute to education for democracy. Citizenship education ought not, therefore, to be confined to a specific range of subjects, but all adult education should be citizenship education. They were the more sensitive about this, since it was felt that the Weimar democracy had collapsed because the German people had not learnt at that time to 'live together in freedom and responsibility, criticism and tolerance' and it had been partly the failure of educational provision that they had not.

So one finds Professor Borinski insisting some years after the war that citizenship education 'does not come in as one subject among others, but is set in the middle of the whole folk high school work, it should fill and permeate the courses and community life of the folk high school'.[25] It should not only, however, set the tone for all adult education, provision should also be made specifically to furnish citizenship education. The collaboration of the Folk High School Association and the German Trade Union Federation in *Arbeit und Leben* was directed to this end. As has already been seen, it was the prime purpose and justification of the residential folk high school.

In the early post-war period the main effort was directed towards young adults, who had never learnt any better than National Socialism. Even many of those employed by the occupation forces were still strongly Nazi at heart. These, and the thousands of wandering young people who were gathered in camps, received some education in democracy. Partly out of this experience, partly from lessons learnt from abroad and from previous experience of residential folk high schools, residential courses came to be considered extremely valuable for citizenship education. The living together with other students and educators created a miniature society in which to practise 'freedom and responsibility, criticism and tolerance' and in which to develop by experimental learning responsible social attitudes. Having students there twenty-four hours a day, undistracted by claims of family or job, permitted very intensive study. Rejecting for the most part the long courses of the residential folk high schools, many groups and associations set up centres, under a number of names, in which young people and later, to a growing extent, older adults could stay together for short periods in order to further education for citizenship. In 1959 the majority of these institutions formed the Working Group of Youth Educational Centres. In 1962, as the importance of work with adults became more apparent, the name was changed to the *Arbeitskreis deutscher Bildungsstätten* (Working Group of German Educational Centres). Nearly ninety institutions are members,[26] with differing political or religious allegiances, or in some cases disclaiming any at all. Among them are centres of the Friedrich-Ebert Foundation, linked to the Social Democrat Party, the Konrad-Adenauer Foundation, which belongs to the Christian Democrats, and the Friedrich-Naumann Foundation (Free Democrats). The Evangelical Action Fellowship for Employee Questions in Germany is an associate member. Many of the member organizations exist to promote international understanding and co-operation, such as the Sonnenburg International Working Group, and several to treat matters relating to European unity. The age groups for which centres cater vary; some work only with young people, others with both adolescents and adults, yet others only with adults.

The Working Group of German Educational Centres does not direct or co-ordinate the educational work of its members. 'It advises its members on educational, organizational and administrative questions. In its co-operation with its members special emphasis is laid on the exchange of experience, further education of personnel and mutual assistance in educational and organizational matters'.[27] It also participates at Federal level in the Working Committee for Education in Citizenship, which, among other tasks, represents the interests of the field in dealings with public authorities.

Because the field is so ill-defined, the bodies working in it so disparate and no umbrella organization covers them all, comprehensive data about the nature and extent of citizenship education in the Federal Republic are unavailable. Just over a decade ago, however, the Educational Centre of the German Folk High School Association published what it called a contribution towards a stocktaking of the institutions engaged.[28] One hundred and sixty institutions completed a questionnaire, which sought information about their status, organization, finance and links with other bodies, their facilities, teaching staff, students and the kind of activities they undertook.

The responses showed that fifty-nine per cent were independent organizations, the rest were dependent on some other body, mainly religious or public. Many of the independent institutions maintained links with other organizations, accepting financial assistance, including representatives of outside interests on their management committees, exchanging specialists, or taking advice. Over half co-operated in publicity with other bodies. Thirty-nine per cent drew their students from surrounding districts and towns, twenty per cent from distant parts of the province in which the institution stood, nine per cent from neighbouring provinces, twenty-six per cent from the whole Federal Republic and six per cent from abroad. Of the participants thirty-nine per cent attended in their leisure time, twelve per cent in their holidays, sixteen per cent on educational leave paid by their employers, six per cent on unpaid leave, three per cent on leave unpaid by the firm, but with a grant from a third party. Twenty-four per cent were children, students, housewives and others not in paid employment.

There was a strong predominance, among participants, of men and of persons under forty years of age, indeed a considerable over-representation of both these categories compared with their occurrence in the population as a whole. It is also interesting to note that there was a much higher proportion of men and a significantly lower one of those under twenty-five than in adult education as a whole at that time. In previous educational experience there was, as in other types of adult study, an under-representation of those having had only the minimum compulsory schooling and an over-representation of those whose initial education had gone beyond that.

The ten occupations to which participants mainly belonged were: clerical workers; pupils/students; public servants, excluding armed forces; school teachers; manual workers; academic occupations/the professions; housewives; self-employed in commerce; armed forces; agricultural workers and families. The categories that institutions said they most wished to reach were much the same, with the exclusion of housewives and self-employed and the addition of trade unionists.

In size of programme the institutions responding varied

from seventeen per cent which offered between one and four events (courses, lecture, series, conferences etc.) per annum to five per cent which offered over 200. The majority of offerings were weekend meetings of 2—3 days (37%), or were of 4—7 days (35%). Fifteen per cent offered evening classes, lectures, etc., six per cent one-day schools and seven per cent residential events of more than one week. The annual number of students ranged from less than 100 to over 10,000. Most of the events attracted between twenty and fifty participants each. The principal teaching methods used were lecture with discussion, and small group work.

The most popular topics of study among participants (the figures indicate the percentage of institutions mentioning each one) are shown in Table 8.

Table 8 Most popular topics of citizenship education in the Federal German Republic

Politics	%	*Economics*	%
German unity questions	63	Economic questions	45
Communism/Marxism	43	Trade union and related questions	44
International organiza-tions/treaty systems	27	Enterprise/enterprise related	26
Development aid	31	*Society*	
Europe	54	Anti-semitism	15
Basic rights and concept/meaning of democracy	70	Women in society and state	30
Political parties	31	Social policy/health policy	57
Current political questions	28	Family questions	30
Municipal affairs	16	*Education and training*	
The radical right	37	Youth questions/school etc.	69
Nazism	22	Occupational questions	26
Town and country planning	20	*Religion*	
		Religious education	26

In the 1970s there occurred a shift of emphasis. There was less demand for Marxism, more interest in the European

Parliament, disillusionment with political parties and a concern with the question of terrorism. In the economic field unemployment attracted attention, and migrant workers. Young people and the family were still topics of interest and the question of women in society was a popular subject. Ecological and environmental issues were much in demand.[29]

The immediate post-war years were followed in the Federal German Republic by more than a decade in which the country's concern was not only to implant firmly a democratic society, but to make the Republic an integral part of a united Europe, in which it was under constant threat, as the front line of the West in the cold war, in which it was continually attacking Communism, having adopted a capitalist system, but at the same time was quite unreconciled to the division of Germany into two separate states, one socialist, one capitalist. The Nazism and anti-semitism of its recent past still sat heavily on its conscience. Within the democratic system the Christian Democratic Union and the Social Democratic Party were at violent odds with each other and denominational schools remained for twenty years after 1945 a live issue in educational debate. It is therefore not surprising that these topics drew the interest in citizenship education. Most of the others, social and health policy, economic questions, labour relations, questions of youth and schooling, would have figured largely in any other Western European country's provision.

In the 1940s and 1950s the Federal Republic was neither sure of its own internal stability, nor confident of its acceptability internationally, nor secure from outside aggression. In the 1960s these uncertainties faded with the growth of international *détente*, the strengthening of its confidence through its prosperity and a narrowing of the gap between the main political parties. The country became resigned to the division of Germany. It was indeed criticized for complacency, which the general downturn of the world economy in the 1970s had not seriously shaken. This development may well have been reflected in the progress of citizenship education, as the 1968 Report seems to suggest. It notes that most of the institutions included in its survey were founded between 1945 and 1954, that only nineteen per cent were created between 1955 and 1959, a mere sixteen per cent in the period 1960—5. It suggests that this is not unconnected with the dying down of the cold war and the stabilization of political relations in the Federal Republic. It also suggests, as an untested hypothesis, it is true, that citizenship education is considered worthy of promotion in situations of danger. Its value is not always obvious. The Report's author, F. Neubeck, further writes:

> Vocational further education is confronted by constantly changing demands of the world of work and invariably immediately seen as a necessity for coping with existence. On the other hand this is far less true of citizenship education. The subjective impression that one cannot improve one's own life through political participation limits the interest in understanding political connections.

Whatever may have been the reasons, it is clear that the intensive concern for the subject had already dissipated since the Second World War. Judging by the statistics of the German Folk High School Association that decline of interest has continued. They show that the subject area of society and politics fell as a proportion of the total provision, from eight to three per cent between 1963 and 1976. Between 1970 and 1977 the number of people participating in these studies fell in absolute terms, from 181,838 to 141,833, during which time the number of enrolments for all evening folk high school courses rose by nearly sixty-nine per cent.[30]

Of course there is still a considerable amount of citizenship education. In addition to the evening folk high school students, there are all those attending courses in institutions of the Working Group of German Educational Centres, besides those studying with organizations outside these two categories. Moreover, public interest may have decreased, but for public authorities citizenship education remains a major function of adult education. This is demonstrated in the legislation which most provinces have passed in the last decade. According to the Bavarian Law on promotion of Adult Education, 1974, adult education serves 'personal, social, citizenship and vocational education', in the Hesse Act, 1974, it embraces 'general, vocational and citizenship continuing education', in North Rhine Westphalia citizenship education is one of seven fields of activity in which adult education must operate. The several laws on educational leave all specify citizenship education, with vocational education (Berlin, Hamburg, Hesse), or with vocational and general education (Bremen, Lower Saxony), as the purpose for which leave must be granted.[31]

The only other Western European state which singles out citizenship education for emphasis in its adult education legislation, as the Federal German Republic does, is Austria.[32] That country has had a political and social history similar to that of West Germany and similarly had an earlier history of adult provision on which to build after 1945. In terms of political instability and/or extremism, both France and Italy also had incentives to promote citizenship education after the war. They had not, however, an adult education tradition, as the Austrians and the West Germans had. Given the regimes which ruled for most of the post-war period it was hardly to be expected that citizenship education in the democratic sense would be allowed much scope in Spain and Portugal. As for the other Western European countries, the Scandinavian states, Belgium, Holland, Switzerland, the United Kingdom and Eire, they all have enjoyed a basic social and political consensus, which has encouraged confidence about the stability of their internal organization. For them citizenship education is an essential part of adult education, but its importance does not need to be stressed, as it has been in Germany. It is felt, rightly or wrongly, that it can be taken as read.

It is not therefore difficult to understand why the place accorded to citizenship education in the Federal German Republic and, to a lesser degree, Austria, is unique. As the stability of the democratic regime becomes longer and more firmly established, it will be taken for granted as it is in these other countries, indeed this may already have happened. The level of institutional provision and the legal status of citizenship education will protect it, however, from the neglect with which it is threatened in other countries. For in one thing they resemble the Federal Republic, citizenship education in the form of specific courses for that purpose has become less popular. There is probably less concern that it should animate all adult education. A survey conducted some years ago in the United Kingdom indicated that few participants were aware of this dimension of adult education.[33] One may hypothesize, although empirical evidence is lacking, that this is because there are no longer great issues presenting themselves in black and white, as they appeared to do in the 1940s and 1950s, that there are crises, but their nature is not clear and that, as F. Neubeck wrote in 1968, 'The subjective impression that one cannot improve one's own life through political participation limits the interest in understanding political conditions'.[34]

References

1. R. FLENLEY, *Modern German History*, 4th Edition, London, Dent, 1968.
2. For the history of education in Germany, see ADOLPHE E. MEYER, *An Educational History of the Western World*, New York, McGraw-Hill, 2nd edition, 1972.
3. G. KLOSS, *West Germany, an Introduction*, London, Macmillan, 1976.
4. F. BALSER, *Die Anfänge der Erwachsenenbildung in Deutschland in der ersten Hälfte des 19 Jahrhunderts*, Stuttgart, Ernst Klett, 1959.
5. W. PICHT, *Das Schicksal der Volksbildung in Deutschland*, Brunswick, Westermann, 1950.
6. *Adult Education Legislation in Ten Countries of Europe*, Amersfoort, European Bureau of Adult Education, 1974.
7. G. STEINDORF, *Von den Anfängen der Volkshochschule in Deutschland*, Osnabrück, A. Fromm, 1968.
8. PICHT, op. cit.
9. H.L. MATZAT, *Zur Idee und Geschichte der Erwachsenenbildung in Deutschland*, Homburg, Verband der Volkshochschulen des Saarlandes, 1964.
10. PICHT, op. cit.
11. W. BURMEISTER, in A. HEARNDEN ed., *The British in Germany. Educational Reconstruction after 1945*, London, Hamish Hamilton, 1978.
12. Lower Saxony, 1970, see *Adult Education Legislation* op. cit.
13. *Stellung und Aufgabe der Volkshochschule*, Bonn, Deutscher Volkshochschul-Verband, 1978.
14. *VHS der Stadt Oberhausen, Bildungsprogramm, Arbeitsjahr 1979–80*.
15. ibid.
16. H. DOLFF ed., *25 Jahre Deutscher Volkshochschul-Verband*, Brunswick, Westermann, 1978.
17. ibid. and *Statistische Mitteilungen des Deutschen Volkshochschul-Verbandes Arbeitsjahr 1977*, Frankfurt-am-Main.

18. see Report of British Delegation to Western Germany, 1954, in *The British in Germany*, op. cit.
19. Quoted in F. LAACK, *Die Rolle der Heimvolkshochschule in der Bildungsgesellschaft*, Weinheim, Julius Beltz, 1968.
20. Resolution 4, quoted in LAACK, op. cit.
21. *Das Gutachten des Deutschen Ausschusses über die Erwachsenenbildung*, 29 January, 1960, quoted in LAACK, op. cit.
22. K.E. BUNGENSTAB, H. KEIM ed., *Grundlagen der Weiterbildung*, Cologne, J.P. Bachem, 1974.
23. ibid.
24. F. BORINSKI, in *The British in Germany*, op. cit.
25. F. BORINSKI, in *25 Jahre Deutscher Volkshochschul-Verband*, op. cit.
26. *Unabhängige Bildungsarbeit in der Demokratie*, Bonn, Arbeitskreis Deutscher Bildungsstätten, 1977.
27. Bonn, Arbeitskreis Deutscher Bildungsstätten, 1972.
28. H. NEUBECK, *Ein Beitrag zur Bestandsaufnahme der Einrichtungen politischer Erwachsenenbildung in der Bundesrepublik*, Frankfurt-am-Main, Pädagogische Arbeitsstelle des Deutschen Volkshochschul-Verbandes, 1968.
29. Information given in an interview at the offices of the Arbeitskreis Deutscher Bildungsstätten, September, 1979.
30. *25 Jahre Deutscher Volkshochschul-Verband* and *Statistische Mitteilungen*, op. cit.
31. BUNGENSTAB ET AL., op. cit.
32. Bundesgesetz vom 21 März 1973 über die Förderung der Erwachsenenbildung usw.; Gesetz über die Förderung der Kultur (Vorarlberg), 1974; Gesetz über die Förderung der Erwachsenenbildung usw. (Niederösterreich), 1977.
33. COLIN TITMUS and C. GRAEME HELY, 'Collective and individual dimensions in the adult education of working people', London *Studies in Adult Education*, vol. 8, no. 1, April 1976.
34. NEUBECK, op. cit.

CHAPTER 5

France

Since 1789 French history has been a tale of revolution, near revolution, foreign invasion, of extreme conservatism, radicalism, class divisions, within a continuing tradition of strong central administration and weak local authority. Politically for a hundred years a battle was fought between monarchical and republican principles of government, the former identified with reaction and authoritarianism, the latter with liberalism and democracy. For most of the nineteenth century the monarchical was in the ascendant, under various houses — Bonapartist, Bourbon, Orleanist and then Bonapartist again. Invasion put an end to both Bonapartist reigns, the other two were ended by internal revolution, which also followed Napoleon III's defeat by the Prussians in 1870.

Until that date republicanism had been a short-term unstable phenomenon, following the revolutions of 1789 and 1848. Even after 1870 the Third Republic came into being largely by default, because the various royalist groups could not agree among themselves which house should provide the new monarch. In fact it did endure to become the longest lasting regime since the French Revolution, and, despite a long history of internal opposition, it was only brought down in the end by the German invasion and defeat of France in 1940.[1]

The largest country in size and population in Europe after Russia, and economically the most highly developed, France began its industrial revolution comparatively early, after the

United Kingdom but before Germany. It did not, however, pursue its industrialization as assiduously as these two, although there were some periods of rapid advance. Not until 1929 did the number of French people dependent on industry for their living exceed that dependent on agriculture.

By the end of the nineteenth century France had fallen behind both Britain and Germany in wealth and population. The effects of the First World War were to exacerbate both trends. Between the wars the French national mentality was defensive. Economically it sought to retain what it had through cartels and a protective tariff policy, rather than to win more through active competition. This stagnation was a not inconsiderable factor in its downfall in 1940.

Throughout the nineteenth century France was deeply divided socially, having neither a national consensus about its form of government nor a dominant class self-confident in its dominance. Its nobility was diluted and split and lost its influence. Its middle class grew rich and finally predominant, but it was disunited, being monarchist or republican, secularist or clerical. The urban working class was less numerous than that of Great Britain or Germany, but by its revolutionary activities in 1789, 1830, 1848 and 1871 it had made itself feared and detested by the bourgeoisie and the aristocracy. It got no sympathy either from the large socially conservative peasant population.

The influence of the Church was important. It has been assured a privileged relationship with the French State by a Concordat between the Vatican and Napoleon I. Throughout the nineteenth century the Catholic hierarchy, itself rank conscious and authoritarian, naturally supported monarchism. Secularism, republicanism and atheism became identified, by the Church. When the Third Republic was founded the hierarchy threw all its influence into the balance against the new regime. The result was a bitter conflict which led in 1905 to complete separation of the Church and State. It took many years for old animosities to die down and faint echoes may still be heard from old-fashioned secularists.

The rise of an organized working class movement in the last years of the nineteenth century added a new complication to the Church—State, Monarchy—Republic divisions of France. The Church, being anti-democratic, opposed it.

If for no other reason than that, the Republic, believing that it had greater danger to apprehend from the right than the left, tolerated it sufficiently to legalize trade unions in 1884. The latter, however, had revolutionary ideas and not until after the First World War would they work with the bourgeois society. The lingering of this attitude and schism into confederations dominated by different religious and political ideas has reduced the effectiveness of French trade unions over the years.

A striking feature of the Third Republic, in view of its long duration, was the violence of the passions aroused by social, political and economic differences and after defeat in 1940 there was a strong sense that it had occurred because of rottenness in French society. The first reaction was a return to traditional virtues under the Vichy regime: labour, family, patriotism, religious faith, a due deference to rank and authority. The Vichy Government, however, having become identified with National Socialist Germany, was driven out when France was liberated in 1944 by the Western Allies. It was replaced by forces emanating from the Resistance to the Germans, but since the only unifying feature of these was a common enemy, when that was defeated, pre-war divisions reasserted themselves in France. For thirteen years after 1945 the country suffered a succession of short-lived cabinets, always composed of a coalition of conflicting interests, the delicate balance of which was threatened by any attempt at decisive action. It was a period of immobilism on many critical issues, which nevertheless saw France taking a major role in laying the foundations of the European Community, and in which the foundations were laid of the French economic miracle of the 'sixties.

The immediate cause of the Fourth Republic's fall in 1958 was not, however, its failure to resolve the country's social problems, but the stresses imposed by the cost in men and money of the colonial war to keep Algeria French. Faced by a threat of civil war or a military *coup d'état*, the country turned to its wartime hero, Charles de Gaulle, who had relinquished government office in 1946 because, among the warring political factions, he could not obtain the authority to carry through the policies he considered necessary. In 1958 he had no difficulty in doing so. A new constitution shifted the balance of power to the executive, principally the President, to whom both Ministers and Parliament were in effect subordinate. In a short time de Gaulle liquidated the French Empire, made France the chief power in the European Community, asserting its independence against the United States of America, and used his authority to put through a number of social measures, which no government of the Fourth Republic could have done.

Above all the end of the Algerian War put a stop to a drain on the country's resources which had effectively concealed the true extent of the economic progress France had made since the Second World War. After the no-risk policy of the inter-war years the strength of a modern industrial power, exemplified by both Germany and the United States of America, had greatly impressed young French business men during the war. There had been no question of returning to the discredited practices of pre-war years, there had been an enormous task of reconstruction, and the county had opted for a policy of modernization and expansion, with all the risks and rewards it offered, guided by a government-established Commissariat of the National Plan. Both the planning machinery and the policy were highly successful in the 1950s, in spite of government immobilism. In the 1960s, after peace in Algeria, the economy boomed. The standard of living rose, to surpass that of the United Kingdom, and continued to rise, although at a slower rate, into the 1970s.

For whatever reasons, economic prosperity has been accompanied by political stability. A Gaullist coalition has ruled France for the last twenty years. It was put severely to the test in 1968 by student riots and a general strike, largely provoked by the failure of special reforms to keep up with economic advance. It has been strained in the last few years by difficulties of inflation and unemployment, as other governments have been, but it has survived.

One continuing problem, inherited from the past, which the Fifth Republic has faced, has been that of education. This has been a sensitive issue since the French Revolution. Nowhere did the Catholic Church fight more desperately against the forces of secularism, republicanism and democracy than in the battle for control of the schools. A system of State secondary schools, called *lycées*, had been founded by Napoleon I, but the real struggle took place over primary education. In 1881 and 1882 the Republic made primary education compulsory from the age of six to thirteen and set out to ensure that it took place in secular State schools, whose teachers were the spreaders of republican ideology against the already entrenched Church schools. By a number of measures, including the expulsion of Catholic teaching orders from France, the Government sought to exclude the Church from education. It never entirely succeeded, but it established the predominance of the State as the provider of education at both primary and secondary levels.

The considerable educational achievements of the Third Republic's first decades were completed by the reform in 1880 of higher education, which had fallen into disrepute under Napoleon III, and by the creation of apprenticeship schools. In their time these educational achievements were considerable, but they stirred great and enduring animosities, which helped to prevent any major changes in the system until after the Second World War. The school system was a dual one, each part of which was self-contained and largely self-perpetuating. Primary education, for working-class, lower middle classes and peasantry, was taught by people who had themselves gone straight from primary school to training college and back again to teach in the type of school they had left. The *lycées*, the only route to higher education, had in many cases their own fee-paying primary departments and were the preserve of the business and professional middle and upper classes. There was a highly selective entrance examination for the available places left in the *lycée* proper, but only a small minority of primary children managed to get in. This marked separation of the two types of school was believed by many people to have been a major contributor to the social divisions of France.

The Fifth Republic was the first regime with the legislative power to put through major reforms, although there had been pressures for them ever since 1945. From 1959 a number of important measures have been instituted, aimed at furnishing equality of educational opportunity through comprehensive secondary schooling up to a minimum age of sixteen and to provide the kind of workforce needed by the country's modern economy. As in other countries these efforts have been only partially successful. Reform in universities took even longer than that in schools. Impatience at its slowness was a major cause of the 1968 student insurrection. In the same year a law did reorganize higher education, which became more flexibly and democratically administered, to meet the stresses of vastly increased demand for student places. The 1970s have shown, however, that the Ministry of Universities, through its control of the purse strings, still holds and exercises the real power.

In no country is it possible to make a clearer case for the determining influence of political, economic and social history on the development of adult education than in France.[2] The link between political radicalism and adult learning was established early on. In 1792 the philosopher Condorcet presented a Bill to establish a national educational system, in which important provisions were made for adult classes.[3] It and most of the initiatives which were inspired by the revolutions of 1830 and 1848 came to nothing, except to implant the idea that education for the people had dangerously subversive possibilities. The Church distrusted any education not provided by itself and believed that workers should not learn anything that would make them dissatisfied with their proper subordinate station in life, a view shared by monarchists in general.

As in other countries though, liberal intellectuals supported education for working people, because they believed in the value of education for all men, and perceptive employers recognized the economic value of a literate workforce. Republicans considered education a democratic right and a necessity for citizenship. From the 1848 Revolution there was, however, a growing gap between middle-class republicans and the increasingly radical working-class movement, demonstrated by the revolution of the Paris Commune in 1870 and the savagery of its repression by the bourgeois Provisional Government. This divergence of aims had its effect on working-class adult education.

In post-school, if not, strictly speaking, adult education, French governments had been in advance of other European ones. Both the Orleans Monarchy and the Second Empire made provision in primary education for evening classes for older people. Indeed the permissive measures of the Third

Republic's primary education laws in this area were no real advance on earlier regimes. Three types of course were envisaged: elementary education for those who had received none in childhood; complementary courses for young people who wished to supplement their school instruction; and lectures and conferences for the dissemination of general knowledge. Having passed the legislation the State left the organization of these courses to local authorities, making only a small grant to teachers, which was later withdrawn. Considering that education in France is a preserve of central government, it is suprising how many local councils accepted the unwanted task of subsidizing evening classes in primary schools, of which there were 54,351 in 1914, with 632,000 regular attenders out of an enrolment of 800,000. Many councils did nothing, however, and the real driving force was the primary teachers, the republican spearhead.

After the First World War this generation of enthusiasts was dead or had retired. The Republic was tired, the primary curriculum, which had not changed since the 1880s, was out of date, and what was then needed was probably secondary evening classes. The primary ones had almost died away by the early 1920s, never to recover, for, as in other spheres of education, the State was unwilling or unable to take any action.

There was, however, a strong, if short-lived private attempt to offer a higher level of adult education to workers. Influenced to a certain degree by British university extension and university settlements, people's universities were set up throughout the country. At their height there were 260 of them,[4] founded by middle-class liberals, by joint action between bourgeois and workers, or by workers alone. The accommodation varied greatly, from ones with library, reading room, bar and games room, to others which met in barns or had no permanent premises at all. On the whole the movement was republican and secularist, but there were variations of ideology. Some eschewed political questions altogether in order to avoid giving offence, others tried to present controversial topics objectively, still others were forums for militant class ideas.[5]

The first people's university was founded in 1898, by 1904 the movement was already past its peak and by the beginning of the First World War only a few institutions survived. From the first they were opposed by monarchists for their republicanism, by right wing bourgeois for their socialism and by the Catholic Church, then at the height of its battle with the State, for both and for atheism. It created its own rival popular institutes. Within the people's universities middle class and workers found it hard to work together. Where the former took control, the latter ceased to attend, where the latter won, the former withdrew their financial support. This was of great importance because neither the State nor universities as institutions gave any help. A fundamental cause of failure was probably lack of communication. Intellectuals trained in French higher education could not teach workers what they wanted to know in a way they could understand and which they found interesting.

A Catholic attempt to educate a working class élite at this time, the *Sillon* (Furrow) movement, was condemned by its own Church, so that in the first decade of the twentieth century, when in other European countries, such as the United Kingdom, Holland, Sweden and even Germany, the foundations were being laid on which contemporary adult education has been built, in France the potential foundations were being undermined. The only exception was trade union education. After 1918 both secular and Catholic confederations learnt from experience of People's Universities and other pre-war efforts to create an effective structure of trade union education, which has continued to develop, in all the different confederations, up to the present day.

Between the wars French workers had almost no opportunities to continue systematic study into adult life, either in the form of public authority evening classes or through private associations or movements, such as German evening folk high schools, the British Workers' Educational Association, or even Swedish study circles. What is more there was no significant pressure that they should have. After the Second World War, when there was a strong body of opinion to maintain that the urban and rural working class of all ages needed further educational opportunities, formal courses of study were not considered appropriate to their needs, partly because of the failure of primary school evening classes and of the people's universities. Consequently even today there are still in France only the beginnings of a systematic provision of adult classes of a non-vocational kind. Indeed, until about twenty years ago the concept of adult education as a distinctive sector of education was not current in France. For learning opportunities adults had to look to trade union education, some vocational training and socio-cultural animation.

Socio-cultural animation in France

The term 'socio-cultural animation' has come into current use since the late 1950s. It derives from, and in some of its uses is an up-to-date name for, *éducation populaire*, popular education, a name and a concept which go back to the nineteenth century. In its origins education for the people, in France as in other countries which had a similarly-named movement, such as Germany and the Netherlands, was directed at extending education to the lower classes, which had previously been deprived of it. As such its main thrust was to establish universal, compulsory primary schooling for children.

When that was legally created in France, by the laws of 1881 and 1882, the emphasis shifted. The State primary school was by no means firmly founded and the battle for the hearts and minds of local communities was extended into out-of-school activities, which had in most of them been dominated by the Catholic Church up to that time. Popular education became engaged in extra-curricular offerings for children of school age, in social and cultural activities for post-school adolescents and in adult education, because primary school evening classes, people's universities, popular institutes, popular lectures, with or without lantern slides, and the late nineteenth century initiatives in trade union education were all included within popular education and not classified separately as adult education. The intense rivalry between secular and Catholic forces may well have stimulated growth.[6]

After 1918 popular education had lost impetus, for the Church—State conflict had died down and the goal of universalizing basic education had been achieved. There was little interest in systematic courses for adults, except in the trade unions, which went their own way. The emphasis shifted to social and recreational activities for specialized groups. The youth hostels movement began, the scout movement made an important impact, cine-clubs and drama clubs were founded. The Catholic Church came officially to an awareness that it had a duty to concern itself with the social needs of people and the Catholic Working Class Youth and the Catholic Agricultural Youth were set up, among other Church organizations. The *Ligue de l'Enseignement*, Educational League, a spearhead of republicanism and secularism ever since its foundation in 1866, as it still is today, began to form special interest groups, such as the French Union for Secular Holidays, under its umbrella.

The year 1936 was a significant date in the history of popular education. Until then State support for it had been marginal, but in that year the left-wing Popular Front coalition, having increased statutory holidays and shortened the working week, introduced a large programme to encourage both young people and adults to spend their leisure in healthy physical and cultural activities.[7] The impact of this first systematic entry of the State into this field was blunted by the short duration of the Popular Front Government and the approach of the Second World War, but it established a precedent of State subsidy for popular education which has bound every post-war government.

Popular education grew by pullulation of organizations, inspired by diverse ideologies, or indeed professing none at all, having in common only that, for the most part, their efforts were directed at the urban and rural working classes, and that they were engaged in the same general area of activity. It was a very wide one and vaguely delimited. It could be defined to cover all non-vocational group activities of a social, recreational, sporting or intellectual nature, carried on outside home, school, or work, by people of any age from the cradle to the grave. From time to time, however, influences from within or without were sufficiently powerful to touch to a greater or lesser degree the whole field. The battles over the primary school and the initiative of the Popular Front were examples of this.

At the end of the Second World War another one made itself felt. Most of the pre-war associations had been banned by the Vichy regime, but they were nearly all re-established and a considerable number of new ones set up. The impetus came from the wartime Resistance, which had united Frenchmen of all classes. Many intellectuals had become conscious of the cultural deprivation of their working-class comrades and had come to blame the ills of France which had led to the 1940 defeat on the social divisions to which the two-tier school system, they believed, had largely contributed. To the extended educational opportunities which the workers should have, schools could offer little. Instead they were to be provided by popular education. A coherent body of theory and practice, the first, was proposed for this, which introduced some new ideas and elevated to principles some others which had been the product of circumstances.

Its purpose was to provide opportunities for individual self-fulfilment by cultural, social and recreational means, to promote, through communal activities, social co-operation and a sense of civic responsibility, to reduce the divisions between classes by furthering the social and cultural advancement of the under-privileged. Popular education was to be not so much a complement to, but a reaction against, the official school system. Instead of rigid, centralized direction from Paris, it was to have a loose, flexible organization, based on independent local groups. The emphasis was not on formal rote leaning, but informal activities; not instruction, but mutual assistance in learning through clubs and study groups; not mastery of a subject, but the satisfaction to be found in the process of learning.

For reasons partly of finance, but also of principle, the movement depended almost exclusively on voluntary workers. Their dedication was the source of its dynamism. Unpaid organizers and activity leaders from the ranks of the community were more likely to be acceptable and responsive to its needs than professionals. Besides, the opportunity to learn to accept responsibility for its own needs was the most valuable education in community service that the movement could provide for its public. From the voluntary principle it followed that popular education was to be left in the hands of private associations. The State was to make no direct contribution, its role was to make available finance, advice and facilities for training popular educators.

The outcome of this initiative to bridge the gap between the intelligentsia and the working class was comparative failure. In popular education the unity and idealism of the Resistance lasted no longer than in other spheres of national life. The upsurge of activity after the war mainly touched young people and was effective principally in the fields of sport and recreation. Only a few organizations founded after the war, such as the Institute of Working-class Culture and People and Culture, had much influence with adults and in the case of the latter it was with middle-class ones.[8] If adults did participate in popular education, it was in associations whose main clientele was children and adolescents, such as the Houses of Youth and Culture, or the Federation of Leo Lagrange Leisure Clubs, or in ones catering for specialist interests, the School for Parents, the Feminine Civic and Social Union, sporting clubs, or scientific or cultural groups, such as the French Astronomical Society or the French Federation of Film Clubs. The emphasis is demonstrated by the name of the government department made responsible for popular education, now the State Secretariat for Youth and Sports.[9]

The ideas of 1945 may not have been realized as concretely as their proponents would have wished, but they were not discredited and to a large degree they continued to inform popular education in the post-war years. After a period of stagnation in the 1950s the Fifth Republic gave it renewed stimulus. General de Gaulle saw his government as one of national unification after years of disunity, aiming to make France great again, building an advanced economy and the modern social institutions to go with it. Popular education was one of these institutions. Although the State's main concern was with the work it could achieve with young people and with areas where success would redound to national prestige, as in sport and high culture, the whole field benefited from the increased interest.

It still stuck, however, to the principle that the State should not directly or officially make provision of activities. That remained in the hands of the multitude of private associations. Where, however, it wished to support or initiate action, the State could cause to be set up an association, whose governing body was composed of both representatives of private organizations and civil servants, but had the legal status of a private association and thus conformed to the conventions. Even without this device its power increased as organizations became more and more dependent on State subsidies. On the other hand government effectiveness was somewhat reduced by the dispersion of responsibility for popular education over a number of departments. In addition to the Secretariat for Youth and Sports, the Ministry of Agriculture clung to responsibility for rural associations, the Ministry of Culture increasingly took under its wing activities in the arts, the Ministry of Health supported social centres and young workers' hostels and the Secretariat of State for Tourism supervised holiday colonies. This diffusion of competence has continued.

The initiation and control of local action by local people has also remained a basic principle, to which both private bodies and the State have remained attached. For example, in 1968 when the Federation of Houses of Youth and Culture appeared to be concentrating too much authority in its national organization, the Government forced a reversal of policy under threat of withdrawal of subsidy.[10] Until the late 1960s, however, control of State supervision and subsidy still lay largely in Paris. At that time it became a clearly enunciated policy of the Government that responsibility for socio-cultural activities should be laid upon local authorities, which were encouraged to set up organizations to co-ordinate and encourage social and socio-cultural work in their areas — still with some aid from the State.[11]

In theory the voluntary principle is still basic and most workers are part time and unpaid. In practice, many associations have long ago grown beyond the point where they could be run by unpaid volunteers. The number of professionals has been increasing constantly over the last twenty years and, indeed, animation has become a profession, with its own national diplomas — the CAPASE and a new one, the DAPASSE, created and made official by the state.[12] There is an ongoing controversy about this. Activities are still largely staffed by volunteers, could not indeed be run without them, but the influence of these people on associations is decreasing, since they have neither the time nor the prestige conferred by professionalism to match the full-time workers. This development is deplored in many quarters on the grounds that professionalism is contrary both to the spirit of popular education and to that of animation. Nevertheless it is difficult to see the trend towards professional domination being reversed.

In the course of the process discussed in the previous paragraphs the term 'popular education' was replaced in general and official usage by socio-cultural animation. What this expression means, what the change signified and why it took place are not generally agreed. Indeed there is a substantial literature on the subject, of varying, sometimes conflicting views, written by psychologists, sociologists, educators, of a wide range of ideologies.[13] One of the difficulties in arriving at a clear notion of its sense derives from the fact that *animation* in French, like community in English, has become a cosmetic word, it automatically evokes a favourable response when applied to any activity, whether it is appropriate or not. Thus it has spread beyond the socio-cultural sphere to be susceptible of use in the whole range of business and commerce. A salesman, for example, may be referred to as an animator of sales (*animateur de ventes*).

What does seem clear is that its current popularity began in popular education, where, linked to the epithet 'socio-cultural' it began to be used in the 1950s to denote a process, then the technique used to achieve this process and subsequently, by extension, the field in which this process was to take place. There is a wide measure of agreement that the process stimulates communication between people, that this leads to action for the benefit of the individuals and the group in which the communication takes place, for the ultimate purpose of the transformation of society for the better. By implication the communication is an educational process, bringing awareness and knowledge of matters which interest the individuals and the group and consciousness of their potential. The action too is educational, in that people learn by doing, testing the ideas and methods they have evolved by communication. Thus the tenants of a housing scheme may be brought through discussion to an understanding that they have common problems both of a material and psychological nature from living in the scheme, to the identification of these, to a sense that they may by action resolve them. This should lead on to a plan for action and action itself. In the cultural field socio-cultural animation will through a similar series of stages arouse and develop the creativity of people, thereby enriching their own lives and the lives of those around them.

The techniques to be used to set the process in motion, even whether it is a matter of technique, have long been debated. Both the process and the techniques clearly share principles with the methodological approach put forward for popular education at the end of the Second World War.

Animation is not the transfer of knowledge from the *animateur* to the animated. It is essentially a process of learning by mutual interaction in which the *animateur* acts as a catalyst, a non-directive stimulant, a resource person in a democratic process. Indeed socio-cultural animation, it is widely agreed, is self and group development by democratic means to a democratic end, although there is wide disagreement about the sense of *democracy* and *democratic*.

It still has to be explained why popular education, the field in which socio-cultural animation takes place, should have taken on the name of the process. The change of name has brought about no significant alteration in the nature and extent of the field of action, nor in the organizations that operate within it, nor in its structures, except possibly for the devolution of responsibility from central to local government. Perhaps the most plausible explanations are tactical and political, inspired by the connotations of the term 'popular education'. Education itself has strong school associations, implies didacticism, the authority of the teacher over the taught. It was long thought an inappropriate name for something that contained a strong element of reaction against school. In fact some people in the 1950s preferred to call it popular culture.

Popular education, from its nineteenth century origins, saw itself as a movement for the improvement of a specific class, the workers, by means of education. It therefore had a marked political character, which was out of tune with the ideas of the Fifth Republic. Class and party politics were in disrepute, having been blamed for the ruin of the Fourth Republic. De Gaulle saw himself as an apolitical figure, unifying the nation. The role of popular education, as the Gaullist regime saw it, was not a class one, not one of a movement, but it was to be an institution and a technique working with all classes and ages, to help create the unified, flexible body of labour and citizens required by France's resurgent greatness. Socio-cultural animation had no political overtones, it sounded technical at a time when the hopes of all Europe rested in technical advance, and it had the sense of bringing to life, which the Government was trying to do to France.[14]

It may be that the wide variety of definitions of socio-cultural animation derives from its use to denote the diverse field in which, as a process, it is to take place, a field full of its own contradictions and conflicts. It may also spring out of its extension from a technique to become a philosophy. In its extreme form, of complete non-directivity, it is probably an unattainable ideal. Even in a modified form it is difficult to see how a pottery group or a photographic club, two very popular activities, in which people participate to acquire certain technical skills, can operate without an element of instruction. Since they are activities within socio-cultural animation, the latter must be defined in such a way as to accommodate them.

One feature of it as technique or process is that it appears to assume in those to be animated a level of maturity and experience at which they can take responsibility for their own actions. This would seem to make socio-cultural animation more appropriate to adults than children. Since the field devotes, both in practice and by design, more attention to young people than adults, the definition must be further modified to take into account this fact.

Many people in countries such as the United Kingdom, have been inclined to view that part of socio-cultural animation which reaches adults, comparatively small and largely dealing with sport and recreation, as an unsatisfactory substitute for a structured provision of systematic learning opportunities for adults in a country which, for political and social reasons, has not been able to build such a provision. This would be an inadequate view. One has, in fact, to consider two different philosophies. In British evening institutes, the Workers' Educational Association and university extra-mural work, in the evening folk high schools of Federal Germany and Austria, the learning group is collected in a class, pursuing a systematic course of study under a teacher. Although the learning experience itself is important, the emphasis is laid on the outcome in terms of the body of cognitive knowledge acquired, or the change of attitude arrived at. In France and indeed in Belgium, which has developed popular education/animation, the emphasis is laid on the educational value of the experience itself, on the acquisition of learning skills, on personality development, rather than mastery of a body of information. In the Netherlands *vorming* (see Chapter 7) and in Sweden study circles combine to some extent both philosophies.

Over the last two decades the principles of socio-cultural animation have been taken up outside France. It has attracted people for several reasons. As its concern is for all ages, from the cradle to the grave, it is in keeping with the concept of lifelong education's principle of vertical integration throughout life. In those countries which had a structured provision of adult study opportunities, it was becoming increasingly clear that it attracted only a minority, and very few indeed of those most in need, those with least schooling in childhood. Socio-cultural animation seemed to offer activities and methods less redolent of school, more under the control of the participant, and therefore likely to be more appealing to those turned off by formal education. The methods used and the goals bore a close resemblance to those of community development,[15] which was much in vogue in English-speaking countries as an approach to the problems of social and economic underprivilege. Socio-cultural animation differed from community development in that its emphasis was less local, stressed the educational process more than immediate action to improve the standard of social life and covered a rather wider field. It may be said that the influence of the concept and practice of socio-cultural animation played a large part in the decision, taken in Scotland on the recommendation of the Alexander Committee, to combine non-certificate, non-vocational adult education with the youth and community service to form the community education service.[16]

It would seem that socio-cultural animation has been a great success. In France itself many doubts have been expressed about this.[17] For a number of reasons, not least shortage of resources, it has not realized the high hopes placed upon it. In particular it has not reached the socially and educationally under-privileged to the extent it was meant to do. To many of its more radical and impatient proponents, it shows no signs of transforming society. They might, as many do, complain that it is being neglected by the State in favour of vocational training, whose contribution to the economy is more direct. It is certainly clear, that although the Government shows no sign of abandoning socio-cultural animation altogether, it is no longer considered, if it ever was, to provide all the nation's needs in adult education. As other countries have adopted socio-cultural animation, so France has devoted great efforts in the last twenty years to developing a nationwide system of formal adult study provision, to meet the requirements of her economy.

Vocational education in France

The urge to economic enrichment, individual or collective, has from its earliest days been a major incentive to adult education. In France there were numerous examples of initiatives inspired by this drive from the beginning of the nineteenth century, but then, like other forms of adult study provision, it failed to develop until the last few years.

Even at the height of the most reactionary regime that the country has had since the French Revolution, in the 1820s, evening classes for working men, seeking to imitate British Mechanics' Institutes, were set up in Paris, notably at the National Conservatory for Arts and Crafts. They were founded by members of the upper classes. In the 1830s old established trade guilds ran classes for their members, largely because the old apprenticeship system had broken down. Partly through philanthropy, but also because they felt the need for a literate workforce, manufacturers provided instruction for their employees. In 1860 the Lyons Chamber of Commerce organized courses of occupational training for workers.[18]

Under the Third Republic there was a strong contrast

144

between technical and professional education for an élite in the Great Schools, which were harder to get into than universities, and which enjoyed an international prestige, and the low status and comparative neglect of vocational training at lower levels. The First World War gave a certain impetus to the latter. In 1919 the Astier Law prescribed day-release courses for apprentices and young people in commerce, but it was not fully implemented. Some higher education leading to technical qualifications was available for adults at the National Conservatory for Arts and Crafts. Immediately after the war the requirements of returning servicemen and the demands for skilled labour to rebuild war-damaged areas caused occupational training schemes to be created. Later on, in 1936, widespread unemployment by French standards, a result of the world slump, led to new ones being set up, intended to offer training for jobs with prospects of stable employment. It hardly amounted, however, to an occupational education policy for adults.

Even after the Second World War, when France chose a modernizing, expansionist economic policy and therefore needed more trained people and new skills, there was little concerted action on a national level, the inertia of the Fourth Republic saw to that. It is true that to meet the needs of post-war reconstruction a special scheme was developed, as it had been after 1918. By 1947 what is now called the National Association for the Vocational Training of Adults (AFPA) had the capacity to train 30,000 building workers in courses lasting six months each. Evening classes under the Astier Law were opened free to adults as well as adolescents and were greatly extended. These and others like them were palliative measures, however, which became less effective in the 1950s to make up the shortage of trained manpower, as the economy grew and changed in character.

It required the Fifth Republic to undertake the large-scale measures required. It has poured forth what might fairly be called a deluge of laws, orders and decrees on adult training. What is more, they have been implemented to a high degree. Apart from texts relating specifically to agriculture, training for trade union and socio-cultural activity, and the 1968 Law on the Direction of Higher Education, which laid upon universities a responsibility for adult teaching, there were four major laws up to the end of the 1960s, those of 1959, 1963, 1966 and 1968.

All previous legislation was, however, replaced or supplemented by the law of 1971, Organizing Continuing Vocational Training within the Framework of Permanent Education. This is the foundation of current French practice in this area of adult education. The text begins with a statement of principle.

> Permanent vocational training constitutes a national obligation. The object is to permit the adaptation of workers to change in techniques and conditions of work, to encourage their social advancement by access to different levels of culture and professional qualification and their contribution to cultural, economic and social development.[19]

At government level policy was to be determined by an inter-ministerial group under the Prime Minister and administered by a committee of high civil servants, answerable to the ministers. Civil servants, representatives of employers and of trade unions were to form a national advisory council, and at regional and departmental (county) level there were to be further advisory committees similarly composed.

Apart from training supplied by employers to their own employees, vocational education within this supervisory framework was to be organized on the basis of contracts between demanders and providers. The contract might cover a single course, or a number of courses, over one or more years, and involve a single demanding organization or a number. The contract must state the nature, purpose, duration and number of participants of the training provided, teaching methods, means of assessment of performance, and an estimate of costs. The State itself might request provision to be made for individual employees seeking training not of their employer's choice; for priority categories, such as women wishing to return to paid work, migrant workers, young people without qualifications; for family and trade union organizations and works committees. The field of demanders and providers could be very wide, in the words of the law, 'Firms, groups of firms, private associations, establishments and bodies, professional, trade union or family organizations, local authorities, public institutions ...'

146

Employees wishing to undertake training were granted the right to leave from work for the purpose on application to their employer. The latter was protected in that he was not obliged to release more than two per cent of his labour force on educational leave in any one year, but a request for leave could not be refused, only deferred. To qualify for leave an employee must have worked in the firm for at least two years, and the length of leave was to be for the duration of training, up to a maximum, except in special cases, of twelve months. How long he had to wait before he qualified for a further period of release as a right depended on the length of the previous one and whether the latter had been initiated by himself or his employer. At the most he would not have to wait more than twelve years.

Training was classified by the law according to five types. The first category comprised *conversion and prevention* courses, the former offering redundant personnel training for new skills, the latter offering such training to personnel threatened with redundancy. The second category was to be aimed at *adaptation*, training intended to facilitate access to a first job or a new one within the trainee's existing firm, especially for unqualified young people. In the third category were to be *vocational advancement* courses, permitting trainees to obtain higher qualification. Fourth category training, for *maintenance and improvement of knowledge*, was to keep up or complete qualifications and culture. The last category would comprise *induction training* for sixteen to eighteen year olds.

Whether a trainee would be entitled to continue to receive his wages, or some payment in lieu, would very much depend on the training he was to follow. In a *conversion* course, trainees would be unemployed people learning a new occupation and therefore not on educational leave. In this case the State would pay an allowance a little less than the national minimum wage fixed by law. Since *prevention* courses were to avert the threat of redundancy, trainees were employed and the employer would continue to pay wages, but would receive some compensation from the State. Followers of *adaptation* courses would also be paid by their employer, whom the State might reimburse in part. Workers taking *vocational advancement* training would receive a maintenance allowance not less than the national minimum wage, if the course being followed was on a special list published periodically by the Government. For *maintenance and improvement of knowledge* courses employers and the State, either singly or jointly, might make payment in lieu of earnings, but they were not obliged to do so. Young people in the fifth category were to receive payment equal to the grant given to students in technical colleges.

To finance vocational education every employer having at least ten employees, except the State and local authorities, was to pay a tax calculated as a fraction of his total annual wage bill. For 1972 it was to be set at 0.8% and it was intended that it should rise to 2.0% in 1976. To encourage him to provide training for his own personnel, he could deduct what he spent for that purpose from his liability for tax. He could set against tax the cost of courses either given directly by the firm or through a contract with a training organization, and the remuneration of trainees. The State's contribution to capital expenditure on facilities for vocational training and to the cost of training activities would be met by a Fund for Vocational Education and Social Advancement. Like State grants to trainees it would come from the Prime Minister's budget.

The 1971 law is of special interest because it is plainly the product of specific national circumstances and at the same time is shaped by considerations whose influence is apparent in other advanced western countries. Through it and its predecessors from 1959 onwards France was in effect trying to create from scratch a national system of vocational education for adults. This in itself was not unique: by the Industrial Training Act, 1964, and the Employment and Training Act, 1973, the United Kingdom Government did much the same thing, but the British situation was very different in that not only did there exist already a nationwide infrastructure for the public provision of systematic continuing education, but there was a long tradition of participation in adult education. France had neither of these.

The 1971 law was produced in the aftermath of the most dangerous threat to its stability that the Fifth Republic had had to face, the student riots and the general strike of 1968. This crisis had shown that France was still a more divided country than, for example, Federal Germany, the Netherlands, or the Scandinavian states, particularly in the field of industrial relations. The Government and employers had been impelled by fear to make concessions to the trade unions, including an agreement of 1970 between the major employers' associations and principal trade union confederations, which was the basis of the 1971 vocational training law. The State itself had moved more or less willingly to a policy of democratization and decentralization of educational provision, as the 1968 Law on the Direction of Higher Education showed.

These facts may help one's understanding of the legal provisions made for adult vocational education. When one reads in Article I that an object of the 1971 law was to encourage workers' social advancement 'by access to different levels of culture' and their contribution to cultural development, one may interpret this as a praiseworthy desire of lawmakers to conform with the principles of permanent education. It may also indicate their awareness that if vocational training was to be fully effective, France would have to provide for adults the opportunities for general education which were an indispensable complement, if not a pre-condition, of specialized training, and which the country lacked. The French text may not then show a more enlightened attitude to vocational training than comparable legislation in Federal Germany or the United Kingdom,[20] which does not present cultural development as an objective. The difference may be that as they already had a structured provision of general education for adults, these countries did not have to mention it in vocational training laws.

Equally the specific involvement of such a wide range of organizations and institutions in training activities may have been done on principle, to make it a matter for the whole nation and not just a section of it. On the other hand, in the under-developed state of French adult education and training, one may ask how else would the Government find the resources to meet the vastly increased demand for adult vocational education that it hoped to inspire. Similarly the free market approach to training, demonstrated by the contract system, was certainly in accord with the economic principles of the Fifth Republic: it encouraged competition and put the paying customers, mainly employers, in a posi-

149

tion to control the product, but the possibility of negotiating lucrative contracts would also attract people and organizations into training provision, which was very necessary.

Since the right of workers to cultural development and educational leave had already been set out in the 1966 vocational education law, the temporary ascendency won by organized labour as a result of the events of 1968 would appear to have had little effect on the 1971 text. What the agreement of 1970 had done was to obtain a written commitment to these from the major employer organizations and thus make more certain the application of the subsequent legislation. The measures relating to educational leave were unique to France at that time in their apparent scope and the fact that they created an individual right to leave. It is difficult to know whether they should be attributed to Government enlightenment or calculation. French adults were not accustomed to follow courses of study and their response to the 1959 law's offer of free evening classes had been disappointing. State policy required mass participation in vocational training and it certainly had not gone unnoticed that the opportunity to study in the firm's time might constitute a powerful incentive.

Given all its national characteristics, the French policy on adult vocational education was nevertheless using similar instruments to those used by other countries to meet similar circumstances. In treating it as a separate area of adult education France was only following a general practice and in passing special legislation to control it she was in the company of Federal Germany, the United Kingdom and Switzerland[21] among others. Whereas other forms of adult education have been subject to fairly loose direction by the State and such direction has been devolved to provincial or local authorities on the whole, occupational training has been under central government control, as, for example, in Switzerland and Federal Germany, where exceptionally it is under federal law, not provincial. France's conformation to this pattern is in strong contrast to its treatment of sociocultural animation, which has attracted little legislation over the years and increasing devolution of authority.

By bringing other ministries, particularly ones concerned with economic performance, into the direction of vocational training France was conforming with other countries' practice, as it was by taxing employers, thus raising the money to pay for the exercise, and by offering a rebate for the training they did, thus offering persuasion to train their personnel.[22] The special concern shown for the training of unemployed, women returning to paid employment and young unskilled workers, was also shared with most other advanced nations.[23]

In fact, as the 1971 law has been applied, one might say that it has most resembled the measures taken by other countries in proving to be more an instrument of economic planning than of educational policy. This is to be seen in the granting of educational leave. Hardly any worker could afford to take unpaid leave and payment was only guaranteed for those people taking specifically occupational training or State-approved courses, which turned out to be restricted to occupational training too. Therefore educational leave for general education would only be given with pay if employers were willing, and they rarely were. Indeed, events showed that, although the right to leave without penalty was guaranteed, few people would take it without the employer's approval, for fear that they might be made to suffer in some way. With very few exceptions paid educational leave has been an instrument used to attract people to kinds of occupational education of interest to employers and the State.

The State could have encouraged individual applications for general education by making grants in lieu of earnings for *maintenance and improvement of knowledge* courses, as the law envisaged, but it was not until 1978 that it passed legislation to this end.[24] Its policy has been much more obsessed with economic performance than the 1971 law suggested. For example responsibility for State action and supervision has shifted and now lies with the Secretary of State for Vocational Education under the Minister of Labour. How far this has been due to rising unemployment, inflation and recession since 1973 is not clear, but these have certainly had their effect. By 1976 fifty-five per cent of State expenditure for face-to-face training was spent on courses for the unemployed.[25] In that year a law encouraged employers to finance training for unemployed people and in the next year another made it obligatory to devote a sum equal to 0.2% of the total wage bill out of their liability for training tax to such work with people under the age of twenty-five. Since the rate of tax had never risen to the 2.0% envisaged in the 1971 law, indeed only in 1979 has it risen to 1.1%, it has meant that employers are obliged to contribute, either directly or indirectly, only at the rate of 0.9% of their total wage bill to other training.[26] Other legislation in 1977 and 1978 offered unemployed young people and women seeking to return to work a period of training and work experience with pay. This use of training to mitigate the effects of youth unemployment is similar to measures taken by other European countries.

Also like other countries France spends more on vocational training than on any other part of adult education, a sum of 11,000 million francs in 1977.[27] Since the 1971 law the number of adults in vocational education has risen from a little under 2,000,000 to a peak of nearly 3,000,000 in 1975 and then declined to about 2,800,000 in 1977, of whom seventy-three per cent were men and twenty-seven per cent women.[28] At first there was a disproportionate representation of supervisory, technical and managerial staff, but the balance has shifted somewhat in favour of skilled craftsmen, who formed in 1977 forty-six per cent of trainees, while supervisory and technical staff made up twenty-two per cent and engineers and managerial staff fifteen per cent. Unskilled and semi-skilled personnel remained under-represented at seventeen per cent.[29]

Compared with twenty years ago the statistics show that many more adults are engaged in systematic study, although the numbers still remain below those of Sweden or Federal Germany, for example. More extremely than these countries, since there is little competition, the vocational imperative predominates in France, but other countries are moving in that direction. Increasingly adults learn what the State and employers want them to, or not at all. In France it has been shown that, in spite of the law, the individual has little chance to study what he wants if it does not conform to the wishes of these powers. Statistics are lacking, but there is evidence to suggest that adult participation in socio-cultural animation has been affected by vocational training competition. If the intensive propaganda to attract employees to take advantage of training opportunities, which was a feature of the early 1970s, has drawn them away from other forms of education, then France may well end up with as unbalanced a provision of adult education as she had when only socio-cultural animation was available.

References

1. ALFRED COBBAN, *A History of Modern France*, 3 Vol, 3rd Edition, London, Penguin, 1965.
2. COLIN TITMUS, *Adult Education in France*, Oxford, Pergamon, 1967, Chapter 1, Historical Outline.
3. ibid. pp. 1—4
4. RAYMOND LABOURIE, *Les Institutions Socio-culturelles. Les Mots Clés*, Paris, Presses Universitaires de France, 1978, p.17.
5. *Cahiers de la Quinzaine*, Paris, 3rd series, No. 2, 10, 20, 1902: 5th Series, No. 20, 1904.
6. For the early days of *éducation populaire*, see LABOURIE op. cit., TITMUS op. cit., GENEVIÈVE POUJOL, *L'Education Populaire*, Viroflay, Association pour la Diffusion de la Recherche sur l'Action Culturelle, 1977, Vol. 1.
7. TITMUS, op. cit. pp. 35—37.
8. PIERRE BESNARD, *Socio-pédagogie de la formation des adultes*, Paris, Les Editions ESF — Entreprise Moderne d'Edition, 1974.
9. LABOURIE, op. cit.
10. COLIN TITMUS, 'France — current problems and prospects', *Adult Education*, vol. 42, no. 2, July, 1969.
11. Many had already begun to do this on their own initiative, see LABOURIE, op. cit.
12. GENEVIÈVE POUJOL, 'La formation des animateurs', in M. DEBESSE and G. MIALARET ed., *Traité des sciences pédagogiques: vol. 8, Education permanente at animation socio-culturelle*, Paris, Presses Universitaires de France, 1978.
13. P. MOULINIER, *L'animation et les animateurs à travers la littérature spécialisée*, Paris, Secrétariat d'Etat à la Culture, Service des Etudes et de la Recherche, 1976, duplicated. PIERRE BESNARD, 'Le problématique de l'animation socio-culturelle', in DEBESSE and MIALARET, op. cit.
14. GENEVIÈVE POUJOL. *Le Métier d'Animateur*, Toulouse, Privat, 1978.

15. COLIN TITMUS, PAZ BUTTEDAHL, DIANA IRONSIDE, PAUL LENGRAND, *Terminology of Adult Education*, Paris, UNESCO, 1979.
16. *Adult Education, The Challenge of Change*, Edinburgh, Her Majesty's Stationery Office, 1975.
17. MOULINIER op. cit.
18. TITMUS, *Adult Education in France*, op. cit., Chapter 1.
19. *Loi no 71—575 du 16 juillet 1971 portant organisation de la formation professionelle continue dans le cadre de l'éducation permanente.*
20. Arbeitsförderungsgesetz, June 1969, amended December 1975: Industrial Training Act, 1964.
21. Switzerland: Federal Law on Vocational Education, 20 September, 1963.
22. e.g. Industrial Training Act, United Kingdom.
23. e.g. United Kingdom, Sweden, Federal Germany.
24. Loi du 17 juillet 1978.
25. PIERRE BESNARD and JACQUES PERRET, *Le système français de formation des adultes: aspects professionnels*, Prague, European Centre for Leisure and Education, 1978, duplicated.
26. ibid.
27. *La typologie des fonctions dans l'éducation des adultes*, Brussels, Confédération internationale des Syndicats Libres, 1979.
28. ibid.
29. BESNARD and PERRET, op. cit.

CHAPTER 6

Norway

Norway is a long narrow strip of territory on the north-western limits of Europe, a significant proportion of it within the Arctic Circle. Larger than Italy, Federal Germany or the United Kingdom, but with a population of just over 4,000,000, Norway is the least densely inhabited state of Western Europe, having only twelve persons to the square kilometre.[1] Much of its land is uninhabitable and more unsuitable for cultivation. There are serious natural obstacles to communication in that the country runs from north to south, but it is divided by innumerable sea inlets and mountain ridges, running generally from east to west.

After centuries of turbulent independence in the Middle Ages, Norway became a holding of the Danish Crown for over four hundred years.[2] With the fall of Denmark as an ally of Napoleon, many Norwegians hoped to regain independence but the Great Powers awarded the country to Sweden. The Norwegians were forced to accept the Swedish king but resisted assimilation into Sweden, managing to retain their own constitution, which they had voted themselves in 1814, and considerable autonomy outside foreign affairs. The relationship between the two countries became less and less acceptable to each one throughout the nineteenth century and Norway finally achieved complete independence under its own King in 1905.

The Constitution laid down complete separation of the executive, the Council of State, from the legislature, the

Storting, which was elected by men over twenty-five having a property qualification. Gradually the influence of the Parliament increased, until, in 1884, the King accepted that his ministers should have the confidence of the Storting as a condition of office. The suffrage was extended by stages until it was given equally to both sexes in 1913, and the lower age limited was reduced to twenty in 1969. A system of proportional representation was introduced in 1919.

There was a slow movement from the authoritarian government of the early nineteenth century to a more democratic rule. As the century progressed and the vote was given to more people, not only did more peasants and workers achieve political rights, but they began to exercise their influence. As in other countries the Labour movement in Norway professed revolutionary aims in its early years. After the First World War there was a split between revolutionaries and reformists and the Labour Party — which won power in 1935 and effectively ruled the country, except under the German occupation from 1940 to 1945, for the next thirty years — was reformist in its approach to its aim of an economy planned and controlled by the State. It began before the Second World War by a number of social reforms, including old age pensions, holidays with pay and unemployment insurance.

Early nineteenth century Norway lived principally on fishing, much of whose catch had for centuries been exported, and a subsistence agriculture. In the middle of the century fishing was joined by timber products and shipping as the country's chief earners of foreign currency. By the 1880s the Norwegian merchant marine was surpassed in size only by those of the United Kingdom and the USA. The foundations of industrialization were laid in the mid-century, speeded by improvements in communications, but the development of commerce and industry was slowed by the absence until the latter years of the century of banking and insurance facilities. There was a significant increase in population and a move to the towns. In 1845 only 12.2% of Norwegians lived in urban areas, by 1900 28% and nowadays the figure has risen to over 50%.

The transformation of Norway from an agricultural to an industrial and trading state has continued since independence, facilitated by the abundant potential for the production of hydro-electric power. It became vulnerable to world trade fluctuations, so that not only did Norway, although a neutral, suffer from blockade during the First World War, it experienced severe depressions in the 'twenties and 'thirties, one third of trade unionists being unemployed at one time. This no doubt strengthened the support for the Labour Party's drive towards a planned economy and a welfare state.

Since the Second World War the question of State control of the economy has been the major division between Labour and its opponents. But it is noteworthy that, no matter what the government, the country has maintained close control of the oil and gas fields that lie within Norwegian waters. These provide rich resources out of which to continue the generous social policies which all parties support. After the German occupation of 1940—5, Norway decided it needed collective security, broke with its traditional neutrality and joined NATO. On the other hand the country's sensitivity to anything which might threaten its comparatively recent independence played its part in the rejection by referendum of entry into the European Community.

Norway is a Lutheran country, over ninety per cent of the population being nominal members of the State Church. It was not until 1845 that citizens could legally leave it and join other sects. Church questions aroused considerable passions in the nineteenth century. There were conflicts between the rationalism of the orthodox Church line, the happy Christianity derived from the Dane, Grundtvig,[3] and the austere, fundamentalist Pietism, which exerted a deep influence in country districts. Politics, culture, and education all showed the imprint of religious dogmatism. Although its power has declined in the twentieth century, Norway is still the most strongly Protestant country in Europe and fundamentalism is strong.

The revival of nationalism in the eighteenth and nineteenth centuries stimulated native culture, which became both an expression of Norwegian identity and a means of propagating it. The country produced artists of international stature; the writers, Henrik Ibsen, and Bjørnstjerne Bjørnson, the composer, Edvard Grieg, and the painter, Edvard Munch. Under Danish rule a Norwegian-accented Danish had become effectively the only written language and efforts were made to revive native Norwegian, based on dialects still spoken by the common people. Conflict between supporters of the two language forms was long enduring and bitter. Even today it has not been entirely resolved, since literary Norwegian, descended from the first, is still different from New Norwegian, derived from the second, in spite of many government efforts to reconcile the two. They are, however, closer than they used to be.

Under Denmark, Norwegian language and culture were further undermined in that those people who could afford it sent their children abroad to be educated. There were hardly any secondary schools in the country and no institution of higher education. The first university was founded in 1811 in Christiania, now Oslo. It was not until the middle of the nineteenth century that the secondary and higher curriculum was broadened away from a narrow basis of Latin and Greek to given prominence to modern and scientific studies. Not until the end of the century did Norwegian language and literature (including the revived native form) become established, by the education act of 1896, which provided for a four-year middle school, followed by a three-year upper secondary school leading to university.

That kind of education was only for children of the official classes. In Norway, as in other Protestant countries, it was early believed that all people should acquire basic literacy for religious purposes. This was made compulsory by an Act of 1739, which was only partially implemented. Up to the mid-nineteenth century preparation for confirmation was still the basic purpose of primary education and in country districts for many children it was restricted to a few weeks a year given in isolated farms by itinerant teachers. When in 1860 the curriculum was broadened and texts giving an introduction to Norwegian history, geography and culture were provided for reading, in addition to the religious and edifying ones hitherto used, they were strongly resisted at first as too worldly by the fundamentalist church interests which were so strong in rural areas.

All sectors of Norwegian education, including universities, have expanded in the twentieth century. In 1969 nine years of schooling from the age of seven were made obligatory.

Norwegians spend six in primary school and then three years in a young people's, or middle, school. Over seventy-five per cent of young people continue into post-compulsory school, most of them in the gymnasium, which leads on to higher education, or in the folk high school.[4]

The national cultural revival gave adult education in nineteenth century Norway a further driving force, in addition to the common ones of religion, democratization and industrialization. Religion had both a negative and a positive influence. The temperance movement was active in education from 1859. On the other hand the Society for Popular Enlightenment (1851) was partially inspired by the feeling that, to establish a modern democratic state and a national culture, rural people needed education to extend the narrow bounds of their fundamentalist beliefs. The first folk high schools in Norway, influenced by Grundtvig, were condemned for their worldliness by orthodox religious opinion and for their liberalism by the State.

It was the mid-century economic growth that saw the foundations of modern adult education provision laid. As in Sweden, provision was made by voluntary organizations, either of middle-class philanthropy or workers' self-help. The Norwegian Students Association gave classes from 1864, workers' (later, folk) academies functioned from 1885. There was significant influence from Britain, Denmark and Sweden, and from the latter study circles were widely copied early in the twentieth century. The economic troubles of the 1920s and 1930s had a twofold effect. Government subsidies were withdrawn from folk academies in 1924—5. On the other hand public concern to offer the many unemployed means to improve their culture during their enforced leisure, stimulated government action in 1933, aimed at bringing the varied adult education organizations together in closer co-operation. In 1932 the associations offering study circles had formed the Joint Committee on Study Activity and the new proposals were for an expansion of provision, a permanent national council for adult education and greater State administrative involvement. Although approved, most of the proposals were only implemented after the Second World War.

Until the discovery of North Sea Oil and gas Norwegians were conscious of being poorer than their Swedish and

Danish neighbours. Like them they have grown much more wealthy since the war and this has enabled them to develop a social democratic welfare state. Norwegian adult education has major features in common with Sweden and Denmark. By comparison with other Western European states, government support has been generous. For all its similarities to its neighbours, however, Norwegian adult education also retains its individual characteristics, as an examination of legislation relating to it will show.

Adult education legislation in Norway

Up to the middle 1960s a Norwegian author could properly write, 'In Norwegian legislation there is no specific Act governing adult education, but there are a number of laws that in some way or other affect educational activity among adults.'[5] In most cases, as in the university acts relating to Bergen University (1949) and Oslo University (1956), the Library Act (1947), the State Travelling Theatre Act (1948) and the Broadcasting Act (1933), the adult education element was only a small part of the measure. In the case of the Correspondence Schools Act (1948) and the Folk High Schools Act (1949) the scope of the law was restricted to one sector of adult education.

Growth had been piecemeal, private initiative being followed by public authority support, as different forms of provision were introduced to meet different needs. By the late 1950s the cost of adult education to the State and acknowledgement of its importance as an essential part of the national educational system led the State to seek for means to organize the provision of adult learning opportunities in such a way as to meet the goals set for it as efficiently and equitably as possible. In 1965 the Ministry of Church and Education presented Storting Proposition No. 92 on Adult Training. On the basis of an historical sketch and an examination of current provision it made proposals for a future overall policy of adult education.[6]

It recognized and recommended expansion in three main areas: education enabling adults to obtain secondary school examination qualifications, mainly a function of public schools, but in which voluntary study associations might also have a role; non-examinable hobby and leisure courses, the field of the voluntary bodies, to which great importance was attached; and vocational training, in which the Ministry of Church and Education, the Labour Directorate and employers were all engaged, and to which a large amount of space was devoted. The role of the universities, libraries, the mass media and correspondence courses was also examined, attention was given to adult education research, the qualification and payment of adult educators, also to the financial problems of adult learners, including the question of educational leave. Recommendations were also made for a national administrative and advisory structure.

The recommendations were inspired by certain principles and also by economic and social pressures. Because of the prolongation of compulsory schooling, there would be an increased demand from adults for secondary schooling to enable them to keep up with the younger generation. 'A good general education for the whole population is also essential to political democracy'.[7] The economy needed more and higher trained manpower, but also the individual should be enabled '. . . to advance to the positions which correspond to his abilities and experience'.[8] Adult education for qualifications, vocational education and non-examinable activities should be on an equal footing with each other and with the formal school system. Public authorities had a responsibility to offer study opportunities to adults, but the role of voluntary associations was valuable and must be encouraged. Perhaps the most significant statement of principle for a comprehensive policy of adult education was:

> The Ministry feels that there should be no sharp distinction between professional training and general educational training of adults — or between 'useful' and 'useless' knowledge. The very fact that an individual seeks knowledge — that he wants to know more about his trade or profession and about the community in which he lives — is valuable as such.[9]

Although some of the recommendations were put into practice, progress towards legislation appears to have been marked by the same careful preparation and attention to consensus that has been remarked in the case of Swedish reform, and it was not until 1976 that a Norwegian Adult

Education Act was passed. It reaffirmed and expanded the statement of aim made by proposition No. 92. It said:

The purpose of adult education is to help the individual to attain a more satisfying life. This Act shall contribute to providing adult persons with equal opportunities to acquire knowledge, understanding and skill, which will improve the individual's sense of value and personal development and strengthen the basis for independent achievement and co-operation with others in working and social life. [10]

The Act was to apply to non-examinable studies organized by voluntary bodies; to courses leading to primary and secondary education certificates (called fundamental education), specially provided for adults; to alternative kinds of fundamental education, designed to take into account adult life and work experience; to post-work and short courses in institutions of secondary and higher education; to short-term courses in folk high schools; to vocational training for adults organized by the State as part of labour market policy; to training given by or for employers; to other adult education to meet specific needs.

The law laid down what institution should be responsible for the provision of each kind of adult education. Central Government was to be responsible for national development and to provide alternative fundamental education, post-work courses in higher education and vocational training as part of labour market policy. County authorities were to have general responsibility for development in each county and to provide fundamental education and post-work courses in secondary schools. Municipal authorities were to be responsible for development in each municipality and to provide fundamental education in primary schools. Study with no set curricula or examinations would be the responsibility of voluntary bodies, which might also offer some fundamental education. The various levels of public authority had an obligation both to provide and to subsidize adult education.

Both public and private institutions or organizations might qualify for subsidy. In order to do so private ones were to have individual membership, a management elected by the members, adult education as a main field of activity and their students must have the opportunity to influence the content and organization of courses.

At national level the Ministry of Church and Education would supervise all activities falling under the Act. It would be advised by a nominated national Adult Education Council. The law also decreed what agencies of county and municipal councils and of universities and institutions of tertiary education would be responsible for adult education.

The percentage of recognized costs for each form of adult study which would be met by public subsidy was laid down. Fundamental education would be a hundred per cent grant aided and the division of costs between central government, counties and municipalities would be as for primary and secondary schools. Post-work and short courses in folk high schools were to get eighty per cent of costs, as were study circles of voluntary organizations. The latter would also receive specified subventions for other types of course, for some staff, administrative and development costs.

Vocational training within or for industry might receive an eighty per cent subsidy if courses were approved by a representative body of the industry concerned, on which employers and labour were equally represented. Participants would also have to have the right to influence the content and organization of each course. Courses provided by the Ministry of Church and Education and the Labour Directorate as part of labour market policy would be entirely financed from public funds.

As need arose, programmes specially designed for the handicapped, for the seriously under-educated and people with heavy family obligations would be entirely financed by the State. Some shop steward courses would receive subsidies of fifty per cent of approved costs and specific grants might be made for outreach, research and development. Significant latitude, as in the question of staff qualifications, was left for the exercise of discretion by the Ministry and by other statutory bodies, to meet changing conditions.

A study of adult education laws in force in Western Europe, presented some years ago, listed sixty-five measures, of which nearly two-thirds had been enacted since 1970.[11] This spate of law-making, in a field where there had previously been little, reflected a change in the balance of forces within adult education. Whereas historically the State, although approving, had left initiative to private enterprise and had adopted a largely passive supportive role, to an increasing extent in the last few decades it has become interventionist, as has already been remarked about other countries studied. It is this intervention, showing a recognition of adult education's importance, its cost, and its need for promotion and organization, that has inspired so much legislation. In it certain trends may be identified, as reference to laws mentioned elsewhere in this book will show. Norway has followed some of them.

Where formerly, it had been a discretionary power, the duty of public authorities to provide, or secure provision of, adult study opportunities, is now widely laid down. A national administrative structure is created, in which considerable responsibility and power is devolved from central government to local authorities, even in States whose school system is centrally controlled. To balance this increased role of public bodies, the role of voluntary associations in both provision and policy making is affirmed and protected by being enshrined in law. Measures relating to structure, authority and responsibility tend to be so formulated as to permit flexibility of response to meet changing circumstances.

The aim of the State is both to regulate for efficiency and to promote growth. Although it does not forbid by law any form of adult education, it has its own priorities, which it singles out for discriminatory action. Among those forms commonly specified are compensatory primary and secondary school studies, courses leading to higher general educational qualifications, vocational training, especially that intended to offer job opportunities to the unemployed and to provide trained labour in sectors which have a shortage, trade union training and education for the handicapped and underprivileged. The obligation to make provision of adult courses tends to be restricted to priority areas and is only imposed on public authorities. On other bodies, employers, trade unions, professional associations and voluntary study organizations, influence is exerted by the giving or withholding of financial support, and the varying rates of subsidy for different activities. As will have been noted, Norway is not alone in meeting the full cost of compensatory school education, labour market training and education for the handicapped and underprivileged.

Although it is firmly situated within a strong European trend, the Norwegian Adult Education Act contains a number of distinctive features. It is the most comprehensive of any Western European measures. Indeed it is the one that most nearly covers the whole range of what is understood as adult education within the country concerned. The only significant omissions are correspondence education, which is regulated by its own law, and long courses in folk high schools, which are considered to be post-compulsory secondary education rather than adult education.[12] Other countries may be moving to an all-embracing policy in the field, but it is not embodied in a single measure. Those that have such a policy, like Sweden, operate it under several laws and decrees. Others, like Federal Germany or the United Kingdom, do not treat adult education as a unified field.

Norway is unusual, if not unique, in that vocational education is included in the 1976 Act and that no sharp distinction is made between it and general adult education, just as the Storting Proposition No. 92 had recommended. In almost every other State vocational training is treated as a special case, with legislation specifically related to it, its organization is different, usually under the direction of manpower ministries, and considerably larger public funds are devoted to it than to other kinds of adult study. In Norway, although the Labour Directorate has a say in it, it comes under the Ministry of Church and Education, like all other adult education, and the principles of most of its funding are similar to those generally applied in the Act.

Although the position of voluntary bodies is protected, employers and trade unions have a guaranteed role, and a certain flexibility is allowed for, the way in which every agency is given its allotted area of activity and even the freedoms are prescribed leaves a heavier impression of State planning and direction in the Norwegian Act than in the legislation of other Western European countries. The precision with which sectors of activity are specified may suggest that the State is not merely limiting what it will subsidize, but what is adult education. In treating adult education on equal terms with initial education, Norway has produced and has intended to produce a law which is as close a counterpart as possible to school laws.

As in the case of other Western countries — for example, Sweden, Denmark, the United Kingdom, where the State is most deeply involved in adult education — Norway has nothing in its history to arouse fears of the tyrannical State. The country is a homogeneous one and government power is not a threat because it expresses a national consensus. This is probably even more true of Norway than of Sweden or Denmark. National solidarity is strengthened by a greater religious element in society and a national awareness, due to Norway's recent struggle for independence, which have made the Norwegians less open than their neighbours to outside influences which might undermine homogeneity. It has even been argued that Norway has fewer class distinctions than they do.

With that solidarity appears to go a cautious conservatism and, until the last decade, a feeling of being poorer than other States. One might say that, with the confidence born of longish wealth and success and an openness to changes, Sweden has gone in for a series of laws, adapting as need arises. Norway seems to have taken a long time to arrive at a measure that will get it right first time and will endure for many years. This is also a reflection of its care and capacity in so small a population to undertake long consultations with all groups of society, so as to arrive at a generally accepted measure whose implementation expresses the common will.

It might also be noted that comprehensive central government direction and planning of society, which have gone further in Norway than in its neighbours, have become particularly deep rooted in education, so much so that some doubt has been expressed whether the trend is reversible.[13] The Adult Education Act reflects both that centralizing tendency and conversely the recent policy of the State itself to impose devolution of responsibility on county and municipal councils. Because of the participation of so many people in the consultation process that precedes legislation, centralization is not undemocratic or contrary to the principle stated in the 1976 Act that students should be able to influence the content and organization of their studies.

The Act has aroused a significant amount of interest in other Western European countries, where it has been discussed as a model. Whether it will work in Norway remains to be seen. The country's oil and gas resources probably ensure that it can afford the level of provision, but it is a law designed for a largely enclosed, homogeneous people, which is likely to be opened up, with consequent stresses to its solidarity, by the influence of oil wealth.

Correspondence education in Norway

Distance learning and multi-media education are terms which have become quite fashionable over the last two decades, designating concepts that have caught the imagination of the general public as well as of the educational world. The Open University in the United Kingdom, *Telekolleg* in the Federal German Republic and the *Centre National de Télé-enseigne-ment* in France use the most up-to-date educational techno-logy. Basically, however, they rely on a medium which has been in use since the last decades of the nineteenth century: correspondence education. Although Norway was not among the earliest countries in which it was employed, it is highly developed and has several interesting features there.

The oldest (and largest) correspondence school in the country, the Norwegian Correspondence School (NKS), dates back to 1914. Growth was steady until the Second World War, when the partial breakdown of the regular school system gave a significant boost, raising annual enrolments from about 50,000 to around 80,000. After the war there was a period of stagnation, even decline, followed by another rapid rise in the 'sixties and 'seventies, culminating in 1975–7.[14]

Correspondence education is strictly controlled by law and has been since 1948, when legislation was passed which was subsequently revised in 1969. Should there be any doubt about what correspondence education is, it states, 'The term correspondence school used in this Act refers to an insti-tution giving instruction by means of letters requiring written papers to be sent in for correction'.[15] Such an institution must be approved by the Ministry of Church and Education, which shall appoint a Correspondence School Council to assist it in the supervision of correspondence schools. Not only the institution but each individual course offered to the public must also be approved.

By regulations issued by the Ministry, an organization offering correspondence education activities shall keep them separate and under a different director from any other activities it may engage in. Earnings from correspondence education shall be limited to the level necessary for the secure operation and development of the school. Accounts shall be sent annually to the Ministry. Principals and teachers shall have similar professional training to their counterparts in the regular school sector. Each institution having correspondence education as its principal activity shall have a teachers' council of the principal and all full-time teachers, under the chairmanship of the former. Each school must send an annual report to the Correspondence School Council. Approval of a school may be withdrawn and failure to observe the conditions of the Act may result in a fine.

Regulations which came into force in 1977 lay down that correspondence courses in the primary school curriculum, either for ordinary pupils or for adults, shall be paid for by municipalities and the State, in the proportions laid down for primary schooling. Students shall pay no fees. For more advanced education public authorities pay eighty-five per cent of costs and students fifteen per cent. On enrolment the student pays fifty per cent of course cost and on satisfactory completion of the work set (90%) the school refunds thirty-five per cent.[16]

Most correspondence education is conducted at primary and secondary level. It is used by students seeking higher job competence, preparing for public examinations, or simply studying for subject interest. There are three main ways of pursuing correspondence education. The first is the classical one, in which the student works entirely on his own, completing the assignments sent through the post by the school and returning them for correction and comment. This is the most popular method. In a second, called combined instruction, the student not only studies alone, but also attends classes in which he receives face-to-face tuition from a teacher. In a third, the student participates in a study circle, which works on the material sent by the school and returns an assignment jointly prepared. This is called a correspondence circle.

In order to supply this service correspondence schools

must be accepted by and enjoy the co-operation of other institutions in the educational field. They work with the Norwegian Broadcasting Corporation in the production of multi-media courses for the public. In combined courses class instruction is given by voluntary associations and public schools, which recruit the students, while provision of teaching materials and the setting and marking of assignments is done by the correspondence school. A similar division of responsibility with voluntary bodies occurs in correspondence circles. In the field of courses in the regular school curriculum there is close collaboration with the public education authorities and, for vocationally-oriented provision, with companies and organizations representing different sectors of the economy. Correspondence education for armed service personnel, which is free and widespread — it makes up eight per cent of NKS provision — is done with the approval of the Civilian Education Board of the Norwegian Armed Forces.

According to the Annual Report of the Correspondence School Council, 1978, there are thirty-six approved schools in Norway, but only about thirty are active. Many, like the Norwegian Correspondence School, began as private commercial enterprises; others, like the Correspondence School of the State Technological Institute, which specializes in electrical, radio and television engineering, although legally private, have close links with the State; others, like the Norwegian Civil Engineers Association Correspondence School, are agencies of professional bodies. Under the conditions of the law all are now run on a non-profit making basis. Some, as their name indicates (e.g. the Typing Institute), operate in a restricted field, others, of which NKS is the outstanding example, offer a wide range of courses, from hobbies to professional and higher education. The People's Correspondence School (FB) is jointly owned by a number of organizations, including the Co-operative Union, the Workers' Educational Association and various trade unions. Not surprisingly, in view of its connections, it specializes in organizational studies, political and social sciences and is the largest provider of material for correspondence circles. Elingaard Correspondence School (EB), active like FB and NKS in correspondence circle provision, works with business organizations and cultural societies and therefore is particularly active in the field of arts and management education. The Agricultural Correspondence School (LB), owned by farming interests, principally concentrates on subject areas suggested by its title.

The Correspondence School Council takes very seriously its duty to examine new courses before they can be introduced. In 1978 it dealt with 275 courses, of which only 145 were fully approved. The rest were either rejected, or required further inspection, or were approved for a shorter period than the full five years, after which any course must seek re-approval.[17]

The considerable rise in the mid-1970s in the number of students enrolled in correspondence education has been attributed to the new regulations which made courses almost free for students.[18] In 1978 there were 187,000 enrolments, about 4.6% of the country's population (including people of school age), in 1,200 courses. There were 5,000 correspondence circles, with 33,000 participants. The most popular courses of study were general school courses, which had 41,000 participants, commercial school courses, with 31,000, language courses, included in part in the general school curriculum provision (21,000), car and engine courses (12,000).[19]

It has been stated that the proportion of correspondence students in Norway is higher than that in any other country. Japan and the USA have about 2.0%, Finland and the Netherlands about 1.5%, and the United Kingdom about 1.0%[20] There are a number of plausible, but not necessarily correct, explanations for this pre-eminence.

It may be in part because of close public control that correspondence education enjoys such prominence in Norway and, conversely, because of its importance that State regulation was imposed in the first place. It could have been an historical accident, the extent to which it was able to make up for the breakdown of the school system in the Second World War, which demonstrated the contribution it could make to national education, and made it popular, so that the State introduced regulations in order that it should not be misused. Those rules, with the high level of quality control, have maintained and improved its effectiveness. Now it is an integral part of the country's education system, enjoying equal status with other sectors.

This is made clear by the 1969 revision of the Correspondence Schools Act and subsequent regulations. The Act was in a way a fore-runner of the Adult Education Act, in that it asserted the tutelage of the Ministry of Church and Education, advised by a nominated council. The Ministry was in effect to say who would provide and what, by its approval procedures. In fact its powers were made greater than they were to be in adult education as a whole, because, while adult education organizations could operate without ministerial sanction, but without subsidy, correspondence schools could not. The new level of subsidy for the latter, set out in the 1977 regulations, indicates an attempt to keep correspondence education in step with the levels prescribed in the Adult Education Act. The same subject priorities that are to be observed in that act are to be seen in the differential subsidies to be made for different kinds of correspondence course. The fact that central and local authorities share the public finance of school-type courses in the same proportion as they do in adult education and the regular schools is another sign of correspondence education being treated on an equal footing with other sectors. The requirement that schools should have a staff council follows the pattern of democracy within the organization as a condition of public subsidy, to be found in adult education.

Norwegian testimony suggests that geography, scattered communities and difficult communications, have been among the reasons for correspondence education's high place in the country.[21] The fact that of two countries much like Norway in their adult education, Sweden, which is also quite similar geographically, has a strong correspondence sector, while Denmark, whose geography is different, does not, would seem to support this contention. But, as E.G. Wedell has pointed out, the geographical factor is not necessarily determinant, since correspondence education has long flourished in the Netherlands and, in the United Kingdom, has its largest concentration of students in the densely populated south-east corner of the country.[22]

Whether correspondence education flourishes or not seems, indeed, to depend on a number of factors. Inaccessibility of face-to-face teaching is one, whether because of geography, or because such teaching does not exist. Convenience is another, since a correspondence client can study when he is free, he is not bound to a class meeting at fixed hours. He can also work on each part of the course at his own speed, he has neither to keep up with, nor hang back for, other students. Economics is another factor. There may be enough people throughout the country to justify a correspondence course, but not enough in any one place to support a face-to-face class. This, together with the fact that students can continue employment while studying, thus combining practical experience with theoretical learning, helps to explain why training for many professions is done, at least in part, by correspondence.

The quality of the product is essential to the success of correspondence education. Whether the assurance of this is left to market forces or public control varies widely from country to country and seems to depend on the past record of correspondence institutions, the importance attached by government to their work, and the extent of government direction of social and economic life, particularly of education. One finds complete lack of interference in the United Kingdom; non-interference with the private sector, but a strong State institution, the National Centre for Distance Teaching, in France; a law laying down strict regulations for State approval of correspondence schools, but also allowing non-approved schools to operate unhindered, in the Netherlands.

In Norway, as in the United Kingdom and the Netherlands, private, unregulated schools had established a good reputation. They may well have established themselves in the first place because they met a need created by geography. Their service during the war brought a national recognition of their importance which British schools did not achieve, and this, together with the existence of a government committed to direction of national life to a degree not approached in the Netherlands, may help to account for the extent of the State regulation introduced in 1948. The combination of history and the way correspondence teaching has been encouraged and integrated with the rest of education helps at least to account for its strength in Norway compared with other Western European States.

References

1. *Basic Statistics of the Community*, Brussels, Statistical Office of the European Communities, 1979.

2. For the history of Norway see R.G. POPPERWELL, *Norway*, London, Ernest Benn, 1972; JOHN MIDGAARD, *A Brief History of Norway*, Oslo, Johan Grundt Tanum Vorlag, 3rd edition, 1966.

3. See below Chapter 8, Denmark.

4. *Reviews of National Policies for Education: Norway*, Paris, OECD, 1976.

5. INGEBORG LYCHE, *Adult Education in Norway*, Oslo, Universitets-forlaget, 1964.

6. *Storting Proposition No. 92 (1964—65) on Adult Training.* Recommendation by the Ministry of Church and Education of 9 April, 1965, approved by Royal Decree of the same date.

7. ibid.

8. ibid.

9. ibid.

10. Norwegian Adult Education Act, 1976.

11. *Adult Education Legislation in Ten Countries of Europe*, Amersfoort, European Bureau of Adult Education, 1974.

12. *Reviews of National Policies of Education: Norway*, op. cit.

13. ibid.

14. This information is derived from a private communication from Anders J. Gåserud, research officer of NKS.

15. Act of 12 November 1948, and 7 February 1969, Correspondence Schools.

16. Regler for statstilkott til Brevundervisning gjeldende fra 1 Januar, 1977, fastsatt av Kirke — og Undervisningdepartementet.

17. *Brevskolerådets Årsmelding, 1978*, duplicated.

18. Gåserud, cit.

19. *Brevskolerådets Årsmelding*, 1978, op. cit.

20. Gåserud, cit.

21. *The Background and Trends in the Norwegian School System*, Norwegian State Council for Correspondence Education, quoted in E.G. WEDELL, *The Place of Correspondence in Permanent Education*, Strasbourg, Council of Europe, 1970.

22. WEDELL, op. cit.

CHAPTER 7

The Netherlands

The Netherlands became a nation by force of circumstances. It won independence and a strong sense of national identity in the sixteenth century wars of survival against Spain. Its unity was reinforced by struggles against England and, later, France and affirmed by its history as a world power in the seventeenth century and as a major colonial one until the Second World War. A naturally poor country, much of its land has only been won and preserved with difficulty from the sea in a continuing struggle up to modern times. It is the most densely populated country in Europe, with 13,856,000 people in an area of 41,200 square kilometres.[1]

Founded as a republic, it has been a monarchy since 1813. This did not prevent the well-to-do middle classes from establishing a firm monopoly of political as well as economic power, which only began to be challenged in the last years of the nineteenth century by groups which had up to then been disadvantaged — Catholics, Protestant fundamentalists, workers and women. Modern political parties began to be established to promote sectional interests. Industrialization came late to the Netherlands. It lacked natural resources and the wealth of the dominant middle class had been built on international trade and on the exploitation of its overseas empire, mainly situated in the East Indies. It was not until 1912 that investment in industry exceeded that in trade and the colonies. An organized labour movement, which pursued socialism in politics, did not develop until around the turn of the century.

The wars against Spain had begun as a fight to defend local privileges against centralism, but had become also a battle to defend Protestantism against the Counter-Reformation. In the area that is now the Netherlands Protestants of the Calvinist sort won, but there remained many Catholics in the country, albeit excluded from public life. Their legal disabilities were removed by the Constitution of 1815, but, although one-third of the population, they only organized themselves effectively to struggle for social and political equality in the second half of the nineteenth century.

Calvinism, in the shape of the Dutch Reformed Church, was the official religion of the Netherlands, but it had always been torn between dogmatists and latitudinarians. In the nineteenth century the official Church departed too far from its original austerity for some fundamentalists and a number of schisms occurred, some of which led to the formation of a second large Reformed Church, more strictly observant of pure Calvinist doctrine. Strict Calvinists were firmly opposed to the secularist tendencies of both governing middle-class liberals and the socialists.

As a result of these developments Dutch society was deeply divided at the beginning of the twentieth century into Catholic, strict Calvinist, and neutral or secular groups. The divisions ran vertically from the highest to the lowest classes and this no doubt helped to decrease the effect of class warfare. This separation of interests appeared to be irreconcilable and there developed what the Dutch call *verzuiling*, pillarization, by which each group was allowed separate and equal development in political, social and, particularly, educational life. Each set up its own cultural organizations, its own political party, its own trade union, its own newspapers and, later, its own broadcasting organization.[2]

But education was probably most responsible for confirming pillarization as a permanent principle of national organization. In 1901 schooling, for six years, was made compulsory and the system of lower, middle and higher schools was taken under government control. Catholics and Calvinists wanted their own schools, however, and their demands were met by the passage of a law, in 1920, which provided for the operation of private schools (mainly denominational in the event) with one hundred per cent State subsidy. The result is that only about a third of pupils are in State schools today, the rest in Catholic or Protestant ones.

The recognition of these divisions did not undermine the stability of society. The middle class was equally dominant in all three pillars and sufficiently self-confident, unlike its fellows in France, for example, to make concessions to the rising working class without feeling that it was thereby fundamentally threatened, So progress towards democratization was comparatively peaceful and universal suffrage for both sexes was introduced in 1920. The socially divisive effects of pillarization and the traditionally strong local particularism of the Dutch, with which it was associated, were mitigated by the adoption of a system of proportional representation, based on a national party list rather than local constituencies. No single party since has been able to win a parliamentary majority. This has meant that coalition governments have been the rule, so that the necessity of compromise in order to form a government has softened divisions at the level of national leaders.

In the early years of the twentieth century labour relations were bad. The socialist movement was committed in principle not only to abolish *laissez-faire*, socio-economic policies, but to overthrow bourgeois society completely. Between the two world wars, with political emancipation and legislation to improve conditions of work, including an eight-hour day in a forty-five hour week, the socialists became reconciled to working within the existing system of government and unions started to collaborate with employers.

From the 1840s the Netherlands pursued a neutralist foreign policy and thereby escaped, like Sweden, a number of external stresses, including participation in the First World War, which might have threatened its stability. In the Second World War it was less fortunate. It suffered enormous physical and social damage and, to add to its troubles, it lost its far eastern empire, now Indonesia, whose trade and produce had, before the war, provided one-seventh of the national income.

There had to be a complete re-orientation of economic and foreign policy. The last vestiges of *laissez-faire* economics and of neutralism were abandoned. To make up for war damage and lost colonies a policy of intensified industrialization was undertaken, in which international companies, like Shell,

Unilever and Philips, played a crucial role. The economy grew at a rate comparable with that of the German Federal Republic, guided by State planning. All the apparatus of a welfare state was created. The Netherlands became an active participant in NATO, the Council of Europe and the Common Market.

For all that it remained until 1960 a very conservative society. Parental authority was strong and it was only in the late 1960s that the age at which one could marry without parental consent was reduced from thirty to twenty-one. Women were discriminated against in a number of legal ways. People were, and still are, highly conscious of social distinctions, by rank, religion and education, for instance. In the 1960s, however, a feeling that society was out of step with the needs of the contemporary world brought about rapid changes. The Dutch Catholic Church, up to then one of the most reactionary, took a leading role in progressive religious thought, the Provo political movement highlighted a demand for more democracy and less institutionalization and Amsterdam became the centre of the permissive youth culture. Pillarization has continued, but divisions have lost some of their sharpness. Working-class children in the Netherlands had less chance of achieving higher education than their counterparts in many advanced countries. In 1962 the so-called Mammoth Law brought in a major reform of schooling, intended to provide greater equality of opportunity and to meet the educational requirements of the highly industrialized society that the Netherlands had become. It was a much needed advance, but has not realized all the hopes it raised, with the result that increasing attention has been directed to adult learning opportunities.

As in other countries the roots of adult education lie in the Enlightenment at the end of the eighteenth century. Then, the middle-class liberals founded the Society for the Promotion of Public Well-Being (NUT), which still exists today, working to improve citizenship and education according to Christian principles.[3] It was only around the end of the nineteenth century that adult education began to develop on modern lines, in response to the needs of industrialization and largely sponsored by the well-to-do bourgeoisie. Pillarization only became an important factor between the wars, because until then the labour movement was too concerned with political emancipation and industrial relations, and the denominational groups with the school question.

Two kinds of adult education emerged.[4] One, *vorming*, had as its purpose the development of the individual personality, character forming and the acquisition of social skills. Among organizations devoted to these aims were people's houses, modelled on British university settlements, people's universities, quite separate from Dutch universities, inspired by British university extension and serving a similar middle-class clientele, residential folk high schools, and an organization with a national network of branches, formed by the labour movement and now called the Institute of Popular Education (NIVON). On the other hand, in evening schools which offered adults the formal school curriculum, in general, technical and commercial education, the stress was on instruction, the transmission of knowledge, *ontwikkeling*, as it was in correspondence education and vocational training.

After the Second World War most of the pre-war organizations were revived and expanded to meet the increasing demand for education. Popular universities, people's houses, folk high schools (and other short-term residential centres), evening classes, correspondence courses and vocational education all flourished. There was less ideological emphasis in the provision of confessional and labour organizations and increasing co-operation between the pillars. For example secular and Catholic bodies combined to form the Association of Folk High Schools.

Except for help to folk high schools and other short-term residential centres, government subsidy to *vorming* remained limited. On the instructional side, however, evening courses were financed by the State on the same terms as day schools, organized as they were according to the same pattern. After the Mammoth Law there was a great increase in students in evening MAVOs (junior secondary schools), HAVOs (senior secondary schools) and VWOs (pre-university schools), from 6,400 in 1960 to 32,600 in 1975.[5] Adults found themselves under pressure to seek further education because of the rising level of child schooling.

One of the characteristics of the Netherlands' transformation from a socially conservative to an advanced country has been its sensitivity to new ideas discussed in the international organizations, of which since 1945 it has been an active member. This seems to have occurred in adult education. Discussions within the Council of Europe and the Organization for Economic Co-operation and Development have stimulated considerable interest in lifelong education and its principle of integrating all educational experience, in activities to reach the least educated, in adult education's potential as an instrument for the furtherance of equal opportunity, in democratic control and self-management of adult education and in multimedia learning systems.

There appeared to be scope for all these ideas in the Netherlands, where adult education, in spite of growth, still seemed underdeveloped and ill-adapted to modern needs. It had grown up there, as elsewhere, in an *ad hoc* fashion, lacked coherence, was unevenly spread throughout the country. The cohesion of adult education was not improved by the fact that three ministries had an interest in it. *Vorming* was the responsibility of the Ministry for Culture, Recreation and Social Work, formal evening classes and correspondence education came under the Ministry for Education and Science, while occupational training was the concern of the Ministry of Social Affairs. There existed hardly any co-ordination of the multifarious interests and no forum of communication between them. To perform just that function in 1965 the Netherlands Centre for Adult Education (NCVO) was established on the model of the National Institute of Adult Education in England. One of its first acts was to produce a report, *The Future and Function of Adult Education in Dutch Society*, which, although unofficial, has had a significant influence on State policy since. Out of it have come State initiated projects of innovation, intended to bring adult education up-to-date and capable of offering lifelong education.[6]

Perhaps the best known internationally and first established was the Open School Committee. Influenced by the British Open University and by the Bavarian *Telekolleg*, its function has been to explore and advise on possibilities for multimedia provision for adult education. It has gone on its own way, however, in deciding that its first priority was not to be higher education, but education at lower secondary level,

179

particularly for young adults, workers and women with limited schooling. A number of experimental projects have been organized in different parts of the country and the Committee's staff provides training, research and multi-media material. Its idea is not to concentrate courses in a national Open School, but to make it possible and attractive for a range of adult education organizations to use multi-media packages.[7] It will be easier in the Netherlands to do this, because of its unique structure of broadcasting. In both radio and television the State runs the technical transmission facilities, but the programming is done, not by public authority or commercial interests, but a number of non-profit making bodies, representing the main religious and political interests.[8]

Open School initiatives and the Government Committee on Paid Educational Leave are only a few of the innovatory projects introduced into Dutch adult education in the last decade.[9] Some have become a standard part of provision. The private offer of daytime school courses to mothers, for example, has led to establishment of official *Moeder-MAVOs* (Mother-MAVOs), daytime junior secondary schools for adults, state subsidized in the same way as the evening MAVOs. It is intended that local educational networks, another innovation, shall fundamentally change the shape of Dutch provision.

Local educational networks in the Netherlands

In 1975 a Committee for the Promotion of Local Educational Networks was established jointly by the Ministry of Culture, Recreation and Social Work, the Ministry of Education and Science and the Ministry of Social Affairs. It was 'to advise on local and regional structures for formal adult education, vocational training and group work in liberal adult education'.[10] Before the work of the committee had really got started, in 1976, there came into force the Regulation on State Contributions to Local Educational Work for Adults. They were both elements in a policy intended to devolve to local authorities responsibility for deciding adult education provision, on the ground that it would be more democratic and also better adapted to the needs of potential participants.

The Regulation created a radically new situation. Up to then local authorities had no responsibility for adult education, either in planning, provision, or finance. In so far as public subsidy was given, it was made directly by central government to the providing body, in the case of *vorming* by the Ministry of Culture, Recreation and Social Work to the private organizations active in the field. Under the 1976 Regulation each municipality, or, if desired, group of municipalities, was to draw up a four-year plan of adult education and a specific programme of activities for the coming year. It was intended that local people and organizations should be engaged in this exercise and it was to include not only *vorming*, but formal school-type education and vocational training. On receipt of its proposals each municipality would be allocated a subsidy, for the distribution of which it would be responsible. The State would no longer make direct grants to organizations.

By reflection and observation of practice the Committee for the Promotion of Local Educational Networks has evolved, in a series of reports, a coherent theory of educational networks, including reasons for creating them, functions to be undertaken and methods of planning and conducting them.[11] The basic starting point is the principle of life-long education, which lays down the necessity of integrating all parts of education both vertically and horizontally. The State should guarantee access to learning opportunities throughout life to all citizens. The structure of provision should be devised from the bottom up, beginning with an inventory of people's learning needs. These, when determined, should be met by both public and private bodies.

The Committee maintains that every locality must have adequate provision and notes that this is not at present the case. It should not be concentrated on one place or field of activity. It must be varied, linked to the life situation of people. The Committee would divide the field into parts related to work, politics, family, personal development, leisure and culture, although other divisions are considered possible. There must be recognition and guarantees for different levels and multifarious forms of outlook on life and society. There should, however, be a fixed core, unaffected by changes of national policy — basic education, up to the level of the six years compulsory school for children, but adapted to the needs and life experience of adults and emphasizing social skills, literacy, preparation for working life and initial vocational training. Special provision should be made for socially handicapped groups, foreign workers, pre-retirement groups, women, and for economically and educationally backward people.

It is necessary, the Committee believes, to make adult education a coherent whole. People may best learn, not only in the framework of a course or a school year, but in all kinds of activities — work-place ones, socio-cultural activity, social work, library work, health care, broadcasting, the arts. Any activity may be educational and the following criteria are laid down for its recognition as such: it is directed to learning goals; it is a process having a certain duration and continuity; it has a clear shape (work plan and skilled guidance); it is aimed at a defined group.

The Committee, following government intentions, lays primary responsibility with municipalities, who have to draw up appropriate planning procedures. They must also, says the Committee, give support, to providing bodies in the form of resources and opportunities to develop skills, and to participants through promotion and counselling services. At regional level authorities should co-ordinate local plans and organize centres for training adult educators. Central government must ensure security and equality before the law, the soundness and the quality of what is offered, and prevent inequality of provision. A National Institute of Adult Education should concern itself with curriculum development, the co-ordination and stimulation of skill development and research, and the State should have a legally established advisory council of independent experts. Social organizations not immediately engaged in adult education — trade unions, organizations for women, foreign workers, old people, people unfit for work — should be stimulated to take an interest on behalf of their members.

In 1978—9 an enquiry was carried out into the working of the local network planning process in 77 of the 296 municipalities engaged.[12] It showed that between municipalities there was a wide variation in expenditure per head of population, from 0.15 florins to 20.31 florins (average 2.99 florins). About half the municipalities revealed their State subsidy, which amounted to about fifty-three per cent of their adult education budget. Sixty-one per cent of authorities replying said they had expanded their provision in the first year of planning, 1978, by an average of 214 per cent over the previous year's figure. In 1979 the figures were fifty-eight per cent and 166 per cent. Table 9 shows various activities' shares of this expansion and the actual share of the budget allocated to each activity.

Table 9   Dutch municipalities' allocation to expansion of activities

	Share of expansion 1978 (%)	Share of budget 1978 (%)	Share of expansion 1979 (%)
A. Second chance (leading to diploma)	17	8	20
B. Social and political role education	48	28	43
C. Stimulation of creativity and art education	6	26	7
D. Non-certificate general education	28	32	27
E. Information: documentation; guidance	1	6	3
	100	100	100

Clearly nearly half the increase was in B, which includes the area of women's education, conscientization work in political and trade union branches, work with handicapped groups in institutions such as people's universities, Nivon and neighbourhood centres, literacy work, pre-retirement courses and courses for voluntary workers. The small growth of C clearly suggests that there was discrimination in planning. In accordance with the Committee's proposals, the main beneficiary groups were women, illiterates, unemployed and foreign workers. Forty-three municipalities said their new provision was aimed at disadvantaged groups.

It was left to municipalities to decide how they should go about drawing up their educational plan. A variety of choices was made, which could be broken down into four stages; initiation of the process (that is, one or all of the following — advertising that the process is taking place, evaluating previous year's provision, setting up of a planning group, fixing planning procedures); next, collection of data (one or all of — assessment of existing reasons for provision, assessment of educational needs, creation of a social map of the area); then consideration of choices (fixing of criteria and functions, establishing of concrete priorities); and finally the conclusion of the definite plan. In seventy per cent of cases the planning was undertaken by a planning group, composed normally of experts and representatives of the municipality and of educational organizations. There was usually close contact with officials. The Burgomaster and aldermen, who in the Netherlands form the municipal executive, were closely involved, but the town council itself less so. Educational institutions played a large part and nearly half the municipalities made use of outside experts. Individual citizens and community groups played only a modest part. They were rarely encouraged to and when, for example, there were public hearings on educational planning, attendances were not large.

When municipalities were asked for their impression of the Government's decentralization policy hardly any said it had made things worse. Sixty per cent said it had achieved a broader provision, adapted to the local population, seventy-six per cent that there had been more public political discussion of educational work. Only thirty-five per cent, however, said that the existing work was better done, forty-five per cent that more people, especially the disadvantaged, made use of provision, thirty-nine per cent that it was a more systematic and co-ordinated provision and forty-five per cent that the population had more opportunity to influence the content and form of educational work. On each of the points the rest of the respondents believed there had been no change.

With regard to the planning process itself, on the positive side it was said that there was more involvement, co-operation, insight and discussion by institutions, council, population, mayor, aldermen and officials, more structure and clarity of provision, an improvement of content. The planning group, the support provided and more systematic thinking were mentioned by a few with approval, but only two per cent thought the State subsidy a positive point. There was, in fact, more mention of negative factors. They included a lack of time, money and manpower for the exercises, inexpertness and ignorance of planning on the part of the working groups, institutions, officials and population. Institutions, mayor and corporation and the people were said to fail in co-operation and the Ministry of Culture, Recreation and Social Work was criticized for unclear or bad policy and for exerting too much control.

To the outside observer there seems to have been some justification for complaint. In the first place, although a comprehensive plan for adult education was to be prepared, the subsidy from the Ministry of Culture, Recreation and Social Work could only be used for a limited number of activities in the field of *vorming*. Little time was allowed to draw up plans, despite the fact that municipalities had no previous experience and lacked resources. Then Government policy changed and no programme was required for 1979. Instead a plan embracing all socio-cultural activities, not only adult education, is to be presented by 1981. The decentralization policy was introduced at a bad time, when the national economy had been in difficulties, so that municipalities did not receive subsidies adequate to fulfil the programmes they had prepared, or of a size they had expected. After the first year therefore, there was a certain amount of cynicism.

The criticisms are essentially about the mechanics, however, not the principles, of educational networks. They appear at the moment to offer some promise that they will justify themselves. It is, though, far too early to evaluate them. Their interest for this study lies mainly in the example they present of innovation, seeking systematically to apply certain concepts widely discussed and approved in Western Europe, but closely constrained by the historical, social and political contexts in which they are to be applied.

In one way or another most of the elements of Dutch local networks may be found in other countries' practice. Other countries, the United Kingdom and the Scandinavian states for example, have decentralized responsibility for adult education on to local authorities. They, however, have a long tradition of involvement of municipalities in educational administration. The Netherlands, a centralized government since Napoleonic times, has not. To make municipalities responsible for adult education planning has been, therefore, a more drastic step than it would have been in the countries mentioned.

The nearest parallel to what has happened in the Netherlands is probably the decision of the French government to make local authorities responsible for socio-cultural provision. It was a new role for French communes, but they were not called upon to concern themselves with vocational training or school-type courses, or to devise a plan. On the other hand this last was required by the Education Act (England and Wales) 1944, but, mainly for economic reasons, the procedure was soon abandoned. The outstanding feature of the Dutch reform has not been devolution to local authorities in itself, but the efforts they have made, and were intended to make, to bring a wide range of local interests into the formal planning process. No doubt it is in part to be explained by their inexperience and consequent need for advice, but in some part it was a genuine effort to democratize the process beyond the local bureaucracy. Where the local adult education bureaucracy has been strong there have been obstacles. Dutch municipalities, unconstrained by precedent, may feel freer in their response to their new duty.

Compared with other states the Netherlands local network procedures have been only a tentative approach to co-ordination of adult education. But those countries like Norway, which have made significant progress in the last decade, have built on a structured provision of long standing, existing in a homogeneous society. Local networks are in effect the Netherlands' first attempt at national structure. The State, partly because of a long attachment to *laissez-faire* principles and mainly because of the limitations imposed by pillarization, did not until recently interfere in adult education policy. Collaboration between private organizations, which, as we have seen in Sweden, has caused problems in other countries, has been especially hard in the Netherlands because of pillarization. In more recent years, when central government has begun to take an interest, the fact that different sectors of adult education became the province of three different ministries and that these distinctions were compounded by conceptual differences, so that the Ministry of Culture, Recreation and Social Work was engaged in *vorming* and the Ministry of Education and Science in *ontwikkeling*, cannot have made co-ordination any easier.

The only means of coercion the Dutch Government has decided to use to get local educational networks established has been the power to grant or withhold financial assistance. This is, in fact, standard practice in most western countries, employed to get certain areas of study into programmes and to encourage outreach efforts to attract and provide for the needs of disadvantaged groups, as it is in the case of educational networks.

The real interest does not lie, therefore, in the elements of the Dutch innovation, but in the total package. In one fairly simple administrative act the Government appears to be trying to expand, integrate, decentralize and democratize adult education and shift the emphasis both in subject matter and target population. On its own the change may appear to be incredibly radical, given the history of adult education in the Netherlands. If one considers the economic transformation since the war and, particularly, the social one which took place in the 'sixties, together with the avid eclecticism which adult education has subsequently displayed in adopting new ideas from abroad to render it capable of fulfilling the national role to which it is now called, then the change is not so surprising. It is in keeping with other far-reaching, sudden alterations on which conservative societies have embarked throughout history, when pressure of external change could no longer be resisted. In a land so marked as the Netherlands by religious thought it may not be inappropriate to speak of a conversion. In such a situation, in a field untrammelled by previous progressive attempts, the erstwhile conservative not only needs, but is often able, to make a longer leap forward than those who have been trying to advance for years.

References

1. *Basic Statistics of the Community*, Brussels, Statistical Office of the European Communities, 1979.

2. FRANK E. HUGGETT, *The Modern Netherlands*, London, Pall Mall Press, 1971.

3. C. STAPEL, *Dutch Adult Education on its way to an 'Open School' System*, Bergen, January, 1976, duplicated.

4. ibid., p.31: W.A. HOUTKOOP, *Enige Ontwikkelingslijnen in de Nederlandse Volwasseneducatie sinds 1900*, doctoral dissertation, Amsterdam, January 1977, duplicated.

5. HOUTKOOP, op. cit.

6. D. GOEZINNE, 'Policy Making in Dutch Adult Education', *The Development of Local Educational Networks*, Amersfoort, European Bureau of Adult Education, 1978.

7. ibid.

8. HUGGETT, op. cit.

9. *Experiments in Dutch Adult Education*, Amersfoort European Bureau of Adult Education, and the Netherlands Centre for Adult Education, 1977.

10. D. GOEZINNE, op. cit.

11. Commissie Bevordering Plaatselijke Educatieve Netwerken, *Vijfde Advies, Educatieve Netwerken in Opbouw*, Amersfoort, May, 1979.

12. A. VAN DIEMAN and R. KRAAN, *Evaluatie van Educatieve Planning, Verkorte Verslag*, Amersfoort, Studiecentrum NCVO, 1979.

CHAPTER 8

Denmark

Geographically Denmark is very different from its neighbours, Norway and Sweden. Its land area is small, only thirteen per cent of that of Norway and ten per cent of that of Sweden, but, with a population of 5,088,000, it is more densely populated than either.[1] It is a flat, intensively cultivated country.

Like its neighbours in the ways that the foundations of its contemporary society and adult education were laid in the nineteenth century, it was unlike them in the vicissitudes which it suffered during that period.[2] It lost Norway in 1814, as a result of having been on the losing side in the Napoleonic Wars. Then for two-thirds of the century its foreign policy was obsessed by the struggle to keep the duchies of Schleswig and Holstein, to the south of the country. After two bloody wars against Prussia it was forced to give them up in 1864. This was a staggering blow to national self-confidence, which had taken some time to recover after 1815. It was a salutary lesson on the status of a small country in power politics and led to the adoption of a policy of neutrality, successfully followed in the First World War and attempted with less success in the Second. Its experiences in that conflict have led Denmark to seek safety during the post-war years in the NATO alliance.

Denmark's progress to parliamentary democracy was neither rapid nor smooth. Until 1849 it was an absolute monarchy, albeit benevolent. Under the pressure of liberal ideas and the demands of its rising farmer class for agrarian reform, a constitution, including a parliament of two chambers, of which the lower was to be elected by universal male suffrage (over the age of thirty), was granted by the King, who was still to nominate his own ministers. As a result of the loss of Schleswig-Holstein, for which Liberals were blamed, there was an anti-democratic reaction and ministers ruled for a number of years without the support of the lower house. Indeed it was not until 1901 that the principle of rule by the party commanding a majority in the lower house was reluctantly accepted by the King. In 1915 constitutional change fixed the minimum voting age at twenty-five years, but extended the suffrage to women and introduced proportional representation. In 1953 the upper chamber of Parliament was abolished, thus removing a conservative force, and the age of suffrage was lowered to twenty-three. From the 1964 election it has been twenty-one.

The rise of the Danish economy from bankruptcy in 1815 was principally due to the development of its agriculture. The basis of this growth was a class of freehold farmers which emerged at the end of the eighteenth century. They began the modernization of agriculture in the first half of the nineteenth century and in the second half, showing shrewdness and enterprise under the pressure of a European crisis, combined into producer co-operatives to establish the pattern of intensive cultivation of dairy and pork products for export that has been the hallmark of Danish farming ever since. The growth of agricultural productivity was accompanied from the mid-nineteenth century by industrialization, as in other countries. At first in the hands of small firms, industry later developed a number of large combines producing mainly for the home market and it was not until after the Second World War that it began to rival agriculture as an export earner.

For the first half century of parliamentary government in Denmark the struggle for power was mainly between the farming interests on the left and the conservative owners of large estates, with liberal intellectuals mainly favouring the former. Farmers struggled, successfully in the long term, to have leasehold tenure of land completely replaced by freehold, and to have its ownership transferred from large landlords into the hands of those who tilled it. Urbanization, which raised the town population from twenty-five per cent of the total population to forty per cent in 1910, was a concomitant of industrialization and gave rise to a new force, the urban working class. There was the usual conflict between the new trade unions and employers marked, very early compared with other countries, by an agreement, in 1899, between the two sides to regulate the conduct of industrial disputes. Despite the stresses to which it was subjected by the recessions between the two world wars, it remained in force until 1960. In politics a Social Democratic Party was founded in 1876 and was already a significant force before the First World War, forming with the Conservative People's Party, the Left (a moderate liberal party) and the Radical Left (more accurately radical liberals), the parties which have dominated Danish politics ever since. From 1945 the Social Democrats have been in power most of the time, but their authority has been less stable than that of their counterparts in Sweden, as they have either ruled as a minority government or in coalition with other parties. They have never formed a majority on their own.

There has not been State direction of the economy and society to the same extent as in Norway or Sweden, perhaps because of the continuing influence of farming interests, whose contribution to national wealth remains crucial, although only nine per cent of the labour force now works on the land, compared with 30.4% in industry and sixty per cent in services. Denmark has, however, continued progress towards a welfare state, begun tentatively at the end of the nineteenth century and developed between the wars to the Social Reform of 1933, which made help to those in need a right, not an act of charity, and offered them a reasonable standard of living, not bare subsistence. Since 1945 it has expanded in keeping with increased expectations of citizens.

Denmark, like its neighbours, has a State Church, the Lutheran, of which the vast majority of Danes are nominal members, in that they do not opt out of paying church taxes. The actual level of regular attendance has been calculated at between two and seven per cent. In the eighteenth century the Church had been much affected by the austere doctrines of pietism and then by the rationalist ideas of the Enlightenment. It became dessicated, its beliefs barely more than a code of ethics. At the beginning of the nineteenth century there came, however, a religious revival, in part within the official Church — Grundtvig with his Romantic christianity remained within it — but mainly in nonconformist sects imported, like the Baptists and Methodists, from abroad. This renaissance of belief had a significant effect on the democratization of the country and, as will be seen, was crucial to the growth of adult education.

Pietism, for all its austerity, encouraged education, but the first great school law, which laid down compulsory education for all from the age of seven until confirmation, at the age of fourteen, had to wait until 1814. It took time to implement, but by the middle of the century nearly all Danes were literate. Until 1903 there was a primary school system and a secondary one and little chance of workers' or farmers' children rising from the former to the latter, which opened up entry to higher education. In that year a middle school was introduced between the primary and secondary, which children entered at twelve and from which they could move at fourteen into the secondary. It eased the transition into higher education. This system remained essentially unchanged until 1958, when middle schools were abolished and all children were to pass their seven years of compulsory education in comprehensive schools. For those who wished to stay on there were two-year or three-year post-compulsory options, or the full secondary course ending in the Student Examination, the entry ticket to university. In 1972 the period of compulsory education was increased to nine years.

Adult education in Denmark goes back to the eighteenth century and provision for it is found in the 1814 Education Act. Essentially, though, the foundations of the system as it is today were laid in the nineteenth century. To a large extent it was inspired, as in other countries, by religious convictions, the growth of the labouring classes to political and social influence, and the needs of an economy in the process of industrialization. The Danish development was unlike that of other states, however, in the importance of the initial impetus given to adult education by the aspirations of the freehold farmers from the first half of the century and the continuing influence of principles and traditions evolved in that context.

The roots of adult education today lie in the popular

movements of a century ago. From Bishop Grundtvig even earlier comes adult education's long dominant concern for illumination of the spirit and stimulation of the mind, rather than the acquisition of cognitive knowledge and skills. The former aspect is still strong, but the balance between the two is now more even. Some would say it has gone too far towards the second aspect. Among the most notable of voluntary organizations which still play a major role are the Workers' Educational Association (AOF), the largest, linked with the trade unions and the Social Democratic Party; the Popular Education Association (FOF), related to the Conservative Party; the Liberal Educational Association (LOF), linked to the Liberal Party; the Farmers' Educational Association (LOK); and the Churches' Association for Adult Education (KOK).

Since the Second World War adult education has assumed an increasing importance in response to the same circumstances experienced in other lands — higher living standards and expectations; increased productivity and restructuring of industry; changing consumer patterns; obsolescence of skills; increased leisure; the need to break down barriers raised by growing specialization; and, not least, the generation gap exacerbated by the fact that in 1972 three-quarters of the workforce had only seven years schooling, whereas today's young people get nine.[3] Denmark has not gone, however, as far as Norway in comprehensive planning of adult education, nor used it so enthusiastically as Sweden as an instrument of social engineering.

It still makes a distinction between non-vocational and vocational adult education. The major legislation in the field, the Leisure-time Education Act 1968, covers the former. Under the Ministry of Education county and local authorities have both policy and providing responsibility. Voluntary bodies are to offer non-vocational, non-qualifying courses, but if they fail to do so, and only if, then the municipality must. Thus the position of private initiative is preserved. Courses leading to certificates of general education and vocationally-oriented qualifications are available in a variety of public schools and colleges.[4]

The fact that a number of different government departments have responsibility for different parts of adult education shows that it has grown up and still exists without much central direction. Labour Market Training, under the 1960 Act on the Training of Semi-skilled and Other Workers, comes under the Ministry of Labour, with some contribution from the Ministries of Commerce and Education. Courses are provided to raise semi-skilled workers to skilled status, to retrain skilled workers and to reconvert to new ones those whose skills have become obsolete. It is not possible to say accurately what proportion of Danish adults participate annually in education but figures for 1972—3 enable one to estimate the figure at about twenty per cent.[5]

Danish folk high schools

There is one manifestation of popular education in Denmark, whose fame has spread throughout the world; the folk high school. It has been imitated throughout Scandinavia, in Poland, Germany and Holland, in Africa, Asia and North America. It inspired long-term residential colleges for adults in the United Kingdom. Its effect on Danish life is incalculable. Yet some people doubt whether the long courses, on which the high schools were founded, are adult education at all. In Norway they are included in youth education, situated between secondary and further and higher education, and by the terms of State grant in Denmark they are aimed at youngsters between the ages of seventeen and twenty-one. As Danes are quick to point out, in proportion to the total number of participants in adult education high school enrolments are small, between one and two per cent in long courses and less than five per cent if one includes the many short courses they offer.[6]

The Danish folk high school owed its creation in the form we know to the inspiration of one man. It succeeded because it was uniquely suited to the social, cultural and political circumstances of its time. Fed by a prevailing European trend there was a strong movement to restore Danish self-confidence after 1815 by encouraging nationalist ideas. It sought strength in a romantic identification with Norse myths and legends. Encouraged by events abroad a liberal political movement aimed at replacing absolutism by democracy and

194

there already existed in Denmark a freehold farmer class, growing in economic and social importance, which was well placed to enjoy power and responsibility under such reforms. It was also a strongly religious class, ready to appreciate the value of education.

Nikolaj Severin Frederik Grundtvig was an author, clergyman and popular educator, who combined within himself nationalism, inspired by the Nordic past, a romantic belief in the self-realization of the individual spirit and a somewhat unorthodox Christianity. He put the development of the human being, to which for him a consciousness of one's Danishness was essential, before that of a Christian. He was aware of the revolutionary dangers of the democratic movement and believed they could be averted by educating people into social and political rights and responsibilities. He condemned the dead rote learning of the traditional secondary schools, was much impressed by the college system he had seen in Cambridge, and wanted to create residential high schools in which teaching would not depend on textbooks but on the oral communication of ideas, through conversation and discussion rather than lecture. Such teaching was to illuminate before it informed.[7]

Grundtvig, however, founded no high schools. Other hands set up the first, in 1844, and it was Christen Kold who, adding elements of his own, laid down in 1851 the pattern of the high schools and whose use of the 'living word' established its position in them as the chosen means of teaching. They were private institutions, their character marked by the personality of the principal. They were founded to meet the needs of the farming community, although they were open to all. They brought together in residence the late teenage sons and daughters of the farm for a period of months in the winter, when their work on the land was least needed. Students lived, ate, worked and spent their leisure with the teachers and their families, learning as much by this continual social intercourse as by formal lessons. Their triple purpose was: 'Firstly to make students love and understand their national history, culture and art; Secondly to open their eyes to the wealth of spiritual life; Thirdly to help render the ordinary man fit for civic and democratic responsibility'.[8] There were no examinations and no certificates were awarded.

The folk high schools' great period followed the defeat of 1864. New ones were founded all over Denmark and by 1876--7 there were nearly 4,000 high school students. By 1894—5 there were 5,100 students in sixty-five high schools, a figure which had risen to 8,000 in fifty-seven schools in 1919—20. Seventy-five per cent of these young people were children of freehold farmers.[9] The schools contributed greatly to the recovery of national morale after the loss of Schleswig-Holstein. Identified as they were with farming interests high school men disapproved of the anti-democratic governments which ruled in the 1870s and 1880s, and some of the most outspoken lost for their schools the State subsidy which had been granted from the very early years. By opening the mental and spiritual horizons of farmers, folk high schools, it is widely held, made possible the producer co-operatives to which Denmark owed so much of its prosperity.

Not that they were vocational schools, although they may have inspired the growth of agricultural colleges. There was no fixed curriculum, each principal followed his own ideas, but the core of teaching was in most cases Danish history and literature, although there were schools, more wedded to the material and social progress of the farmer class, which emphasized more utilitarian studies. The choice of curriculum did not represent a refuge from the present, but on the contrary, was meant to help in the understanding of it.

In the years between the world wars Danish folk high schools extended their eyes across the world, seeing the future well-being of mankind in international co-operation, along the lines indicated by the League of Nations. Those ideas were taken up again after 1945 and help has been given to developing countries in particular, both in the form of places in Danish folk high schools and in aid in the establishment of high schools in their own countries. Because the economic crises of the 'twenties and 'thirties hit agriculture hard and because there was a continuing move of population from the country to the town, the folk high schools seemed to have passed their peak in Denmark. There was a further decline after the Second World War. From the early 1950s, however, and in spite of a social, economic and educational system very different from the one in which they were born and first flourished, the folk high schools have grown again in number of institutions and of students.

Table 10   Danish folk high schools: Students in long courses[10]

Year	Number of FHS	Number of students	Number of females	Number of males	Average age
1950—1	55	5,866	3,674	2,192	
1960—1	62	7,309	4,698	2,611	67—8% under 20 years
1965—6	69	8,732	5,869	2,863	
1970—1	80	9,030	5,700	3,330	
1975—6	82	9,764	5,406	4,358	20.9
1976—7	83	9,483	5,367	4,116	24.2
1977—8	84	9,846	5,740	4,106	24.2

The statistics in Table 10 show an increase since 1951 of fifty-three per cent in the number of high schools and sixty-eight per cent in the number of students. For most of the period there was a clear preponderance of female students (about two-thirds of the total), but in the 1970s the balance of the sexes became much more even. At the same time as this has happened the average age has gone up considerably. No doubt a number of factors contributed to this change, but one may note that, up to about 1970, long courses remained, as they had since the nineteenth century, mostly of four to six months duration. Nowadays they show much greater variations in length, from one to ten months, and older men in employment may have found it easier to take time off work to attend the shorter courses. On the other hand rising unemployment in the 1970s may have caused older people to choose a folk high school as an alternative to idleness.

Whatever the intending student's reason there is a wide choice. The foreigner gets the impression that the average folk high school is a private residential institution, with a capacity for between seventy and one hundred students, aged about nineteen or twenty. Typical subjects of study are Danish, arithmetic or mathematics, a foreign language (most commonly English or German), social sciences

197

(particularly psychology, sociology and world affairs), and, increasingly, natural sciences. Arts and crafts and practical skills are widely offered, often as optional activities. Teaching is informal, in study circles, working groups and by lectures. They are not, however, vocational schools, no examinations are set and no certificates are awarded.

In reality it is doubtful whether any single folk high school conforms entirely to this picture. There are exceptions to every characteristic in the stereotype. Borups High School, in Copenhagen, is not even residential. Capacity ranges from 32 (Tølløse) to 250 students (Askov). There are youth high schools, aimed at sixteen to nineteen year olds, others which fix their minimum age limit at nineteen or twenty, yet others which aim at older adults. There may be no vocational schools, but some train leaders and gymnastic coaches for voluntary youth work and others specialize — in music, the arts, home economics, journalism — thus providing at least pre-professional study. There are workers' folk high schools, linked to the labour movement, and concentrating on trade union and industrial relations studies. There are also Home Mission Schools, with a strict evangelical Christian inspiration.[11] The Skaergarden Family High School takes on its courses parents and their children, for whom there is also a school. They are all, however, private institutions, they do not set examinations. Because having attended a folk high school confers status when applying for a job or for entry to vocational training, certificates of attendance are given, if requested.

Most high schools also offer short courses of one to three weeks. Indeed there are some, for example the Jutland Pensioners' FHS, which advertise only short courses for elderly people. In the last decade the number of short courses offered throughout folk high schools has risen from 109 to 330 and the number of participants in them from 2,862 in 1969-70 to an estimated 25,000 in 1977-8.[12]

All recognized folk high schools receive state grants, under the Folk High School Act of 1942, which now cover up to eighty-five per cent of running costs. Cheap government loans under this law have made possible the modern, comfortable and well-equipped buildings that currently exist. Despite this financial dependence, folk high schools remain free — that is, the State does not interfere in any way with the activities of the school, except that the appointment of principal must have State approval. This freedom was won in the 1850s.

Students may also receive grants from the State, and the majority do. To receive a grant a student must be at least seventeen and a half years old, and from then until his or her twenty-first birthday the amount of grant is calculated according to parents' income. From the age of twenty-one the grant is related to the student's own income, plus that of his or her spouse. In the year 1979—80 the maximum grant for a twenty-week course (for an income of 36,590 kroner) was 4,320 kroner. For an income of over 116,990 kroner no grant is made. All students of any age, attending courses of at least two weeks in length, are eligible for grant under the above conditions.

Folk high schools were designed originally in curriculum and timing of their courses, to meet the needs of the children of farmers. In the period 1894—1919 these still made up between seventy and seventy-five per cent of all students while workers' children accounted for only three per cent.[13] In 1945—6 freeholders' children made up sixty-one per cent of the student body. The figure has dropped significantly since then, thirty-eight per cent in 1962—3, and even further in the 1970s.[14]

One reason lies in the declining proportion of the population engaged in agriculture. Another lies in the changing nature of the folk high school, as it seeks to find itself a place in the contemporary education system. It began by offering further education to a section of the population which had hitherto been limited to the village primary school. It then offered a continuation to the middle school (often used as a preparation for agricultural college) to youngsters who had no chance of secondary and hence higher education. Since the Second World War, with, on the one hand, the prolongation of compulsory schooling and also the common extension of the period of initial education to twelve years, and, on the other, wider access to further or higher education, leading to general or vocational qualifications, the traditional function of the folk high schools has become less and less necessary, the competition they have had to meet more and more severe. In the struggle to survive youth high schools were founded in the 1960s, and since then the pensioner high schools and the Family High School. Variation in length of courses, the notable growth in short courses and the increasing effort made to attract adults of all ages are actions in the same battle. So far folk high schools are holding their own, but in the process there is some indication that it is becoming increasingly hard to speak of them as institutions having a core of characteristics in common.

In Denmark the impact of the folk high schools has been so great in stimulating the minds and self-confidence of succeeding generations that it is almost inconceivable that they should disappear. The number of distinguished people in all walks of life who were folk high school men, teachers or students, is legion. In 1964 twenty-five per cent of members of Parliament had either studied or taught in a folk high school. Every party had at least one.[15]

Without being so deeply rooted in national life, folk high schools are to be found in large numbers in Norway, Sweden and Finland.[16] They have their own characteristics. For example, in all three countries they are more closely and clearly integrated into the education system at secondary level than they are in Denmark, where their position is outside the formal continuum. In Norway and Finland the normal minimum age for entry is sixteen. In the former their operation has been closely regulated by law since 1949. In the latter they are of two kinds, folk high schools, and folk academies for slightly older young people. Sweden has about 110 folk high schools and from their beginning, in 1868, in keeping with national inclination, teaching in them has stressed cognitive learning, made much use of textbooks, and shied away from the 'living word' of Grundtvigian romanticism.

Danish inspiration spread and adapted over the border into Germany, as has already been seen, and also had some success in Poland and the Netherlands. Long-term residential colleges for adults in the United Kingdom also owe their foundation to the Danish example, but they are far from the folk high school pattern. In fact, outside Northern Europe and areas of the mid-west of America, the folk high school has been much imitated, but not really successfully. It was well adapted to a certain type of farming people, following a certain working year, at a particular stage of social and educational development. Only in Denmark and other Northern European countries do these conditions appear to have been met. That they have continued to flourish in these lands owes more, one would suggest, to the power of the tradition they have created for themselves, than to either the survival of the original conditions or their suitability to the present day. Their reason for existence has been in question in all the states where they are found. Not only in Denmark, but in other countries, including the Federal German Republic, as we have seen, they are seeking a new public, switching to short courses, even offering courses leading to certificates of general or vocational education. These indeed, may be the ways ahead for residential adult education in Western Europe. Institutions going this way may call themselves folk high schools, but they will retain only the name.

References

1. *Basic Statistics of the Community, 1979*, Brussels, Statistical Office of the European Communities.
2. For more detailed accounts of Danish history see W. GLYN JONES, *Denmark*, London, Benn, 1970: STEWART OAKLEY, *The Story of Denmark*, London, Faber and Faber, 1972.
3. *Adult Education in the Nordic Countries*, Stockholm, Nordic Council.
4. ibid.
5. ibid.
6. Based on information supplied in a private communication by Arne Andresein, High School Secretariat, Copenhagen.
7. THOMAS RØRDAM, 'The Danish Folk High Schools,' Copenhagen, Det Danske Selskab, 1965.
8. PER HIMMELSTRUP, 'The Danish folk high school', paper presented to the annual conference of the Universities' Council for Adult Education, University of Kent, Canterbury, 1978.
9. RØRDAM, op. cit.
10. Arne Andresein, cit.
11. *Danmarks Folke Højskoler 1979—80*, Copenhagen, High Schools Secretariat.

12. Arne Andresein, cit.
13. RØRDAM, op. cit.
14. ibid.
15. ibid.
16. *Adult Education in the Nordic Countries*, op. cit.

CHAPTER 9

Italy

In Italy, as in France, one is outside the tradition of adult education represented by the United Kingdom, Sweden and the Federal German Republic. One is in a land where there does not exist a systematic, nationwide provision of opportunities for adult study, a country where the term 'popular education' has been in current post-war usage, as in France and Belgium, and which is a Catholic country, as they are. It has other similarities to France, but also characteristics which make it unique among members of the European Community.

After the Napoleonic Wars Italy became once again, like Germany, a cluster of sovereign states, as it had been before the French Revolution. It had, however, been marked by the liberal and nationalistic ideas the French invasion had brought with it. There was a series of uprisings in different states over the years, until the north-western state of Piedmont succeeded from 1859 to 1870, with the initial assistance of Napoleon III, in imposing on the rest of the peninsula its own monarch as the King of a united Italy. Somewhat shakily the country was ruled as a parliamentary democracy until the First World War. The result of the war, in which Italy's territorial ambitions had not been fully satisfied and in which it had sustained heavy losses in men and material, was to exacerbate its social and government instability to such an extent that in 1922 Mussolini was able by force to overturn the parliamentary system and replace it by an authoritarian Fascist regime, still nominally under the Monarch. The Second World War destroyed that regime in turn and since 1946 Italy has been a parliamentary republic.

Except during the period of Fascism, Italy has had difficulty since its unification in achieving a government which combined stability with effectiveness. It has been an even more polarized society than that of France. A large part of that polarization derives from geography and history. The North of the peninsula had been a European centre of trade and investment in the Middle Ages and, after a period of decline, has since the nineteenth century again shown enterprise and been responsive to the social, economic and political developments of Western Europe. The South, for long a battlefield and economically neglected for centuries, not only was poverty stricken and almost feudal in its social organization, but has remained at all levels of society resistant to change.

After unification all Italy was ruled as though it was Piedmont. That was contrary to the traditions of the South and, as the administration was highly centralized, it was insensitive to its needs. Nor was it efficient enough for the task. The parliamentary form of government, adopted by the Kingdom of Italy, did not work well. There are a number of possible reasons: lack of basic national political consensus, the intractability of the country's social problems, the inexperience of responsible political participation, endemic corruption, among others.

Repeatedly violent extremes of left and right have attracted active support. The Fascist regime followed the triumph of one side and the current spate of urban terrorism is an indication that extremism still threatens the State. Such manifestations are probably only symptoms of deeper and enduring conflicts. The divisions between capital and organized labour have always been profound, more deeply marked by ideology and the class struggle, even today, than in any other country of the European Community. The strong current of nationalism, which brought about unification, led Italy into costly colonial adventures, inspired by recollections of Imperial Rome, and contributed to both the rise and fall of Fascism. There are signs that it still lives, if only in the ideas of the far right.

There remains also the Catholic Church. The Popes, autocratic temporal as well as spiritual rulers until the forcible occupation of Rome in 1870, have exerted and continue to exert an influence on Italian life unequalled in any other of the countries discussed in this book. The Church has been on the whole a conservative influence, however conservatism has been measured at any given time, and radical forces have been anti-clerical to a degree not found elsewhere. Since the war the dominant political party, the Christian (Catholic) Democrats, who have participated in every government since 1946, have been largely prisoners of their Catholicism and their dependence on the Catholic vote, just as anti-clericalism has bound the left. Religious influence has been as strong as that of the capitalist/socialist division in preventing moderates of left and right working together, for fear they split their parties.

At the beginning of the twentieth century the poverty of Italy was such that the average income per inhabitant was only a third of that of the United Kingdom or France. Of the active population forty-seven per cent were engaged in agriculture. To offset the developing industrialization of the North was the dead weight of the stagnating South, to whose problems were added those of over-population. To these last, migration was the only answer. Thousands sought new homes abroad, thousands moved from the country to Italian towns, principally in the industrial North. This demographic problem has remained, even since the Second World War. In spite of active government encouragement to emigration the population of the country has risen from about 25,000,000 in 1871 to 56,500,000 in 1977.[1]

Many attempts have been made in the last century to overcome the economic, social and health difficulties of the South. In every case progress has been disappointing. The statistics of advance in agriculture, industrial development, health and living conditions since 1945 are impressive until one compares the condition of the South with the North. For Italy, like France and Federal Germany, has had its own economic miracle. The gross domestic product has risen from 7,800 milliard lira in 1951 to 97,600 milliard lira in 1974.[2] It is, indeed, a curious phenomenon that, as fears that Italy is becoming completely ungovernable increase, its economic advance continues at a high rate. But in that progress the share of gdp per head in the South is only about half that in the North.

The country's demographic, social, economic and political problems have marked its education system and, in return, the latter's imperfections have had their effect on them. The battle between clericals and anti-clericals has found its expression in the continuing controversy between those who press for freedom of education, which would allow the Church to run its own schools, and those who maintain that it should be a secular provision of the State. All-embracing legislation has not been implemented, or has tended to perpetuate social divisions. The Casati Law of 1859 made primary education free and compulsory, reformed higher and secondary education and created technical education. A Piedmontese law imposed on the whole of Italy, it made communes responsible for setting up free primary schools, and in those areas where the need was greatest, in the South, they frequently had neither the will nor the money to do so. It was not until 1911 that an attempt to remedy this situation, which left the country with 17,000,000 illiterates at the end of the nineteenth century, was made. The State itself took over the supervision of the primary school.[3]

The next important measures, the Gentile Reforms of 1923–9, may have been more effective in their application, but they did little to open educational opportunity beyond the primary level, or to modernize the curriculum. Nevertheless they survived in essence over thirty years, for, after 1945, educational reform was blocked by the recurring controversy over Church schools, until the current school system was introduced in 1963. It provides for eight years of comprehensive compulsory schooling, the last three in the middle school or lower secondary level, leading in principle to the lower secondary certificate, considered to be the minimum acceptable leaving qualification. Beyond this are upper secondary institutions of various kinds, leading to further and higher education.

Partly because of insufficient resources and facilities, but mainly because of the practice of making pupils repeat a year if their performance is considered inadequate, over ten per cent of young people leave at the end of compulsory schooling without a leaving certificate. Also, in spite of some modernization (competence in Latin and classical Italian is no longer required of all candidates for university entrance) the curriculum is still restricted and basically foreign to youngsters with working-class backgrounds.[4]

At the end of the Second World War, in spite of compulsory schooling there was still much illiteracy, especially in the South. The Government initiated a major campaign to eradicate it, setting up Popular Schools, '. . . to combat illiteracy, complete elementary education and guide to lower secondary or professional education'. They offered daytime and evening courses to both adults and young people. In the decade 1947—57 of 2,679,543 participants, 1,950,688 received a certificate of completion of course.[5] Alongside the State effort a National Union for the Struggle Against Illiteracy was created, a private initiative with State subsidy, whose Centres of Popular Culture, of which there were ninety by the middle 1960s, became models of popular education, linking it with lifelong education. In addition to adult basic education they offered workshops and cultural, recreational and social activities.

The literacy campaign has been the State's most persistent and successful initiative in adult education. The combined efforts of school and the campaign have reduced the number of illiterates in the population to 5.1% (1974). Other efforts, a programme of courses completing the compulsory school curriculum, the creation of Centres for Permanent Education, and provision of vocational training programmes, have achieved much less. Under-financed to begin with (only 0.53% of the Ministry of Education budget was devoted to adult education in 1974), when they failed to reach the hoped for goals, support was reduced.[6]

Over the years the burden of adult education in Italy has been borne by private, non-profit making organizations. Some, like the Humanitarian Society (*Societa Humanitaria*), the Italian Union for Popular Culture and people's universities, of which there exist a number, have a history, interrupted by Fascism, which goes back beyond the First World War. They have always been handicapped by shortage of funds and lack of State support. They have also found it impossible to present a common front, since they are divided by ideological differences, particularly the Catholic/secular quarrel, which have affected so much of Italian life.

In view of the generally low level of education in the mass of the population, it is understandable that adult education has concentrated on basic education. But that has been a means to an end, to make adults capable of earning a living and acting as informed and responsible citizens, to make them masters of their environment, rather than victims of it. Beyond the basic level, unfortunately, adult education, in spite of devoted efforts, has made little impact, and the range, level and density of provision over the country as a whole are lower than in any of the other countries examined in this book.

The '150 hours'

The working class movement in Italy was aware from its earliest days that a primary obstacle to the emancipation of the masses was ignorance. Trade unions were associated, at the end of the nineteenth century, with the people's houses, one of the first examples in the country of working-class self-help associations, which had an educational as well as a welfare aspect to their work. But organized labour was largely ineffectual at that time; its divisions — between Catholics and secularists, those who would compromise with the bourgeois State and those who would have no truck with it — helped to pave the way for Fascism. That regime abolished independent trade union activity for more than twenty years. As a result the educational achievements of the labour movement up to the end of the Second World War were very slight.

For many years after that they were nothing to boast of. The trade union movement was once more divided, into three, the Italian General Confederation of Workers (CGIL), the Italian Confederation of Free Trade Unions (CISL) and the Italian Workers' Union (UIL). They were closely tied to political parties and their independent functions were largely restricted to negotiations over pay and conditions of work. On wider social and political matters they acted as appendages of the parties. In the last decade they have loosened their links with the latter and have thereby become more independent over a wider field. They have also come together in a federation, which has greatly strengthened their power.

Given their priorities, and the narrow view taken of their responsibilities, it is not surprising that, as with the British trade unions, education was only a marginal concern. This applied even to the training of their own officials. The CSIL created a training school in 1951, but it was not until 1966 that the CGIL followed suit, and it was only in 1975 that the UIL did.[7] Only in the last ten years have the trade unions taken a major initiative in adult education.

The Workers' Statute of 1970 may have pointed the way. It laid down the right of workers to paid leave from work in order to attend examinations, and the right to a rearrangement of working hours in order that they might attend classes and prepare for examinations. The big step forward was, however, not a product of law but of collective agreement between unions and employers. Italian trade unions do not represent workers performing particular functions, but all workers within a particular industry or area of economic activity, whatever their function. Between 1973 and 1975 in upwards of twenty industries contracts were signed between unions and the employers, giving employees the right to some degree of educational leave.[8]

The arrangements vary. Some, for example local government workers, can get only unpaid leave. Others may have paid leave, which may be obtainable only on condition that the worker also devotes some of his leisure time to study, as in the ceramics industry, or it may have no such strings, as for the glass workers. The length of leave that an individual may receive varies greatly and is calculated, according to industry, on an annual, biennial or triennial basis. The right to leave may be individual, that is each person accumulates a personal entitlement for his or her own use. This is the case in the glass industry. It may be collective, that is the employees within a factory or establishment acquire a group entitlement to leave, which is calculated as a function of their numbers, and this pool of leave hours is allocated to individuals up to a (usually) fixed maximum. In, for example, the food retail business, the right lies with the workers as a group. Establishments are usually protected in that they do not have to release more than a limited number of employees, ranging from two to three per cent according to agreement, at any given time.[9]

The metalworkers were the first to negotiate a right to leave, they have been the most enthusiastic in making use of it and the pattern of their agreement has been the most commonly followed, with some variations in the figures, by other unions. In each establishment the number of hours of leave to which the work force is collectively entitled is calculated on the basis of a three-year period at a rate of ten hours for each person per year, so that in an establishment of 100 workers they will have a right to 3,000 hours of leave over three years, but no more than two per cent of them may be absent on educational leave at once.[10] When first negotiated, the metalworkers' agreement stipulated that an individual might have up to 150 hours of paid leave, but in order to obtain this he or she had to spend an equal number of hours of course attendance in his or her own time. In 1976 the maximum was raised to 250 hours and the compulsory leisure time class attendance was reduced to equal half the time spent on paid leave.[11] It is the works council, composed of representatives of employers and labour, that decides which individuals should benefit from leave and in practice the decision is left to the workers' representatives on it.

Not only that, the trade unions have decided what study the '150 hours' (the name, applied to the original metalworkers' contract, is applied to educational leave agreements as a whole, whatever the industry or the length of leave entitlement) shall be used for. In their view the primary handicap of the working-class movement is the low level of culture of its members. In 1971 32.8% of the population aged sixteen or over did not have the certificate of completion of five years primary schooling and 76.6% did not hold a lower secondary school certificate.[12] It was therefore decided that priority should be given to bringing people up to the level of the latter. Moreover they have rejected the idea that such courses should be conducted in special workers' schools and asserted their right to have them conducted in the State school system.

General guidance as to the duration of the courses and broad outlines of the syllabus are set out in directives from the Ministry of Education. There is a compulsory core: mathematics and natural sciences; geography, civics and history; Italian; one foreign language. The details, however, are worked out by teachers, students and, often, trade union officials. The teaching methods avoid magisterial instruction, the passing of information from the teacher to the taught. They have concentrated on an interdisciplinary approach and collective management of learning, in which the starting point is the students' experience and group discussion plays an important part.

Teachers have been specially recruited on fixed contract to teach the courses. They are given four weeks initial training and they are mostly young people under the age of thirty. This has had the disadvantage that they lack experience, but also the advantage that they are less likely to be bound to the formal methods of the State school. Teachers collectively decide which students shall be allowed to sit the lower secondary school examination, which, for the '150 hours' students, is based on what has been taught in the course they have followed, rather than on a standard syllabus.

There was a rapid increase in participation in these courses once they began, from 14,237 in 1974 to 89,367 in 1977, followed by a drop to 83,543 in the following year. Whether this last indicates a tapering off of the initial enthusiasm, one cannot say. The proportion of women participants rose from 15.3% (1974) to 36.4% (1977) and of adults over the age of thirty from 39.0% to 43.5%. In the beginning the scheme was dominated by metalworkers and semi-skilled personnel, but both categories have declined, not absolutely, but proportionally, from 77.7% to 19.1% in the case of the former and from 60.9% to 24.7% in the case of the latter. According to Ministry of Education figures the examination pass rate has been between 98 and 99%, which means that once selected for the examination students are almost guaranteed a pass.[13]

In addition to middle school level courses, trade unions have used leave under the '150 hours' agreements to permit individuals to attend single subject courses in universities. The Ministry of Education has refused to support these so they rely on independent action and finance by individual institutions of higher education. The subjects chosen, for example, economics, pollution, are related to workers'

211

everyday concerns and it is estimated that about 5,000 persons attended courses of this kind in 1977.[14]

It should already be clear that paid leave under the '150 hours' agreements is not intended to be used to further education for education's sake. It is an instrument for the promotion of the collective interests of the working class, as seen by the Italian trade unions. Their attitude is influenced by the polarized nature of industrial relations in Italy. The interests of employers and labour are seen to be fundamentally opposed. This is not unlike the British situation, but Italian unions are more deeply Marxist in ideology than British ones. They believe the working class can only defend itself against the power of capitalism by collective action, to which they are prepared to sacrifice the right of the worker to individual self-fulfilment to a degree that British unions, still marked by liberal democracy, are not. Or rather they believe that only through the collective can the individual worker achieve full self-realization.

In their negotiations they therefore rejected the use of paid educational leave for vocational training, because that would serve the interests of the employers, and for the most part they also rejected the individual's right to leave for his or her own purposes. They saw it as a means to the achievement of equality between workers and of increased 'power of group control over working conditions and resistance to the hegemony of the employer in the organisation of work'.[15] Hence their insistence that they should choose who should get leave and what should be studied. The criterion for choice was not, which individual would benefit most, but the level of culture and awareness and the state of the workers' struggle in each establishment. It was on egalitarian grounds that the middle school curriculum was chosen.

There is much talk of working-class culture. Although it is vague, it seems to mean understanding and mastery of the socio-economic conditions of working class life and the historical determinants of it. It is in pursuit of this culture that the methods, the inter-disciplinary approach which attempts to relate subjects of study to the learners' experience and the introduction of topics of discussion relevant to their life situation have been chosen.

That the whole exercise is to be seen in a socio-politcal

context is further demonstrated by the unions' insistence that the middle school level courses shall be conducted in State schools. Their purpose has been, through the insertion of these courses, to contribute to the reform and democratization of the public school. At present, and in spite of the reforms of the 1960s, it does not offer to working-class children an education relevant to their needs. It is authoritarian both in its methods of teaching and in its teacher—pupil relations. Its curriculum bears no relation to working-class life and is in fact informed by the standards of high, or bourgeois, culture. By bringing schools into contact with courses and methods of the kind to be found in the '150 hours' provision, the unions hope to move the schools to look critically at their current procedures and to change them. There has certainly been friction between schools and the Ministry of Education on the one hand and unions, teachers and workers on the other, but apparently little sign of change.[16]

The '150 hours' agreements are plainly a product of distinctive Italian circumstances. They are also manifestations of an international trend towards educational leave for adults. The idea that it is both a right and a need that people continue to study in adult life for their own and society's benefit has become widespread, if not universal. To make it practical and desirable to study it is increasingly believed that opportunities should be given to do so in working hours, rather than only in leisure time. In order that adults are enabled or become willing to take these, wages, it is argued, should be maintained during study, or payments made in lieu.

Even where it is agreed that some paid educational leave should be made available, a number of points of disagreement arise. Should it be an individual right, or should it be the State, the employer, or representatives of organized labour who decide who should have it? The answer to this last question depends on what the purpose of leave is thought to be — self-development of the individual, social or economic welfare of society, or of employers, or the working class movement — and on that in turn depend any prescriptions concerning what may be studied. There is also some debate about who should meet the cost of leave, employers or the State, and whether leave arrangements should be regulated by law, by collective agreement, or left to the grace and favour of employers.

In principle governments and trade unions have generally approved of leave as an individual right. In practice they and employers have emphasized their own interests more, employers wanting leave restricted to vocational education of their choice, governments laying priority on vocational or social role education, and unions wanting leave used for the benefit of the workers' movement. Conflicts of interest and principle and concern for cost are among the main reasons why a number of countries, including the United Kingdom, the Netherlands, Denmark, Norway — and Italy — have no general paid educational leave provision.

Where there has been legislation the trend has been towards the establishment in principle of educational leave as an individual legal right. However, either by law, as in Belgium or Austria, or by conditions governing the payment of cost of living allowances, as in France, the individual's choice has in practice been limited to studies approved by employers or the State, usually vocationally-oriented ones. Even in Federal Germany and Sweden, where a genuine effort appears to have been made to assure individual choice, it is restricted by the shortness of leave entitlement in the former and by limited funds for student grants in the latter.

In these countries, whether they accepted educational leave laws willingly or not, the State and employers have succeeded in protecting their interests. Trade unions have also done so in most countries, either by special laws or collective agreements, which accord to workers' representatives the right to paid leave for training in the exercise of their functions, either as union officials (e.g. Norway), or as members of works councils (Federal Germany), or as members of works health and safety committees (United Kingdom). Basically, allowing for the fact that the needs of the working class movement in Italy are seen to demand that priority be placed on the general education of members, rather than the training of officials, the '150 hours' agreements fall into this category of leave.

The differences between the Italian and the British and French trade unions is one of degree, rather than one of kind. The French have argued for over twenty years that the exercise of an individual right to leave was an illusion, the pursuit of which would allow capital and the State to subvert it for their own ends. They wanted leave to be used for the collective good of the working class and therefore the 1971 law is seen by them as unsatisfactory. The British Trade Union Congress's priorities in the matter of leave would be similar. In all three countries labour relations are conflictual, the interests of labour are seen as fundamentally opposed to those of employers, and generally to those of the State, because employers are seen to exercise a predominant influence over it. It is interesting to note that, where an individual right to paid educational leave may be seen to exist to a significant degree, in Sweden and Federal Germany, labour relations are founded on a basic consensus of interest, which may in turn derive from both sides' concern to defend the highest standards of living in Europe.

On one point trade unions have been shown to be justified. An individual right to paid educational leave, even if guaranteed by law, cannot be ensured by the individual alone. It needs at least the acquiescence of the State, employers and organized labour and is unlikely to be exercised meaningfully without the active support of the trade unions.

References

1. *Basic Statistics of the Community, 1979*, Brussels, Statistical Office of the European Communities.
2. ibid.
3. L. TRICHAUD, *Education et développement en Italie*, Paris, Jeune Europe-Etinco, 1970.
4. K. VON MOLTKE and N. SCHNEEVOIGT, *Educational Leaves for Employees*, San Francisco, Jossey-Bass, 1977.
5. F.M. DE SANCTIS, *L'educazione degli adulti in Italia*, Rome, Editori Riuniti, 1978.
6. VON MOLTKE and SCHNEEVOIGT, op. cit.
7. DE SANCTIS, op. cit.
8. VON MOLTKE and SCHNEEVOIGT, op. cit.
9. ibid.
10. ibid.

11. M. RISK and B. CROSSMAN, 'The right to continuing education and the Italian initiative', *Adult Education*, vol. 52, no. 4, November, 1979.

12. VON MOLTKE and SCHNEEVOIGT, op. cit.

13. F. M. DE SANCTIS, *Dopo le 150 ore*, Universita degli Studi di Firenze, n.d., duplicated.

14. G. PISANO, *The Organisation and Structure of Adult Education in Italy*, Prague, European Centre for Leisure and Education, n.d., duplicated.

15. F. M. DE SANCTIS, A Victory by Italian Workers: the '150 Hours', Paris, *Prospects*, UNESCO, vol. III, No. 2, 1977.

16. ibid.

CHAPTER 10

Postscript

This book is not one of those which start with a premise from which the author proceeds, by reasoned argument backed up with evidence, to a logical, if not inevitable, conclusion. It began, it is true, with a number of assertions about the nature, purpose and significance of the machinery of adult education provision. To that extent it had a basic premise. The assertions were not, however, supported by argument, but illustrated by cases, twenty of them, taken from eight countries of Western Europe. If they were well chosen, this book has no need of a conclusion. There does, however, seem room for a postscript.

It is a thesis of this book that adult education practices can only be understood as products of the national culture in which they exist. It is another thesis that they contain within them elements which have a significance for people beyond the boundaries of their own country. The text has been arranged to bring these out. Each chapter has begun with a sketch of the aspects of national culture that conditioned the form of each phenomenon examined within the chapter. Consideration of every case has ended with some effort to relate it to other European practices.

There has been no difficulty in producing evidence to show the conditioning effect of national factors upon cases. For example, in Italy a low level of general education among workers, a politically divided society and government inaction all played a major part in the creation of the '150 hours' scheme. In the German Federal Republic citizenship education has been given so much attention, because of the perceived need to create an informed, responsible citizenry, capable of exercising democratic rights and fulfilling responsibilities which previous generations had neither understood nor appreciated. France has opened the field of vocational adult education provision to all and sundry partly because of the free market philosophy of the Government, partly because of employers' distrust of the formal education system after 1968 and partly because it seemed the only way to achieve the scale of provision desired, since there was no existing nationwide machinery of adult vocational training.

The lessons of these instances will surprise no one. The national specificity of their work is a commonplace among adult educators. It grew up in an *ad hoc* manner in response to precise needs, not only of a national, but even of a local kind. It was not, like school education, imposed in a uniform pattern by government, although that stage may yet be reached if the 1976 Norwegian law turns out to be a harbinger. So deeply rooted and moulded by its national origins has adult education appeared to some practitioners, so necessary does it seem to others to return attention to local needs, that they question whether it is possible to undertake worthwhile comparisons between countries, or desirable to do so.

This is a widely, but not generally, held view. For many years people have been comparing what they do with what is done abroad, in an attempt to improve their own practice. In the 1820s the experience of Mechanics' Institutes in Great Britain inspired evening classes in France. University extension and folk high schools have exerted an influence far across the borders of their countries of origin. Today the relevance of foreigners' practice to one's own is increasingly appreciated. British community colleges and the Open University, French paid educational leave legislation, Dutch educational networks, have all attracted international interest, not as an intellectual exercise alone, but from policy makers considering their options.

So it is growing more clear that phenomena of adult education are to be evaluated not merely in their national context but in that of neighbouring states and even of all Western

218

Europe. They draw from and influence their national environment, but they also draw from, and have something to offer to, neighbouring countries and the whole region. It is possible that some aspects of a country's practice have nothing to tell foreign educators, that the practices themselves are so peculiar to that country that nothing which is done abroad has any relevance to them. If such exist, however, on a national scale, they are not known to this author. Certainly none of the cases discussed in this book is of that kind.

There is in every example of structure and organization something which springs from purely national conditions and needs, and parts which are wider in their relevance. How much can be learnt abroad from that example depends on the balance between the purely national and the wider elements. It is likely that only those parts of it that are not nationally specific will take root in other states, and if those parts are too few, it may not be translatable. Transferability will also depend on the specificity of the culture in which it is to be transplanted. British university extension was very influential, but only stripped of its specifically British forms and clothed in foreign ones. When in France uniquely British conditions met peculiarly French ones, it left no enduring mark at all.

Some features of practice, although not characteristic of one state only, have limited application outside. Folk high schools spread through all the Scandinavian countries, because they all had a freehold farming class, needing education to make use of its growing political power, working a similar farming year and living in the same Lutheran tradition. The example was not followed further afield, or was transformed, because other countries did not have sufficient common elements with the schools' Danish homeland for it to be borrowed in its original form.

To an increasing extent, however, there are features of adult education provision which all Western European countries have in common. This development is only occasionally obvious in the externals of structure and organization, because these are still strongly shaped by history, but there are signs that it will be. It shows at present in countries' preoccupations. Broadly, Western European countries are at a similar level of economic and social advance. They subscribe to the same principles, they are confronted by the

219

same problems, share a view of adult education's contribution to solving them, are equally aware of the difficulty of achieving general participation in adult study, and have access to similar levels of technology.

The cases examined in the foregoing chapters have within them a European dimension in that they reflect these concerns. However foreign the environment or the form of provision, attempts to achieve more equal educational opportunity through adult education, in municipal adult schools, the Open University, or the '150 hours' programmes, will offer the possibility of insights or experiences to other states. The situation of adult education in France is widely different from that in the Federal German Republic, in the United Kingdom, in Norway, in the Netherlands, but all these countries look to adult training to produce the skilled manpower they need, and so French vocational training has something to tell them. All countries fail, to a greater or lesser degree, to involve sections of their population in continuing study, all believe it to be socially desirable, so they are all concerned with outreach activities to non-participants and measures to facilitate attendance at courses, such as paid educational leave. Even though the purposes to which it is put are not those which other countries would set as priorities, they are interested in the technical and organizational lessons to be derived from the Open University's experience of multimedia education.

Since the Second World War a number of international organizations have made a major effort to promote and facilitate the dissemination of information relating to practices in adult education. In a number of cases they have sponsored or themselves conducted analytical studies of what individual countries do. The United Nations Educational Scientific and Cultural Organisation has been prominent in providing tools by which access may be obtained to documents and publications. Its directories of adult education periodicals and documentation centres, its *Terminology of Adult Education* are meant to meet worldwide needs, but they provide important data concerning Europe.[1] UNESCO has sponsored the project 'Organisation and Structures of Adult Education Systems in Europe', co-ordinated by the European Centre for Leisure and Education, Prague, which has produced the largest series of studies of adult education provision in individual countries, both capitalist and socialist, that has ever been published.[2]

The Organisation for Economic Co-operation and Development also has interests extending beyond Europe, but has published studies which have an important European content. Its concern for adult education is more recent than that of UNESCO and has concentrated on aspects of economic relevance, particularly recurrent education and paid educational leave. The Council of Europe has been active nearly as long as UNESCO, deals purely with European matters and has over the years produced a number of studies of practice, notably in the field of informal adult education and sociocultural animation.

The membership of all these organizations is confined to governments, whose priorities for adult education do not always coincide with those of bodies working in the field. In a number of countries the latter have formed national institutes or associations, such as the National Institute of Adult Education, in England and Wales, which represent the views of the field to public authorities. They also act as collaters and publicizers of knowledge concerning practices and principles, both within and beyond their own countries. European institutes of this kind come together in a non-governmental association, the European Bureau of Adult Education.[3] Because not only such bodies, but also individual agencies and organizations at national, regional and local level, both public and private, may belong to the Bureau, it is possible for a wider range of adult educators to participate actively in its work than in that of UNESCO, OECD, or the Council of Europe.

Since 1953, in its work to encourage mutual awareness and stimulate contacts between people in adult education, it has promoted a wide range of conferences and working parties — on residential adult education, paid educational leave, the disadvantaged and local learning networks, for instance. Several of its publications, notably the periodical, *Notes and Studies*, *Adult Educational Legislation in 10 European Countries*, *Experiments in Dutch Adult Education*, have provided authoritative information for the preparation of this book.[4]

All the organizations mentioned have shown a particular interest in spreading knowledge of innovations in adult education. They have demonstrated thereby their awareness of the need for new approaches to meet changing circumstances and to reach that large proportion of the post-school population hitherto untouched by continuing education. As adult education becomes increasingly structured and institutionalized, the accommodation of novel ideas in established practices becomes more complex and it is fortunate that the adult sector remains more open to change than the formal school system.

The development of women's studies in the last decade provides an interesting example of innovation working its way into practices. The feminist movement argued that, to a significant extent, inadequate opportunities for education helped to perpetuate and reinforce the subordinate status of women in relation to men. It also contended that action to remedy the situation would only be taken if women were made sufficiently aware of their position and the factors which produced it to press for change. Out of this thinking there has emerged through Europe a number of initiatives in women's studies, that is, 'programmes devoted to the situation of women and to the nature of women's role throughout history in the social, cultural, political and intellectual development of a particular society or group of societies'[5] — and usually aimed exclusively at women.

These initiatives fall roughly into two classes, first those taken independently by groups of women or through feminist associations and second those taken within existing adult education institutions. On the whole the second class appears to have predominated as women activists have tried to change the system by working inside it. Because, in part, of the nature of the subject-matter, women's studies appear to have been more easily accommodated in certain sectors of adult education than others, but the phenomenon is also in part due to the different degrees of openness to new practices shown by different sectors. By the nature of their tradition and principles Scandinavian study circles, evening institutes and university extra-mural programmes in Great Britain, evening folk high schools in Federal Germany, have all been open to women's studies, on the initiative, mostly, of women within these organizations. In the Netherlands feminist bodies are able to operate within local education networks and in France in socio-cultural animation. The vocational sector, formal further and higher education, have, however, been less ready to offer study directed specifically to women in their role as women.

Like most developments in adult learning, women's studies have grown as an unco-ordinated scatter of national and local actions. They are still a marginal and not totally integrated element in provision. But they are an international phenomenon, of which individual manifestations may present features of value to people working in the same subject area throughout Europe. As was to be expected, international organizations, in particular the European Bureau of Adult Education, have done valuable work in disseminating knowledge of these.

It is an important goal of these bodies to help the rank and file educator to recognize that, behind nationally specific trappings, foreign practices are conditioned by concerns which he shares, so that he may find value in studying them. They invite him to consider that there may be other ways of doing things than his own. They may not suggest precise alternatives, viable in his circumstances, but they may lead him to review his existing procedures with a more critical eye, to realize habit for what it is and not to take it as behaviour immutably imposed by the very nature of the adult education process. What more than anything else prevents adult educators from profiting by consideration of foreign provision is probably their inability, or at least their failure, to distinguish its purely national or local elements from those which have a wider resonance.

Hitherto the publications of international bodies have not greatly helped them to achieve this. The comparative dimension has largely been missing. This book was designed to begin to set that right. If it has succeeded and thereby helped those engaged in any way in the education of adults to understand and learn from the rich and varied range of Western European practices in that field, it will have justified itself. The real goal, of course, is that out of this extended knowledge will come, however indirectly, improved and augmented learning opportunities throughout life for those who have completed their initial education.

References

1. *Directory of Adult Education Periodicals,* Paris, UNESCO, 1977. *Directory of Documentation and Information Services in Adult Education,* Paris, UNESCO, 1980. COLIN TITMUS, PAZ BUTTEDAHL, DIANA IRONSIDE, PAUL LENGRAND, *Terminology of Adult Education,* Paris, UNESCO, 1979.
2. In the series, *Adult Education in Europe,* monographs have so far been published on Czechoslovakia, France, Poland, Hungary, the German Democratic Republic, Yugoslavia and Austria.
3. The permanent offices of its secretariat are at:
   Nieuweweg 4, P.O. Box 367 — 3800 AJ Amersfoort, The Netherlands.
4. See Bibliography.
5. *Terminology of Adult Education,* op. cit.

Glossary of non-English terms

(Da=Danish; Du=Dutch; Fr=French; Ge=German; It=Italian; No=Norwegian; Sw=Swedish)

animation socio-culturelle (Fr) — socio-cultural animation

Arbeitskreis Deutscher Bildungsstätten (Ge) — Working Group of German Educational Centres

Arbeit und Leben (Ge) — Work and Life

Arbetarnas Bildningsforbund (ABF) (Sw) — Workers' Educational Association

Centre National de Télé-Enseignement (Fr) — National Centre for Distance Education

Deutscher Volkshochschul-Verband (Ge) — German Folk High Schools Association

éducation des adultes (Fr) — adult education

éducation permanente (Fr) — lifelong education

éducation populaire (Fr) — popular education

Erwachsenenbildung (Ge) — adult education

folke højskole (Da) — folk high school

Folkuniversitetet (Sw) — folk university

formation continue (Fr) — continuing education

FÖVUX (Sw) — Committee on Methods Testing in Adult Education

Frikyrkliga studieforbundet (Sw) — Educational Association of Free Churches

Gymnasium (Ge) — upper secondary school

HAVO (Du) — senior secondary school

Heimvolkshochschule (Ge) — Residential folk high school

KFUK-KFUMs studieforbund (Sw) — Educational Association of the YMCA-YWCA

Ligue de l'Enseignement (Fr) — Educational League

lycée (Fr) — upper secondary school

MAVO (du) — junior secondary school

Moeder-MAVO (Du) — mother-MAVO, junior secondary school for adults

Norsk Korrespondanseskole (No) — Norwegian Correspondence School

Nykterhetsrorelsens Bildningsverksamhet (Sw) — Educational Association of the Temperance Movement

ontwikkeling(Du) — education (in the sense of instruction)

Pädagogische Arbeitsstelle des Deutschen Volkshochschul-Verbandes (Ge) — Educational Centre of the German Folk High Schools Association

politische bildung (Ge) — citizenship education

Riksdag (Sw) — Parliament

scuola popolare (It) — people's school

Sillon (Fr) — Furrow (educational association for young men, of Catholic inspiration)

Studieforbundet Medborgarskolan (Sw) — Educational Association of the Citizens' School

Studieforbundet Vuxenskolan (Sw) — Adult Schools Association

Studieframjandet (Sw) — Study Promotion

Sveriges kyrkliga studieforbund (Sw) — Swedish Churches Educational Association

Telekolleg (Ge) — Distance Learning College

Tjänstemännens bildningsverksamhet (Sw) — Salaried Employees' Educational Association

verzuiling (Du) — pillarization

Volksbildung (Ge) — popular education

Volkshochschule (Ge) — folk high school

vorming (Du) — education (in the sense of personal development)

VWO (Du) — senior secondary school

Weiterbildung (Ge) — further education

Bibliography

Adult Education: A Plan for Development, London, Her Majesty's Stationery Office, 1973.

Adult Literacy in Scotland, Edinburgh, HMSO, 1980.

Adult Education in Sweden, Stockholm, Swedish Institute, 1970.

Adult Education in the Nordic Countries, Stockholm, Nordic Council, 1976.

Adult Education Legislation in Ten Countries of Europe, Amersfoort, European Bureau of Adult Education, 1974.

Adult Education: the Challenge of Change, Edinburgh, HMSO, 1975.

BALSER, F. *Die Anfänge der Erwachsenenbildung in Deutschland in der ersten Hälfte des 19 Jahrhunderts*, Stuttgart, Ernst Klett, 1959.

BARRY, CHARLOTTE, 'Adults brace themselves against legalised assault', London *Times Higher Education Supplement*, 7 March, 1980.

Basic Statistics of the Community 1979, Brussels, Statistical Office of the European Communities, 1979.

BERGEVIN, P. *Adult Education in Sweden*, Bloomington, Indiana University, 1961.

BESNARD, PIERRE and PERRET, JEAN, *Le système français de formation des adultes: aspects professionels*, Prague, European Centre for Leisure and Education, 1978, duplicated.

BESNARD, PIERRE, *Socio-pédagogie de la Formation des Adultes*, Paris, Les Editions, ESF — Entreprise Moderne d'Edition, 1974.

BUNGENSTAB, K.E., KLEIM, H., ed., *Grundlagen der Weiterbildung*, Cologne, J.P. Bachem, 1974.

Cahiers de la Quinzaine, Paris, 3rd series, no. 2,10,20, 1902; 5th series, no. 20, 1904.

CHARTIER, NICOLE, *Multi-purpose Schools and Centres in Europe*, Paris, Foundation for Cultural Development, n.d.

COBBAN, ALFRED, *A History of Modern France*, 3rd edition, 3 vol., London, Penguin, 1965.

Commissie Bevorderung Plaatselijke Educatieve Netwerken, *Vijfde Advies, Educatieve Netwerken in Opbouw*, Amersfoort, May 1979.

DAHLÖFF, U. *Reforming Higher Education and External Studies in Sweden and Australia*, Uppsala, Uppsala Studies in Education 3, 1977.

Danmarks Folke Højskoler 1979—80, Copenhagen, High Schools Secretariat, 1979.

DEBESSE, M. and MIALARET, G., ed., *Education permanente et animation socio-culturelle*, *Traité des sciences pédagogiques*, vol. *8*, Paris, Presses Universitaires de France, 1978.

DE SANCTIS, F.M., 'A Victory by Italian Workers: the '150 hours', Paris, *Prospects*, vol. III, no. 2, 1977, UNESCO.

DE SANCTIS, F.M., *Dopo le 150 ore*, Universita degli Studi di Firenze, n.d., duplicated.

DE SANCTIS, F.M., *L'educazione degli adulti in Italia*, Rome, Editori Riuniti, 1978.

DOLFF, H., ed., *25 Jahre Deutscher Volkshochschul-Verband*, Brunswick, Westermann, 1978.

EDSTRÖM, L—O., *Struktur und Reform schwedischer Erwachsenenbildung*, Bonn, Westermann, 1969.

Experiments in Dutch Adult Education, Amersfoort, Netherlands Centre for Adult Education, Study Centre NCVO and European Bureau for Adult Education, 1977.

Extended Adult Education, Stockholm, Liber Tryck, 1974.

FAIRBURN, A.N., *The Leicestershire Community Colleges and Centres*, Nottingham, Nottingham University Department of Adult Education, 1978.

FLENLEY, R., *Modern German History*, 4th edition, London, Dent, 1968.

FORDHAM, P. ET AL., *Learning Networks in Adult Education. Nonformal Education on a Housing Estate*, London, Routledge Kegan Paul, 1979.

GLYN JONES, W., *Denmark*, London, Benn, 1970.

GOEZINNE, D., 'Policy Making in Dutch Adult Education', *The Development of Local Education Networks*, Amersfoort, European Bureau of Adult Education, 1978.

HAMMARBERG, P., 'The situation and tasks of the voluntary organisations', *Notes and Studies 49—50*, Amersfoort, European Bureau of Adult Education, 1971.

HEARNDEN, A., ed., *The British in Germany. Educational Reconstruction after 1945*, London, Hamish Hamilton, 1978.

Higher Education in Sweden, Facts and Figures 1978, Stockholm, National Board of Universities and Colleges, n.d.

Higher Education into the 1990s, London, HMSO, 1978.

Higher Education: Report of the Committee under the Chairmanship of Lord Robbins, HMSO, 1964.

HIMMELSTRUP, PER, 'The Danish folk high school', paper presented to the annual conference of the Universities Council for Adult Education, University of Kent, Canterbury, 1978.

HOUTKOOP, W.A., *Enige Ontwikkelingslijnen in de Nederlandse Volwasseneducatie sinds 1900*, doctoral dissertation, Amsterdam, January 1977, duplicated.

HUDSON, J.W., A History of Adult Education, 1851.

HUGGET, FRANK E., *The Modern Netherlands*, London, Pall Mall Press, 1971.

JEPSON, N.A., *The Beginnings of English University Adult Education*, London, Michael Joseph, 1973.

JONES, H.A. and CHARNLEY, A.H., *Adult Literacy, a Study of its Impact*, Leicester, National Institute of Adult Education, 1978.

JOHANSSON, B., *Adult Education in Sweden*, Stockholm, Swedish Institute, 1973.

KELLY, THOMAS, *A History of Adult Education in Great Britain*, Liverpool, Liverpool University Press, 1970.

KING, E.J. ET AL, *Post-Compulsory Education: a New Analysis in Western Europe*, London/Beverly Hills, Sage, 1974.

KLOSS, G., *West Germany, an Introduction*, London, Macmillan, 1976.

LAACK, F., *Die Rolle der Heimvolkshochschule in der Bildungsgesellschaft*, Weinheim, Julius Beltz, 1968.

LABOURIE, RAYMOND, *Les Institutions Socio-culturelles. Les Mots Clés*, Paris, Presses Universitaires de France, 1978.

LESNE, M., COLLON, C., OECONOMO, C., *Changement Socio-professionnel et Formation — Etude d'une Situation de Crise dans le Bassin de Briey*, Paris, INFA, 1970.

LOVETT, T., *Adult Education, Community Education and the Working Class*, London, Ward Lock Educational, 1975.

LOWE, JOHN, TITMUS, COLIN, SAVICEVIC, DUSAN, 'Widening access to university adult education in Europe', *International Congress of University Adult Education Journal*, vol. XV, no. 3, November 1976.

LYCHE, INGEBORG, *Adult Education in Norway*, Oslo, Universitetsforlaget, 1964.

MATZAT, H.L., *Zur Idee und Geschichte der Erwachsenenbildung in Deutschland*, Homburg, Verband der Volkshochschulen des Saarlandes, 1964.

MEE, G. and WILTSHIRE, H., *Structure and Performance in Adult Education*, London, Longman, 1978.

MEYER, ADOLPHE E., *An Educational History of the Western World*, 2nd edition, New York, McGraw-Hill, 1972.

MIDGAARD, JOHN, *A Brief History of Norway*, 3rd edition, Oslo, Johan Grundt Tanum Vorlag, 1966.

MORRIS, H., *The Village College*, Cambridge, 1924.

MOULINIER, P., *L'animation et les animateurs à travers la littérature spécialisée*, Paris, Secrétariat d'Etat à la Culture, Service des Etudes et de la Recherche, 1976.

NEUBECK, H., *Ein Beitrag zur Bestandsaufnahme der Einrichtungen politischer Erwachsenenbildung in der Bundesrepublik*, Frankfurt-am-Main, Pädagogische Arbeitsstelle des DVV, 1968.

OAKLEY, STEWART, *The Story of Denmark*, London, Faber and Faber, 1972.

229

PERRY, WALTER, *Open University*, Milton Keynes, Open University, 1976.

PICHT, W., *Das Schicksal der Volksbildung in Deutschland*, Brunswick, Westermann, 1950.

PISANO, G., *The Organisation and Structure of Adult Education in Italy*, Prague, European Centre for Leisure and Education, n.d., duplicated.

POPPERWELL, R.G., *Norway*, London, Benn, 1972.

POUJOL, GENEVIÈVE, *Le Métier d'Animateur*, Toulouse, Privat, 1978.

Recommendation on the Development of Adult Education, General Conference of UNESCO, 19th session, Nairobi, 26 November 1976.

Report of the Committee on Continuing Education, Milton Keynes, Open University, 1976.

Report of the Vice-Chancellor 1978, Milton Keynes, Open University, 1979.

Reviews of National Policies for Education: Norway, Paris, OECD, 1976.

A Right to Read, London, British Association of Settlements, 1974.

RISK, M. and CROSSMAN, B., 'The right to continuing education and the Italian initiative', *Adult Education*, vol. 52, no. 4, November 1979.

RØRDAM, THOMAS, *The Danish Folk High Schools*, Copenhagen, Det Danske Selskab, 1965.

Scottish Education Statistics 1974, Edinburgh, HMSO.

Sharing and Growing; a short account of the growth and activity of community colleges in Devon, Devon County Council Education Department 1977.

SIMPSON, J.A., *Today and Tomorrow in European Adult Education*, Strasbourg, Council of Europe, 1972.

STAHRE, S–V., *Adult Education in Sweden*, Stockholm, Swedish Institute, 1966.

STAPEL, C., *Adult Education on its way to an 'Open School' System*, Bergen; January 1976, duplicated.

START, K.B. and WELLS, B.K., *The Trend of Reading Standards*, Slough, National Foundation for Educational Research, 1972.

Statistics of Education 1975, vol. 3, Further Education, London, HMSO.

Statistische Mitteilungen des Deutschen Volkshochschul-Verbandes Arbeitsjahr 1977; Frankfurt-am-Main, Pädagogische Arbeitsstelle des DVV, n.d.

STEINDORF, G., *Von den Anfängen der Volkshochschule in Deutschland*, Osnabrück, A. Fromm, 1968.

Stellung und Aufgabe der Volkshochschule, Bonn, Deutscher Volkschochschul-Verband, 1978.

TITMUS, COLIN, *Adult Education in France*, Oxford, Pergamon, 1967.

TITMUS, COLIN and HELY, C. GRAEME, 'Collective and individual dimensions in the adult education of working people', London, *Studies in Adult Education*, vol. 8, no. 1, April 1976.

TITMUS, COLIN, 'France — current problems and prospects', *Adult Education*, vol. 42, no. 2, July 1969.

TITMUS, COLIN, BUTTEDAHL, PAZ, IRONSIDE, DIANA, LENGRAND, PAUL, *Terminology of Adult Education*, Paris, UNESCO, 1979.

TITMUS, COLIN, 'Proposed theoretical model for the comparative study of national adult education systems in Europe', *Society and Leisure*, vol. VIII, no. 2, Prague, European Centre for Leisure and Education, 1976.

TRICHAUD, L., *L'éducation populaire en Europe, 2, Scandinavie*, Paris, Editions Ouvrières, 1969.

TRICHAUD, L., *Education et développement en Italie*, Paris, Jeune Europe-Etinco, 1970.

Typologie des fonctions dans l'éducation des adultes, Brussels, Confédération Internationale des Syndicats Libres, 1979.

UCAE Annual Report 1978—79, Universities Council for Adult Education.

UDDMAN, R., New Developments in Swedish Adult Education, *Notes and Studies* 45—46, Amersfoort, European Bureau of Adult Education, 1970.

Unabhängige Bildungsarbeit in der Demokratie, Bonn, Arbeitskreis Deutscher Bildungsstätten, 1977.

Universities Council for Adult Education, *First Statement Submitted on Behalf of the Council to the Committee on Adult Education*, 1970.

VAN DIEMEN, A. and KRAAN, R., *Evaluatie van Educatieve Planning, Verkorte Verslag*, Amersfoort, Studiecentrum NCVO, 1979.

VHS der Stadt Oberhausen, Bildungsprogramm, Arbeitsjahr 1979—80, Oberhausen, 1979.

VON MOLTKE, K. and SCHNEEVOIGT, N., *Educational Leaves for Employees*, San Francisco, Jossey-Bass, 1977.

WEDELL, E.G., *The Place of Correspondence in Permanent Education*, Strasbourg, Council of Europe, 1970.

Index

236

237

University Grants Committee (UK), 44
University Technological Institutes
    (Fr), 87
updating education, 21, 147
urbanization, 57, 58, 61, 156, 190, 205

Vichy régime (Fr), 129, 137
village colleges (UK), 29
vocational adult education, 38, 75, 80,
    101, 106, 135, 144–53, 178, 180,
    181, 182, 214, 220, 223; *finance of,*
    148, 152, 163; *government role in,*
    10, 11, 20, 102, 146, 147–151,
    179, 194, 207; *laws,* 14, 21, 40,
    103, 123, 124, 145, 146–49, 150,
    151; *providers of,* 12, 24, 61, 76,
    102, 146, 149, 161, 169, 172, 193,
    218; *status,* 6, 20, 24, 67, 117, 164,
    165
vocational advancement, 13, 146–47,
    194
Vocational Training Act (FGR), 103
voluntary organizations, 26, 52, 110,
    111, 134, 178, 181, 186, 193;
    finance, 24, 25, 159, 163; *profes-*
    sionals in, 9, 139; *role in adult*
    education, 27, 28, 47, 48, 52, 161,
    162, 164, 165, 169, 181, 193, 207;
    Swedish, 2, 12, 60, 61–68, 70, 71,
    75, 76, 81, 92, 94; *types,* 102, 105,
    113, 120, 136, 138, 146, 193;
    volunteers, 9, 49, 52, 137, 139
vorming (Ne), 143, 178, 179, 181, 185,
    187

welfare provision, 19, 57, 58, 99, 156,
    157, 160, 191
Wilpert, Professor, 40

Wilson, Harold, 41
women in adult education, 32, 35, 38,
    50, 51, 80, 90, 92, 120, 122, 146,
    151, 152, 180, 182, 197, 211;
    women's studies, 183, 222–23
Work and Life (FGR), 104, 118
Workers' Educational Association, 11;
    Denmark, 193; *Norway,* 169;
    Sweden, 63, 64, 65, 89, 90, 91;
    United Kingdom, 11, 21, 24, 25, 27,
    35, 36, 73, 111, 134, 142
Workers' Institutes (Sw), 60
Workers' Statute (It), 209
working class, 36, 41, 98, 128, 132,
    134, 138, 150, 156, 174, 176, 191,
    207; *attitude to education,* 39;
    collective interests, 210, 212; *edu-*
    cational level, 35, 137; *education*
    for, 60, 66, 103, 113, 131, 133,
    134, 135, 136, 159, 177, 180, 192,
    194, 208, 213; *organizations,* 17;
    participation in adult education, 21,
    45, 115
Working Committee for Education in
    Citizenship (FGR), 119
Working Group for University Adult
    Education (FGR), 40, 119
Working Group of German Educational
    Centres, 11, 12, 13, 119, 123

young adults, 117, 122, 148; *educa-*
    tional level, 77; *education for,* 112–
    116, 118, 119, 136, 138, 145,
    146, 147, 151, 152, 180, 194–96,
    197, 199, 200, 207
youth and community service (UK), 22
youth hostels movement, 136